# THE BROAD SPECTRUM
# PSYCHOTHERAPIST

# THE BROAD SPECTRUM PSYCHOTHERAPIST

## Wyn Bramley

FREE ASSOCIATION BOOKS   LONDON / NEW YORK

First published in 1996 by
FREE ASSOCIATION BOOKS LTD
Omnibus Business Centre
39–41 North Road, London N7 9DP
and 70 Washington Square South
New York, NY 10012–1091, USA

99 98 97 96    5 4 3 2 1

A CIP record for this book is available from the
British Library

ISBN  1 85343 328 4  hardback

Designed, typeset and produced for the publisher by
Chase Production Services, Chipping Norton, OX7 5QR
Printed in the EC by T. J. Press, Padstow

*This book is dedicated to my patients and supervisees.*

# Contents

*Preface*                                                                    ix

PART ONE: REASSESSING THE THERAPIST'S FUNCTIONS

1.  Reassessing the Therapist's Functions: 1-3                               3

        Function 1: Fitting Therapy to the Patient                          5
        Function 2: Checking the Therapeutic Context                        5
        Function 3: Scanning the Session as it Happens                      8

2.  Reassessing the Therapist's Functions: 4-8                              11
        Function 4: Classifying the Process Interactionally                 11
        Function 5: Working With the Transference                           31
        Function 6: Making Interventions                                    33
        Function 7: Making the Assessment                                   33
        Function 8: Getting Supervised                                      34

3.  Reassessing the Therapist's Functions: 9 and 10                         35
        Function 9: Operating as GP to the Mind                             35
        Function 10: Getting Rest                                           60

PART TWO: MAKING THE ASSESSMENT

4.  Making the Therapeutic Alliance                                         65
        The Therapeutic Alliance                                           67
        Opening the First Session                                          70
        Using Silence                                                      74
        Finding a Common Language                                          80
        Separating Out the Transference                                    84

5.  Making the Dynamic Formulation                                          93
        Setting Achievement Goals                                          95
        Using the Psychiatric Background                                   97
        Forecasting the Future and Measuring Resources                    102
        Making Trial Interpretations                                      104
        Restricting Exploration                                           108
        Attending to Patients' Questions and Anxieties                   112

6.  Making the Dynamic Formulation: Short Examples    114

7.  Making the Contract    130

PART THREE: FOLLOWING ASSESSMENT

8.  Making Interventions in the Longer Term    141
    What is the Intervention For?    146
    Who is Making the Intervention?    148
    The God    148
    The Friend    150
    The Surgeon    150
    The Teacher    151
    The Parent    153
    The Sage    155
    The Setting as Constant Intervention    159

9.  Making Interventions: Clinical Illustrations    162
    Reserved Interventions    164
    'Acting In' Interventions    165
    'Acting Out' Interventions    168
    Reconstructing Interventions    169
    Translating Interventions    173
    World-Assumptive Interventions    175
    Other Types of Intervention    180
    'Fingers Crossed' Interventions    183

10.  Dealing With Transference in the Longer Term    185
    The Reciprocated Transference    186
    The Attitudinal Transference    191
    The Mediated Transference    193
    The Allowed Transference    195
    The Split Transference    198
    The Confronted Transference    200
    The Cross Transference    205
    Transference to Things    206
    The Dissolved Transference    209

Afterword    211

Further Reading    213

Index    216

# Preface

This book is addressed to qualified and qualifying psychotherapists and counsellors whose training and subsequent clinical supervision have been primarily psychodynamic: in other words, based on and developed from psychoanalytic theories.

I am assuming key concepts such as 'The Unconscious Mind', 'Mechanisms of Defence', 'The Therapeutic Alliance', 'Transference', as well as the developmental ethos in which these are rooted, are accepted and understood. The aim is not to tell readers what they already know, nor introduce a new body of theory, but rather to raise some queries about, share some examples of and look afresh at ways of dealing with therapeutic encounters which fail to fit neat technical or theoretical categories. Wherever possible, clinical material from my own or supervisees' patients illustrates points raised.

I imagine interested readers to represent a wide spectrum of psychotherapeutic services; GP surgeries, hospitals and day centres, church and voluntary agencies, as well as private practice. The book therefore looks mainly at short- and medium-term treatment, psychoanalysis proper being a specialized form of private practice suited to a comparatively small number of the population seeking psychological help.

Like me, readers may include group and couple work in their practice, concentrating on one or two sessions a week, while referring for full psychoanalysis those who are psychologically-minded, motivated, and rich enough in time and money to benefit. Most readers will be coping with a wide range of personal problems which have then to be fitted into the short, medium and occasionally long vacancies available, as well as having to be matched with therapists possessed of the appropriate level of skill. Some senior therapists' jobs include acting as Assessor to patients who will then be referred for therapy elsewhere. For all these reasons the text stresses the importance of, and goes into considerable depth about, skilled Assessment.

I take for granted also that readers have perused 'the sacred texts' during their training, so there is no need for a discussion of them here. My further reading list at the end of the book aims to provide more pleasure and some enlightenment to readers who have found themselves in sympathy with my approach to psychotherapy.

I would like the book to come over not as some erudite tome to be dutifully struggled with at the end of a tiring day, but more as a written down, if one-sided conversation, one long-in-the-tooth practitioner sharing experiences, thoughts, and occasional worries with another.

A note on terminology. To avoid the tedium of 'his/her' all the time, I use the female gender when referring to the therapist and the male when referring to the patient. This in no way implies gender bias; being a women therapist myself it just comes easier to me.

I use the term *patient* deliberately. A patient *suffers* (Latin root): this entitles him to *treatment* (therapy). He has a right to expect understanding, exemplary respect and sensitivity and, where appropriate, relief from duties and responsibilities that make him worse – a very special status in fact. True, some parts of society associate the word *patient* with infantility, dependence, worthlessness. This says more about society's debasement of language and the politics of manipulation than the word itself. I, for one, should like to rehabilitate it.

Finally, a note on the case material used. Like most therapists I feel uncomfortable about using private material in a book, even though care has been taken to disguise every patient's identity. But I feel equally strongly that patients are our best teachers and it is impossible to pass on learning acquired in clinical practice without the use of actual cases.

The majority of patients in these pages have completed their therapy, some many years ago. One or two are about to finish and a few were patients of colleagues. By the time the book is published, no current patient need feel he or she has been written about.

Some life crises, personality types and symptoms are very similar and during a career in the psychiatric services spanning more than thirty years there is bound to be duplication of clinical pictures. Occasionally, where two or more patients' lives have followed similar patterns and where the psychodynamic principle or issue under discussion is not affected, I have combined biographical details from more than one case in order to further protect the patient's identity. In every case, name and occupation have been altered, though I have tried to give people invented jobs that make sense in terms of the problems, relationships and lifestyle presented.

# PART ONE

# Reassessing the Therapist's Functions

## CHAPTER 1

# Reassessing the Therapist's Functions: Functions 1–3

It is the year 2000. The latest technological miracle has brought Freud back from the grave. But the experiment went a bit wrong, so the great man of middle years finds himself in London instead of Vienna. The government, wishing to take full advantage of his famous brain, makes him General Inspector of Psychiatric Services. They issue him with a security pass, travel allowance and a limitless supply of luncheon vouchers, so he can visit anywhere at any time throughout the country.

Off he goes then, peering in puzzlement at the tokens in his hand, wondering what can have happened to civilization since his demise, to make such passes, allowances and vouchers necessary.

But these are the least of his problems. Imagine. What is the founding father of psychoanalysis to make of the very existence of a National Health Service, let alone its marketplace philosophy? What is he to make of concepts like community care, focal psychotherapy, therapeutic community? What of family, marital, Group Analytic therapy? How does he react to the proliferation of drugs unheard of in his day, of people having to rely on them while enduring a year-long wait for psychotherapy on a limited contract? What is he to make of nurses, social workers and some strange creatures called 'counsellors' using his ideas in their daily work, not to mention the institutes sprouting up everywhere, that purport to train them?

The culture shock is phenomenal. Whatever conclusions he finally draws, one fact is immediately clear: psychoanalysis as practised in old Vienna is unsuitable, unaffordable, impractical and unstaffable for the nation as a whole.

Yet I am constantly amazed by fellow psychotherapists who talk as if they are second-rate healers because they do not practise 'pure analysis'. They attend lectures and conferences where eminent analysts speak, returning home full of clinical aspirations and enthusiasm, only to deflate the moment they are back at work, complaining they are referred the wrong sort of patients, they have to work miracles in a few short sessions, their training is inadequate to assist with high levels of disturbance, and they are fed up with doing lip-service psychotherapy when the real thing is out there somewhere, if only mad 'management' could be made to see sense and purchase the 'proper' training for them.

However, Freud's 'talking treatment' was developed in and to some extent fashioned by the scientific, philosophical and social ethos of his time. So why do so many therapists working today, in a radically altered culture, feel they are not really 'kosher' unless they are equipped to do as Freud and his contemporaries did? Most medical doctors revere Hippocrates and keep his oath, but they'd find themselves in a pretty pickle if they copied his medical practices today! Is this sanctification of 'pure analysis' (perfect but conveniently unattainable) a way of dealing with clinical doubt or failure, blaming and passing the buck to parental management for not feeding (that is, training) us properly?

Is it good old sibling rivalry I hear when therapists confined within the NHS, the church, social services or a charity moan that it's all right for them (the private analysts): *they* have the money and time to train properly; *they* see only five patients a week – look at *my* caseload; *they* can pick and choose their customers, while I have to take every Tom, Dick and Harry?

It seems not to occur to these practitioners that they themselves could be 'frontier-busters'; that, while retaining the best of psychoanalytic thinking, a new approach is called for that more patients can use and more therapists can practice. The new approach does not have to mean a lowering of standards, the deployment of diluted and inferior analysis, but it does require a radical rethink that results in tailoring psychodynamic treatment to the patient and not the patient to the treatment.

The advent of focal theory went some way to meeting this need, but its great shortcoming was that in order to avoid making people more ill (sometimes no therapy is better than half a therapy), patients were carefully screened for suitability to the method and large numbers were excluded. In a GP surgery, at Relate consulting rooms, and in NHS clinics, therapists have to use their knowledge and clinical experience to deal with a wide population, many of whom have never heard of and couldn't care less about psychodynamics and suitability criteria – all they know is they hurt and they want it made better.

And where are we supposed to refer all those patients deemed insufficiently psychologically-minded for such rarefied treatment? Shouldn't we train more patient-oriented therapists rather than resort to the prescription pad so easily and so often that what in the correct circumstances are powerfully effective drugs become discredited and distrusted palliatives, a sop to the 'rejects'?

*Function 1: Fitting Therapy to the Patient*

Our chief function as modern-day psychotherapists must be to find treatments appropriate to modern-day patients, deliverable via public and charitable agencies by properly trained and supervised practitioners. 'Properly trained' does not have to mean 'trained in psychoanalysis'. Nor does it have to be a second-best affair. We must of course desist from 'chucking out the baby' of psychodynamics with the 'bathwater' of psychoanalysis, but we must also resist the temptation to gaze constantly backwards to the idealized past. While acknowledging our debt to the originator of psychoanalysis and his followers, we must, Janus-faced, look also to the future and find a treatment approach available not just to the affluent and the educated, and not restricted to those for whom self-reflection is second nature, but to ordinary people, in ordinary jobs, who could not afford or make use of pure psychoanalysis even if it were offered.

I hope to show, especially in the chapters on Assessment, that such an approach is feasible, although it sometimes takes more skill, experience and personal risk-taking to work successfully and for a relatively short time with a 'low suitability' patient than to conduct an elaborate and meticulous classical analysis where the traveller is eager and speaks the language, the signposts are clear and getting lost occasionally is all right because the journey is being taken at leisure.

*Function 2: Checking the Therapeutic Context*

The psychoanalytic context consists of one quiet room, one couch, and the analyst and analysand. Psychoanalysis is a private transaction between two people, whereas psychotherapy takes place (except for private practice, which is pretty rare outside the major cities) in the public sector. It may be carried out in anything but a hushed environment by a community nurse, a university counsellor, a registrar in a hospital, a specially-trained priest or a therapist attached to a general medical practice. These settings impinge on the therapy and the therapist, not only because of the less salubrious physical surroundings, but also in terms of money and training available to the practitioner, whether supervision is paid for by the employer, how long the waiting list is and what policy prevails with regard to the nature and length of therapy offered. Whether other sources of referral are available is another key factor.

A training in psychoanalysis equips a practitioner with the necessary theory to treat such patients, but does not assist in any way with the management of dynamics within the supporting psychiatric team, which (see example below) has a direct bearing on their treatment. Neither does it teach specialized techniques for working in the short term or doing intermittent therapy, where the patient makes a contract for a given number of sessions – say twelve to sixteen – and may come back if needed at agreed intervals – say six-monthly, or annually.

As we all know, proper psychoanalytic technique is slow and thorough and takes as long as it takes. The psychoanalytic attitude is one of sphynx-like inscrutability (the so-called 'blank screen'). Transference phenomena are cultivated and revered, however long they take to develop, and great potency is attributed to interpretation. In psychotherapy all these ingredients have to be modified and adapted to suit the needs of public-sector patients and the constraints imposed by political, financial and institutional realities. The training of all psychotherapists should, but very often does not, reflect this fact, and instead merely replicates or imitates chunks of the psychoanalytic training. The result is a sorry mismatch between treatment offered (that is, truncated, pseudo-psychoanalysis by resentful and guilty therapists with inferiority complexes) and the treatment setting (no money, too many referrals, too few therapists, and patients who don't fit comfortably into the suitability criteria for psychoanalysis, even in miniature form). And that is just *inside* the room!

Much training also fails the public-sector psychotherapist in not equipping her to deal with issues outside the consulting room that psychoanalysts never have to tackle: 'the treatment team' and role of 'key worker', cross-referral procedures, patient allocation, being 'purchased' and having to prove cost-effectiveness, working with other professionals representing incompatible ideologies and sometimes even sharing patient care with them, not to mention the conflict inherent in practising good therapy while pleasing line management with the necessary throughput of patients.

A recently-appointed Student Counsellor who was still in therapy training came to me for supervision. The first case she brought was a student she described as needy and frightened, but with whom she felt she had made an authentic if tenuous relationship. He missed sessions and was seeking help from various other sources. The counsellor strove valiantly to contain him in the one setting, declining to grant mini-sessions or discuss personal matters in the college grounds.

The trouble seemed to be that as there was no coherent treatment plan the tutor, college GP and psychiatrist of the region's community mental health team all became involved, without any reference to my supervisee, in spite of the student being quite open about his sessions with her. Such was the paucity of communication among the professionals that the young man could not be pinned down in any one place long enough to make a calm Assessment, which meant that neither the supervisee nor I could begin to understand any unconscious determinants in his behaviour. We looked glumly to a future when all the exhausted helpers would dismiss or avoid him, seeing him as 'manipulative' or 'attention-seeking'.

In the supervision session we ignored the student's pathology as being for the moment unknowable, and instead concentrated on how the supervisee saw and related to her new colleagues and how they used, misused or ignored her. Though she'd made clear she was in the dynamic camp, the GP treated her like 'the welfare' and was always too busy to talk (but not too busy to refer on her patient), while the nurse in the mental health team to whom the GP assumed the psychiatrist would refer 'did a bit of cognitive therapy', having just completed a quick course. She was also emigrating in a few weeks!

Before any patient is offered therapy, lines of clinical responsibility must be clear and back-up clinical support at the ready (how much more usefully could this psychiatrist have been deployed?). Having worked as consultant to various mental health teams, my informed guess was that much of the 'snubbing' from them was due to their own time- and mind-consuming struggles to work together in an unfamiliar interdisciplinary way. Rivalry between them and feeling professionally undermined or left out by other team members would be rife. They would be looking inward to their team, trying to find a comfortable niche for themselves: relations with the Student Counsellor were not even on the agenda yet!

The supervisee and I played with lots of ideas about initiating team-building activities among academics, the general practice and the mental health group. Given the tact and diplomacy required, these were of necessity long-term plans. Meanwhile, what about the student?

Of all the supervisee's new colleagues the psychiatrist seemed the most approachable, but she could never get him on the phone. The psychiatric assessment was due within days. Because the student was hyperanxious and often muddled, the supervisee feared he would not himself demand to be sent back to her. We decided on a damage limitation exercise. She would write formally to the psychiatrist explaining her work with the student so far, and include in particular the student's butterfly habits. The tone of the letter would show her as wanting him to have the background information to help him in his assessment, and her preparedness to have the student back if he (the student) agreed. Her first priority then would be to establish some clear boundaries and make a proper Contract with him.

A copy of the letter would be sent to the GP, modelling the courtesy and professionalism he seemed bent on discounting. This case could then be used as a basis for discussion when she began her bridge-building policy.

This case also demonstrates the need for a confidentiality-within-the-team policy. Being sworn to secrecy obliges one to lie or suffer manipulation such that one cannot maintain the freedom necessary to do the best for the patient. Many patients worry about confidentiality, but I have never heard one object to the policy that anyone in the same treatment team trying to help him might need to have discussions from time to time.

## Function 3: Scanning the Session as it Happens

I picture the well-functioning psychotherapist with a huge swivelling third ear on her crown and a third eye dead-centre of her forehead that sees in all directions like a fly's. She wears an easily detachable (but real) spare heart on her lapel, the tube linking it to her internal heart via her buttonhole making it look rather like an enlarged version of the TV newsreader's microphone. Through her translucent skin I see right into her head, where sits a big filing cabinet (I was born long before the computer generation). The top drawer is open; the lower drawers kept for refinements of the filing system in the top one. The front folder in the top drawer is huge but empty – not even a speck of dust; the second crammed and in need of sorting; the third orderly and relatively unchanging; and the last, right at the back and barely reachable, is marked: 'PRIVATE BUT VERY IMPORTANT'.

While ordinary eyes and ears go about their business, the third ear scans noise and silence as if carefully listening to music. The individual instruments and notes (sentences, facts, historical reports) are not so vital as the meaning, mood and intensity of feeling the totality of communication conveys. Likewise the third eye sees not just a fidgety squirming man who can't return its gaze, but, along with what the swivelling ear is receiving, recognizes the bullied, shamed and humiliated child in the playground, no hope that mum will come to his rescue.

The extra heart assists the therapist in identifying with the patient's emotional states, then and now, and lets her experiment with actually being there, while leaving her other heart to beat normally and undergo feelings from a safe distance – so-called 'empathy'.

The filing cabinet? The front empty folder is the clean uncluttered space in the therapist's attention that is made unconditionally available for the patient to put the 'documents' of his story in. The next bulging jumbled file is a copy of all these documents and, appended to them in no particular order, all the therapist's associations to what he has presented, all her hunches, hypotheses and half-made links, as well as notes on her own reactions and her predictions about any future therapy. This is the file she will take to supervision, removing sorted papers to a lower drawer afterwards, before meeting the patient again and cramming the second file once more.

The third orderly file represents her training (including her own therapy), which is used neither as a reference book nor a bible, but more like a familiar map that stays basically the same, but from time to time clinical experiences with patients make her take it out and add or subtract details. This map is not a copy of her training but a map of what she has made of her training. It can be reinspected in times of trouble, but in the main has been so absorbed into her system that finding her way around her patients has become second nature. She is using the map unconsciously and automatically, without the need to have the real thing in front of her. Needless to say, it should never be placed, even for a moment, in the front file!

Right at the back is her very own patient file – the little girl she was and in part still is, her pre-analysed, troubled self, her needs and problems that have defied analysis and can still haunt her. In that file also lies her reserve of hope, her own belief in the value of living, brought about by all her life-conflicts and their full or partial resolution; also her own pain and her belief in her capacity to bear further pain. She accepts, as so many of our patients do not or cannot, especially at the start of treatment, that the pain-free life has yet to be invented, and that pain not only bravely borne but also understood can go hand in hand with new learning and new strength.

And so it is to this dusty folder she must turn when she is stuck with a despairing patient, and neither turning her scanners on herself, nor the consulting of her map, nor her supervision have helped.

What has been scanned must then be sifted and sorted. I will examine this procedure in Chapter 2.

# Reassessing the Therapist's Functions: Functions 4–8

*Function 4: Classifying the Process Interactionally*

That which the patient produces behaviourally, linguistically and visually, plus all the observable reactions and speech from the therapist, I call the 'material' of the session. (Some therapists prefer to call it 'content'.) The interactional 'process' of the session is the conscious, half- and quarter-conscious, and *un*conscious way this material is arranged, delivered and then responded to by both therapist and patient.

Material is self-evident, measurable, video-able. Interactional process cannot be caught on a screen, cannot be quantified, can only be intuited and translated, with more or less accuracy. On video we may see the materialistic result of process but no amount of photographic jiggery-pokery can record the busy exchange between two interior worlds. The couple are constantly generating, then inhibiting, distorting, redirecting or maintaining the process occurring between them according to their respective conscious and unconscious translations of it, as it develops. Invisible yet always on the move, sometimes graspable or partially graspable by one or both, sometimes by neither, the meaning and purpose of any piece of interactional process is a matter of opinion not a matter of fact.

Interactional process means that process which occurs *between* the therapeutic couple, as distinct from, even though occasioned by, processes *within* each individual (for example, the various deployments of their well-established 'internal object relations' and 'mechanisms of defence').

Schematic presentations are always simplifications, but with that caveat let me say that the interactional process in therapy can be broadly categorized under six headings: reciprocal cueing; mutual trial identification; identification with the aggressor; projective mechanisms (in both directions, though it is devoutly to be hoped that the therapist becomes quickly aware of hers, even if she has to dive into that dusty file at the back of her cabinet to realize it); working through; and transference with all its variants.

The therapist uses her ideas (unprovable) and feelings (untestable) about the process (invisible) to guide her toward interpretation (debatable) of what might 'really' (whose reality?) be happening. Small wonder that much of the general public regard our profession with suspicion!

CUEING

The public, however, may not realize that we arrive at most interpretative conclusions with the overt or unconscious connivance of our patients; we have after all spent many hours talking together and so, as with most couples, we get to know what hints to drop, how to warn each other off without causing offence, how to dodge awkward questions, how to tone down or prevent conflict with each other and how to couch tactfully that which might be construed by the other as hostile criticism.

Both parties may also resist the interpretation that is forming and growing: the patient reluctant to face some truth about himself that though potentially liberating isn't worth the blow to his self-esteem; the therapist resisting her own conclusion because she feels it is too soon, or too powerful an insight for the patient to cope with at this time in his therapy when other pressures are upon him. Perhaps she resists because she lacks confidence in her ability to cope with the aftermath of this interpretation, or perhaps it is just that the evolving interpretation could equally well apply to herself!

Resistance shown by the patient is there for a reason; it is not just a psychological accident. So great care and much thought is needed before resistances are challenged. Both patient and therapist, if they are in tune with the session's process, will find ways of sending and receiving one another's clues, telling one another without words when they are ready to speak or hear, or when they are frightened and need more time. They also develop mutually acceptable ways of showing each other when they are barking up the wrong tree.

Cueing is a delicate and subtle affair. It takes time for both parties to crack one another's codes, to 'speak without words' to each other. In short-term or intermittent therapy the treatment period is often over before either has deciphered the other's cues, and much valuable intimacy is lost. For in addition to repairing the wounds of 'then', a new and deep experience with his therapist 'now' – new growth on top of the repair – is needed to give the patient the confidence to move forward in his relationships, rather than settling for a mere restoration of his old functioning.

This experience of being so close to another human being that you can 'read' each other, especially for patients who can't remember ever having had it, is arguably one of the greatest healing elements in psychotherapy, although we professionals tend to see it merely as a means to some greater end.

What we don't know yet is how much the therapist's concentration on transference provides freedom from old relating habits such that the patient can commence cueing, and how much the accurate sending and receiving of cues makes it possible to stand otherwise threatening revelations from the transference. Chicken or egg?

Working short-term with cueing requires a therapist brave enough to take risks and confident enough to admit mistakes and put them right in the same session. She must be swiftly, almost instantaneously self-monitoring, and more prepared than the classical analyst to interact with her patient. She needs to selectively allow her personal responses to show, make informed guesses to offer for confirmation, amendment, modification or correction by her patient, while simultaneously maintaining the therapeutic distance necessary to allow for transference to develop and for the patient to consult with himself uninvaded and uninterrupted. This is quite a balancing act, and one which no therapist can get right every time.

Mrs Miller had been in weekly private therapy with me for three months. Diagnosed as depressed by her GP, she was working hard on her unhappy girlhood with an overanxious, suffocating mother and a distinctly chilly father. Her problems were far from solved, but the insight gain made her feel she was now doing something positive and her depressive symptoms had gone.

Then disaster struck. Her only daughter, aged thirteen (a year older than my own son), contracted meningitis and was dead within the week. She took two weeks off therapy (I told her to ring me at any time) to deal with the funeral, her distraught parents and her stunned husband, which she did heroically before collapsing herself and spending the second week under sedation.

She returned to therapy haggard, thin and unkempt. Her remorse was terrible to witness. She constantly blamed herself for being a bad mother. Now she knew why her own mum had been so protective. *She* would never have let a child get ill. She continued pitilessly blaming herself and crying, while I found myself becoming upset and in danger of weeping also. A rapid self-monitoring brought me up short. It was all too easy to identify with her. I couldn't help it; what if it had been my son? I prayed he'd put his crash helmet on that morning while trying to pull myself together.

Then came my cue. Till now her body had been hunched, eyes cast down. Suddenly she looked up at me. The pain in her face made me want to run a mile. Yet in her eyes I saw terror too, terror and pleading. Using trial identification I put myself in her place for a second (a second was all I could bear), saw myself as she must see me – on the edge of tears, panicky perhaps, impotent certainly. Her fear was that like her, I too would not be able to stand her pain. The plea was that I should at least have one more shot at it.

I don't know how, but I managed to dredge up some vestige of professionalism and shoot her a look as I raised my chin: 'In control now. Please use me as you need to.'

Wringing her hands she continued the self-laceration, while I tried to offer comfort occasionally by making remarks of the don't-be-too-hard-on-yourself variety.

Then came the second cue which it would have been criminal to miss. After one of my 'supportive' comments she said sharply, 'That's not the *point!*' before crying more, this time in apology.

I could have kicked myself. 'Please,' I said gently, 'tell me what I have missed. Help me understand.'

When the daughter had been just four, they had had a quarrel over some naughtiness, and being depressed and somewhat out of control at the time, my patient had hit her hard so that she stepped backwards, falling over a milk bottle and badly cutting herself. At the hospital they asked the child how it had happened and she never said a word about her mother hitting her. Neither Mrs Miller nor her daughter ever mentioned it again, and now it was too late to put it right.

At this there was a positive storm of self-recriminatory tears.

It had not occurred to me that she would be concerned with anything other than the immediate, tragic present, but what she had come to me for that day was not comfort or support, but confession. Despite all attempts to bury it, this incident and what she saw as her cowardice over it had tormented her for years. Now at last it was in the open. If we had not already developed an effective cueing system this material might never have surfaced, long delaying the self-forgiveness Mrs Miller so badly needed.

TRIAL IDENTIFICATION

From the therapist's side this is a deliberate technique to attempt a more precise understanding of the patient's feelings by momentarily *being* the patient. Identification is much more potent than empathy; indeed many trainees are cautioned to avoid it at all costs. But as long as the therapist has a spare 'heart' as described above, one of them can be completely given over to the patient from time to time. It is a risky business for beginners who sometimes believe one heart is enough, and having adopted the patient's emotional stance cannot return quickly enough to normal functioning. The experienced practitioner is less confident and knows it can only be done by using the second heart to take over while the 'identified' heart can resume normal operation in its own time. In other words she uses what therapeutic jargon calls 'splitting' mechanisms, but doing so consciously, whereas when the patient 'splits' it is usually a defence against having to face the two sides of his ambivalence simultaneously: this needs to be seen as material for interpretation.

But it isn't always defensive. Patients too can simultaneously stand in two persons' shoes.

During the termination period there is usually nostalgia, a picking over of the whole course of therapy, and this is when patients often tell me how they trial-identified with me.

I could see at once that, though kind, you were a call-a-spade-a-spade sort of person, so I decided to spill the beans right away.

This had not been transference, for I suppose I am like that (though I wish it hadn't shown so much), and there were no key figures in her life in any way similar.

This woman had been to three therapists in the preceding three years, and none of them had gained access to the guilty secrets she longed and feared to tell. She 'read' them all as not wanting to disturb her (or themselves?) too early and had therefore, as she put it, 'piddled about'. With me she had imagined herself in my place and immediately divined that, all other things being equal, I like to get down to business straight away, and in any case I had 'sussed her', as she put it. We paced ourselves accordingly, presumably via unconscious or half-conscious mutual cues, and her treatment took off very quickly.

She always knew before a holiday if I was particularly tired (it wasn't just guesswork for I am not always fatigued then, but she was right every time). Once she stopped mid-monologue, peered closely at me and announced: 'You've got the curse bad, poor lamb, haven't you?' She was right.

Trial identification can sometimes linger and haunt. Supervision or one's own therapy can be very helpful here, sorting how much the therapist's reaction to the material she has identified with belongs to the patient and how much is hers, long buried maybe, but now exhumed by the contact with the patient's interior world.

A failure or unwillingness to trial-identify can prove harmful to one's sense of professional competence when it turns out that one's guess at the patient's state, based on external observation only, turns out to be wrong. A perhaps distressing but nevertheless accurate trial identification can also alert the therapist to the particular patient with whom it is unwise for her to work.

Adam was referred to my Student Counselling Service many years ago by a very worried tutor. He was studying philosophy and, though the brightest student on the course, was turning in hardly any work. However, he attended each tutorial eager to discuss 'the meaning of life' type of questions relevant to the present day, scoffing away essays as irrelevancies.

In our first session he scowled at me suspiciously, answering in monosyllables, until I told him I wasn't a doctor and had no authority to prescribe pills or ECT. Relieved, he launched into a long, beautifully worked out and utterly unassailable argument about the futility of human existence. My heart sank. His suicidal impulses were as clear as the proverbial bell. Every day he harangued other students, his brother and his tutor with these arguments as if in triumphant defiance, but I guessed that underneath he was pleading with them to give him a reason for continuing to live.

I made it clear I was no philosopher so I was not going to do business with him on those terms. I said I felt he was not so much trying to prove a philosophical premise as find a meaning and a hope for his own personal life. He gave me a guarded look then muttered his willingness to come and see me 'for a bit'.

Having trial-identified with him in his first session (I use this technique a lot during the Assessment period. It is one of the reasons why Assessment is so emotionally taxing and why therapists are wise to regulate how many new patients they see at any one time), I was dismayed to realize that he had already adopted me, albeit on probation.

Psychotherapists, like all self-reflective people, have at times meditated on suicide. Although far more eloquent than I could ever be, his ideas touched me where it hurt. I almost feared contamination; or put another way, was downright reluctant to have my parallel despair stirred up. Thank goodness for that spare heart, which I had to call on often during my time with him, and not always in the session either. I would sometimes find myself inside his (and my denied) private hell, when dropping off to sleep, sometimes in the bath, or taking a solitary walk. Thank goodness too for my great appetite for life that compensated for the dark side. Tragically I could find no counterweight in Adam. If I tried to create one he would ruthlessly reject it with a display of philosophical karate that left my head spinning.

Adam refused to see doctors or psychologists as he had been sent to them throughout his childhood and hated them. He was perfectly, indeed frighteningly, rational and calm, and never declared his suicidal intent openly, so there were no grounds for putting him in hospital, which he would fight anyway. I discussed the case with the consultant psychiatrist who was head of the Student Health Service and we hatched a plan where I would see Adam weekly on condition he agreed to a one-off psychiatric assessment. For his part, the psychiatrist would be free to make recommendations but undertook not to prescribe or attempt hospitalization. Adam wearily and cynically agreed, sighing 'bureaucracy, bureaucracy'.

The consultant's diagnosis was 'schizoid/narcissistic personality, probably suicidal'. He found no clinical evidence of depression or thought-disorder that might have been susceptible to medication if Adam could be persuaded. As Adam would see no one else and the psychiatrist was in agreement, I made a contract with him to start straight away.

After three months I felt exhausted by his constant, carefully argued nihilism. I too found no conscious awareness of depression. Trying to help him access any emotion about anything or anybody at all proved impossible. His parents and family were dismissed as good, simple people, but as much duped by religious, social and political myths as the rest of humankind. He'd had no special relationships with any peers, saying none of them could 'take the pace'; that is, give him any satisfactory answers. They gave up on him when he refused to stop asking the same questions.

After much cogitation and doubt, wondering if it was the right thing, I invited him to join a student Group Analytic group which had already been running a year and was very cohesed, patient with its members and highly sensitive to individual needs. This would be in addition to our individual meetings. To my surprise he agreed.

As expected, he used his first meeting as if it were a debating chamber. Members talked to him in much the way his tutor, then I, then the consultant had done, trying to get the discussion into a more personal zone. One or two brave souls tried to argue with him on his own terms but were roundly defeated.

However, as the weeks then months wore on, there seemed a subtle change in his behaviour. It seemed to dawn on him that group members needed to hear something other than the same old record if he was to maintain their interest. They had begun a pattern of politely listening to his diatribe against the universe each week before turning away to their own concerns. Adam started to alternate between missing sessions and attending but remaining silent throughout. No one could induce him to talk – unless it was about *that*, but it was clear he was listening with great concentration to others' accounts of their relationship with partners.

I dared to hope. We were all rewarded some weeks later when he mumbled almost bashfully that a girl he'd met briefly at a conference and who'd lived then in a distant city, was coming to London and ringing him up on the excuse that she needed information about housing, university courses and so on. The group were jubilant but tried to hide it so as not to embarrass him. Each time he condescended to turn up they would ask him about her and offer advice about how to cope with his tongue-tiedness. (He had not subjected her to his usual lecture but plainly did not know what else to do.) To our amazement he admitted he was very taken with her, but naturally, like everything else it was futile.

Soon after, he missed a session. This was not unusual; I generally wrote to him after he had missed two, or took it up with him in his individual session, after which he would invariably 'come home'. In the middle of the working day before the evening of the group meeting his brother, with whom he lived, rang to tell me that he had killed himself in his bedroom the previous night and he had left a note which I might want to see.

I arranged to meet the brother at once. I read the note saying sorry to myself, the group, his tutor and his brother. He wrote while the paracetamol and beer were taking effect that dying was not so bad really, but he seemed puzzled that a wistful feeling kept coming over him ... here the note petered out. If only ('if only, if only') I had been able to find and use that wistfulness, that echo of hope.

Then the horrible aftermath began: accounting to deans, tutors, parents; the funeral to be attended; the brother to support and the group to tell. We were all terribly shaken. How to participate in their shock and grief without abandoning them to join my own group as a member?

Worst of all was the self-reproach. Hadn't I worked as a sister in mental hospitals long enough to remember always to be extra vigilant with a suicidal patient the minute he seemed to be getting better? Why hadn't I realized the brief candle of hope he'd held up to us was bound to be cruelly snuffed out by his dark view of the world, and indeed may have spurred him on to end his life?

Looking back now, I see that had I not trial-identified as much and as often as I did, I might never have taken the suicide threat so seriously as to refuse help without him agreeing to see the consultant. I saw the need to cover myself, medically and legally, as well as getting a second opinion from a respected source. Luckily his parents were full of gratitude for my attempts; they would certainly not sue. However, understandably needing someone to blame, another set of parents might have.

I always knew, deep down, that he would do it. In a way that is what made it possible (just) to work with him. If I refused, he would die the sooner, so there was nothing to lose in trying.

Trial identification, then, is a valuable diagnostic tool, as well as a therapeutic technique. Sometimes, if it proves all too easy to identify, it might be wise to question whether one is the right therapist for this patient.

## IDENTIFICATION WITH THE AGGRESSOR

**This is where the patient (usually) does not or cannot *say* what his childhood experiences were like, but unconsciously *shows* the therapist by treating her the way he was treated. On the receiving end, the therapist is made to feel in no uncertain terms just what he went through.**

Harold, a private patient I was seeing at home, seemed constantly on the edge of breakdown, wringing his hands, breaking into stifled sobs, blaming himself for being a useless person. My heart went out to him when he was like this.

But there was another less attractive side to him. A perfectionist but critical of others, he was always in trouble at work, either told off for overlong reports, for being late at the office (due to an obsessional breakfast ritual), for working unpaid at weekends against office policy, or having 'personality clashes' with management as a result of embarrassing them with accurate but hairsplitting criticisms in meetings and performance assessments. He was incapable of 'rubbing along' or 'turning a blind eye' or of following office practices that didn't make absolutely 100 per cent sense to him. After a formal warning from his exasperated boss, he'd gone to the union yet again. Clearly they were fed up with his long and oft-repeated meticulous presentations of his every grievance, and advised him to buckle down and get on with it: this was the age of performance assessment; time was money; we all have to accept it.

His marriage was in a mess, his wife considering leaving, but he would not move her up our agenda. Work was all. He had to get it *right*.

I was perplexed for a long time. Putting myself in his shoes and experiencing his low self-esteem made me feel compassionately tolerant of the irritating obsessionality he mistakenly believed was going to fix everything. I was determined to help him find another way.

Yet at other times I could have cheerfully strangled him. He had what I called 'gripe phases' when nothing in the therapy was right for him. Might he point out the front door was sticking? Had I realized the Harpic in the loo had run out? There were long discussions about our summer holiday dates. Work did not permit him to take them within the three-month period stipulated by the written contract I give all patients, so why should he have to pay if he was forced to take them in term time? In the event he took holidays three years running in August, so it was a non-issue.

It was not the complaints themselves that made me grit my teeth, so much as the polite, almost ingratiating, yet secretly triumphant way they were made. I was always left feeling furious on the one hand and guiltily caught out on the other. I could see why he was scapegoated at work (he complained endlessly about this, but because he was technically correct – they *were* scapegoating him – he was convinced it was all 'their' fault and he had no part in it).

Owing to his dog-walking, fish-feeding, briefcase-sorting, breakfast-eating ritual he was ten minutes or so late for every session. We talked about it often and at length, but he only pointed out yet again that if I didn't take on so many patients (I felt like a mercenary bloodsucker) perhaps I could give him a later session than 9 a.m. He would then cry (having sensed me bristle?) and feel attacked by me and say I was getting at him like the rest. He couldn't understand why no one, not even me, liked him when he was trying so hard.

My practice when people are late is to leave the front door open and sit waiting and ready in the consulting room so they can walk in as soon as they arrive. Harold had not been on time for ten months. One morning I slept late so I had to go without breakfast to have all ready for 9 a.m. I just made it, and knowing Harold would be late, made myself a cup of tea and began loading the washing machine. Harold arrived dead on nine catching me with washing in one hand and tea in the other. He did not say anything, fixing me with a withering but jubilant look before sweeping into my consulting room, pointedly holding the door open for me.

I was technically in the wrong but still felt 'set up'. I was guilty and angry at the same time. I found myself heartily sympathizing with his colleagues and managers. As I was digesting this reaction and willing my flaming cheeks to cool down, I became aware that he was talking about his father. This was unusual. He spoke much more about his mother as a rule. She was a meek and passive woman with high standards of personal conduct and a consuming need to be approved of. Like Harold she was a perfectionist in all she did, but unlike him would die rather than complain. If anything went wrong, no matter what the setting, she would assume it to be her own fault.

I was hearing more of the father, a successful lawyer who, until now, Harold had described as the wonderfully strong and popular man he would like to be but could never hope to follow. They had had a close and loving relationship all Harold's life and their closeness had continued into Harold's married life. He'd insisted there really wasn't much else to say about him. His main problem was trying to cast off his mother's influence and stand up for himself.

Because of the incident with the tea, which I was struggling to make therapeutic sense of, I listened keenly for any new clues. His father, accompanied by his mother, were visiting for the weekend and Harold had cleared out the garage, washed the lampshades and taken the curtains to a 24-hour cleaning service in readiness. I commented that it sounded like royalty was coming. Yes, he said, he'd been most cross that he was behaving just like mum again so had turned on his wife and blamed her for not keeping the house clean, thus necessitating his frantic last-minute preparations when he had all his work stresses to cope with too. 'I caught her reading a damn book,' he cried furiously, 'a silly, sloppy romantic book!'

Light dawned. What if his need to keep his father idealized made him see all his problems as his mother's fault? She'd be only too willing to take the blame wouldn't she? And because criticism of his father was unthinkable and therefore unspeakable, was he showing me how his father made him feel as a boy, by making me feel rebuked, guilty yet resentful, as his wife later said she had felt when he tore the book out of her hands?

I tested this hypothesis with some gentle probing and long-forgotten memories came tumbling out of how his father had always humiliated and undermined him by picking on mistakes and short-comings 'of nitpicking proportions', and how his mother too had been treated this way. It turned out that her placatoriness was a learned way of surviving in the marriage rather than a neurosis she brought into the relationship. Harold was very upset indeed at recognizing his father's feet of clay, but it marked a turning point in his therapy. Interestingly, now I had at last 'got the message', the snide criticisms of me stopped and life at work improved dramatically.

The reason I took so long to see this identification with his father was because the process of his 'needling' and being contemptuous of me, as his father was to him, was interspersed with behaviour and attitudes that were like his mother's. This passive depressive element I had picked up straight away, presumably because patients' material that arouses the therapist's sympathy is easier to accept than material that produces negative responses of which the therapist might disapprove. For far too long I tried to 'make allowances' for his unpleasant behaviour instead of analysing it.

It is to be hoped that the therapist's own treatment during training has made her aware of her own tendencies with respect to identifications of this sort. I have supervised trainees who sincerely believed they were trying to help their patients when what I could see was a need to bully them, make them submit to the therapist's 'interpretations' as they themselves had been bullied by parents or at school or, dare I say it, by their own analysts. The fact that such bullying is meant only for the patient's good makes it all the sadder.

PROJECTIVE MECHANISMS

The patient sometimes unconsciously projects parts of himself onto the therapist who might then explain what she sees and suspects to the patient, with a view to testing its accuracy or eliciting more associations from him that will confirm or negate her interpretation. Alternatively she may let projection rule for a while, providing she can make therapeutic use of it.

James, nineteen, was the shy, rather cowed son of an ambitious, educated, politically active left-wing single mother whom he claimed set impossible standards for him to follow. She never said so directly but he always sensed he had let her down somehow and she didn't rate him very highly as a man. She had left James's father as soon as she became deliberately pregnant. He was dismissed as an 'indecisive wet week' whenever, as a child, James had asked about him.

As therapy progressed it became clear to us that beneath his mother's Superwoman persona was a fragile girl (who had been abandoned by *her* father) who could not afford to be dependent on men and accordingly devalued and denigrated them, including James.

One day there was a mix up over his session time, which he had rearranged so he could attend a conference. I didn't turn up, believing the appointment to be the following week, so I did not know he had been to my house until we next met. (Interestingly, on checking my diary, I remained certain that it was James who had got it wrong, and wondered if he was unconsciously setting up a confrontation by making this 'mistake'.)

He had been fuming all week, yet had not rung to check what

had gone wrong. Although I had never seen him angry before I sensed we were in for a showdown.

It came when I said I had checked my diary but I was sure I had not made a mistake. 'No, oh dear no, it could never be *your* mistake could it?' Taken aback, I said quietly, 'Go on, I'm listening' (an old technique I use to buy time to think).

There followed a three- or four-minute onslaught about my being too big for my boots, (and who did I think I was?) and patients have rights too you know. Suddenly he stopped, turned a ghastly white colour and his eyes filled with tears. I thought for a moment he was going to bolt from the room. I said: 'Don't look so worried. I am not as devastated by your fury as you always imagined your mother would be if you told her what you really thought.'

After that he ceased attributing his mother's hidden vulnerability to me (but could there be a smidgen of truth here? Was it *all* projection?). Most of the transference from mother to me gradually dissolved and he began to experience me as a real person, one he could stand up to and fight with.

And fight we did. Once the showdown was thoroughly talked over, he began to project his younger self onto me, while he himself assumed the position of 'the aggressor'; that is, his mother. Rather than interpret this, I deliberately 'acted in', demonstrating to him how he might have responded to his controlling, critical mother had he been able, by responding to his new-found ability to challenge with a firmness and refusal to back down that he'd not been able to show her. For some weeks he kept provoking me, as if to force me into such a demonstration.

Toward the end of his short treatment he returned to his unprovoking self (withdrew all his projections), and started practising the assertion he had learned from me *on* me instead, a healthy and natural assertion which needless to say I encouraged. The problem of social and sexual impotence for which he had been referred had disappeared without us specifically talking about sex at all.

Projections from the patient can be so powerful that the therapist who takes the patient's behaviour at face value only can be rendered quite helpless, angry or miserable. When I have a wretched supervisee considering terminating therapy long before treatment has finished, the culprit is often relentless projection by the patient which she has failed to understand.

It is unwanted (because disliked) aspects of the patient's own self that are attributed to the therapist – she is subsequently accused of being a bully, or a cold fish, or a constant carper, whatever the unwanted quality is. Having thus disposed of a part of himself he is left relieved but depleted. The solution is to identify with the quality that has been lost (projected), that he now sees as existing in the therapist, and attack it for the nasty entity he believes it to be. What he cannot approve of in himself he can attack in another.

For all his complaints and criticisms he is in no danger of deserting therapy, as many inexperienced therapists fear (or hope!), for once a quality that has been projected is identified with, then wheresoever the projector goes there must go the recipient also, if the projector is to feel at all complete. This accounts for why so many miserable marriages continue: there can be no constructive separation until reciprocal projections are re-owned by each projector.

Alas for the unsuspecting therapist if, as is often the case, there is a grain of reality in the patient's perception. For example, I like to see myself as a gentle understanding soul, but I have to admit that several patients down the years (sweetly obliging, overly polite women mostly, but with an inner rebelliousness representing a longing to 'take over' in their jobs, marriages or friendships) have experienced me as their bossy headmistress. They are often envious of what they see as my career seniority and success, but though I can see the projection for what it is, it always brings me up short and makes me extra vigilant in my professional technique. There just might be something in it!

We all have our Achilles' heel, and patients often have an uncanny knack of finding it. Even experienced therapists are sometimes guilty of introjecting what has been projected, in other words absorbing a patient's projection as if it were a straightforward and accurate perception. The therapy can be seriously jeopardized as a result.

A senior supervisee was assessing a thirty-six-year-old builder. By the end of their second session she felt they had got nowhere and doubted her ability to be of the slightest use to him. Knowing her work well, I was astonished that she had so quickly lost hope. She had handled far more complex cases than this with ease.

The bare facts Tom offered her were these. His wife had a lover she would not give up. She had lost all interest in him and the marriage but liked the money brought in by his successful firm as well as the new house he'd recently completed. Like him, she adored their two children and would not consider leaving them. So he could not leave her, or them, but neither could he tolerate being so openly cuckolded. That was about it. That was his problem.

Whenever the therapist angled for a bit more material, Tom would go over and over these facts in an almost bored way, saying he couldn't elaborate further, he was only a builder after all, not a trick cyclist. There were long silences in which the supervisee felt foolish, while he gazed out of the window. If prompted he would just repeat; '*I* don't know what I should do. That's *your* job isn't it?'

In the supervision session the supervisee was looking distinctly hot and bothered but strove to compose herself. I asked her what she privately felt about him. Invariably she and I had the same emotional reactions to the patients she presented. I wondered what was so different about this one. For I was feeling very sorry for Tom's stuck position, but she seemed too consumed by anger and misery at his treatment of her to feel sorry for him. Then came her uncharacteristically heated reply: 'He's got me cornered, won't tell me anything, won't relate to me. He thinks I'm useless, he looks down on me.'

Already it looked as if he was doing to her what his wife was doing to him. One could hypothesize that as a builder he might hold traditional male views. He might therefore find it impossible to tell a female therapist how impotent he felt, how downtrodden and abused. But he could show her, by projecting such hateful feelings into her, while protecting his 'ego' by affecting a laid-back, superior attitude.

Another idea I tried on for size was that perhaps Tom was intimi- dated by her. (One of the few bits of family history she had gleaned was that his mother had been a very intimidating character.) The supervisee was astonished that anyone could find her remotely intimidating and at first rejected the idea. I asked her had she not realized how impressive her professional image was, how striking the way she carried her body and her briefcase, how she walked with a purposeful important person's air? It seemed to me that it would be all too easy for people as susceptible as Tom to find her evident skill and seniority intimidating. Remember his 'I'm only a builder' statement?

Luckily the supervisee was in analysis so there was little left for me to do. Believing in herself had always been a personal difficulty for her, so when Tom made her feel as he had been made to feel she simply believed she was inadequate and that he had exposed her.

I am delighted to say she continued with the patient after all and proved as competent as ever.

Another common manifestation of projection is where the patient projects his unbearable feelings onto the therapist so she can bear them for him. A good therapist recognizes the mechanism, bears the feelings, then returns them to the patient in more manageable form. At least, that's the theory. In fact, sending back unwanted baggage can prove very tricky.

Gerald, the friend of an ex-patient, was a twenty-five-year-old violinist who consulted me privately. He had been sent down from university through 'lack of motivation', and had then taken up a part-time job in a local orchestra and supplemented this income by waiting at tables in the café he already frequented as a customer. It was a cosy, stress-free life and he could see no reason to change it except that time was marching on and he should be moving to London and making a proper musical career. His girlfriend and his mother constantly nagged him in this regard. He admitted they were right but kept putting it off – had indeed put it off for four years now.

A cognitive psychologist had tried to get him to organize himself by setting graded tasks, starting with the least fearful and least difficult, but he had never done the therapy homework and the therapist eventually gave up on him.

He struck me as genuinely scared that he would never find motivation. Why else go to the doctor for antidepressants, and then get himself referred to a psychologist, and then spend a big slice of his small salary seeing me? He told me that even if his long-term girlfriend were to threaten leaving him (she wanted to marry and have a house and children fairly soon) he felt he still would not accomplish even the first step of finding an agent, even the addresses of agents for that matter. Yet she was clearly the centre of his world; without her his life meant nothing.

Gerald's father was a professor of music who expected his son to do great things automatically. If Gerald got 90 per cent in an exam, all his dad cared about was the other 10 per cent. He was usually too busy to come to a concert in which Gerald was playing but if he did he would always find fault. Whenever I hinted that Gerald might have a lot of feeling about this locked away somewhere he shrugged and said: 'Water under the bridge.' He had left home years ago and just given up on both parents. He now never thought about them except on the rare occasions he was obliged to show up for a family function, or Christmas, and then he slumped in front of the television not talking or being talked to, but occasionally presented by his mother with 'helpful' suggestions about accountancy courses and such.

Months, then a year, went by, Gerald and I finding more and more evidence of malfunctioning in the family, he agreeing that it all made sense but that it didn't change anything. He still felt he must but could not develop, and unless someone (dad?) gave him the right contacts and the right London job on a plate he really couldn't see himself ever doing anything about it. Yet abandoning the project was unthinkable. He had no doubts about his musical talent, and he really did want to be a professional violinist, but he just could not face making the first step, despite the fact that he could see himself in ten years time bitterly regretting this inertia.

Despite all our work on his early life, nothing changed. I began to worry. Was he making me do all the work for him the way he longed for his dad to turn up trumps at last and rush to his aid? He said this sounded right in theory but he didn't feel that way about his father, even when he tried. 'When it comes to him, I am anaesthetized,' he said.

I asked him about life between the sessions and was dismayed to realize that for a year he had been co-operating in the sessions and seeing the sense in what I was saying, but then going away and forgetting all about it till the next session. He never had any reactions to my holidays, just accepted them philosophically, though he could see how another person could, in theory, feel upset about an enforced break in their therapy.

Then the lease on his flat ran out and he was forced to stay with his parents until the new flat was free. I jumped at the chance to help him contact some of the denied emotions toward his family. He understood everything I said about this but on seeing his parents again he just felt empty, and could not manufacture feelings to suit me. I could not get him to see the purpose was to suit *him*, though as ever he saw it 'in theory'.

In order to take advantage of his being at home I tried to speed things up by encouraging him to catalogue once again the incidences of his father's appalling neglect throughout his boyhood, as well as his mother's collusion in it. His stories made me feel furious on his behalf, but he showed no emotion, and could have been discussing the soccer results. Once again I drew his attention to his lack of indignation about what had happened to him as a youngster. He smiled a genuinely sweet smile and said 'Please, don't fret so about it Wyn. You're more upset than me.'

I realized then what must have been staring me in the face for months. The whole unconscious point of his behaviour was to make me feel his denied feelings for him. Therapy was patently not bringing any change, yet he came, regular as clockwork, always on time, always providing lots of interesting material. There was no way he was going to leave therapy because he needed me to contain what for him would be uncontainable feelings. His terror of losing his girlfriend yet refusing to take any practical steps in his career that would mollify and keep her was explained by the fact he had projected all his denied emotions into her also (she hated his family), so they were simply no longer available to him. He was incapable of using his anger and disappointment as others might, to motivate him to succeed *despite* his parents if he couldn't succeed *because* of them.

What remained was for me to find a way of returning the disowned feelings to him in a form he could begin to tolerate, and so help him make a real break, rather than the fake one he claimed he'd made years ago, from the parents to whom he was still enslaved.


WORKING THROUGH (REVISITING)

I shall say little about this except to remind readers of what they already know but doubtless, like me, find easy to forget. Namely, that 'working over and through' constitutes most if not all of the therapy, once the Assessment is done. It is the sometimes tedious, even boring part of treatment that nonetheless cannot be rushed. Material is visited and revisited, first from this direction then that. The therapist makes a well-thought-through interpretation, which is confirmed again and again by subsequent material. Using different words, metaphors, allusions, she tries to get the patient to see it too, but he nods politely and ignores it. Six or seven sessions later, hallelujah, the penny suddenly drops: the patient sees it for himself and of course takes all the credit.

It matters not how skilled and experienced the therapist is. It is in the nature of psychotherapy to be sometimes painfully slow as well as circular and repetitive. It is vital we do not blame patients when they creep and crawl toward insight instead of galloping, which would be much more flattering to our 'egos'. It is important too that newly qualified and none too confident therapists do not come to believe that what experienced therapists call 'working through' is actually evidence for their inadequacy. Lightning cures in the consulting room only occur in films and on the telly.


TRANSFERENCE

If the therapist classifies that part of the interactional process which is transference as anything else and persists in this error she will find herself in deep clinical trouble. On the other hand it is critical that in her eagerness to be 'psychodynamic' she does not classify process as transference before she is really sure. When in doubt, wait for more evidence.

Neither is transference the cut-and-dried entity it is often assumed to be. The perception of the transferred-onto-person by the transferrer (if it *is* a person: it could as well be a place or a set of circumstances) is generally accurate in some degree but special qualities or tendencies of that person or situation are, from an objective observer's point of view, exaggerated, out of sync with other qualities. But this begs the question: what is accurate perception anyway? One man's healthy self-assertion is for another man downright bossiness.

When we speak of transference we are discussing shades of meaning and emphasis that sometimes dominate the foreground of the transferrer's perceptions and sometimes recede, albeit hovering, awaiting a comeback, to the middle- or background. Transference does not refer to some static delusion about a person or situation that the transferrer has dragged into the present, direct from his pram. Transference can be weak or strong and the therapist should be aware of the intensity of transference as it waxes and wanes from session to session, occasionally disappearing and suddenly returning with a vengeance. Too many therapists feel quite smug once they have nailed down the transference, as if from now on it is more or less dealt with, needing only occasional reinterpretation when the patient forgets. But it is they who forget that the word *dynamic* pertains to *movement*. Psychodynamic process is always on the march: now you see it, now you don't; now it is important and now it isn't.

A supervisee was treating Gwendoline, a single thirty-four-year-old university lecturer who was dissatisfied and restless with her life despite great outward success. She was one of non-identical twins and her sister could not be more different. She was married to a busker-cum-pavement artist and lived with him and their two toddlers in a squat. According to Gwendoline they survived on baked beans and pot.

Because of institutional policy this was to be a short therapy. The supervisee accurately assessed the rivalrous relationship between the sisters to be the focus of the work. The father had been a diplomat who took his wife everywhere with him, leaving the girls with a procession of nannies and au pairs. Forced to rely on each other, they became very close. But during teen years when each attempted to assert their separateness, the other twin found herself a string of boyfriends while Gwendoline (in the supervisee's view) became murderously envious, which she coped with by adopting a motherly and condescending role with regard to the 'wayward' sister while she herself studied for endless exams which she effortlessly passed, claiming this, not promiscuity, was the true path to female liberty.

The supervisee reported that she herself was always seen by Gwendoline as a scrupulously neutral referee (perhaps, in part, the fair and kind mother Gwendoline would like to have had?). There was no transference of any note here: all the psychological intensity was between the two women.

In the sixth session Gwendoline related how she'd endured a sleepless night, tossing and turning, furious at her sister's callous disregard of her feelings. The sister had borrowed her car at great inconvenience to Gwendoline who had had to bus in to the university and forgo her weekly shopping trip to Sainsbury's. The car had come back late, dumped at her gate without even a note of thanks. It was littered with toffee papers and there was a girlie magazine on the back seat ('Heaven help their children!'). Worst of all there was a distinct aroma of hash.

The supervisee had heard this kind of thing many times. She saw how Gwendoline always bent over backwards for her sister, ostensibly to be of help, but actually to catch her out and find cause to attack her. The magazine she saw as a painful reminder to Gwendoline of her sister's free and easy attitude to sex, which she always claimed was dangerous to her nephew and niece but of which she really felt envious.

The supervisee's confidence was on this occasion unfounded. The patient did not respond with her usual self-justifying protestations followed by a grudging agreement to think about it: she was sulky and withdrawn rather than indignant. On leaving at the end of the session Gwendoline sniffed. 'It's stale in here. You should open some windows.'

The supervisee had failed to make the links that would have brought her to a transference interpretation of the session's events. Assuming the material to mean what it had always meant, it never occurred to her that today she, not the twin, was in the line of fire.

On the day of the reported session the supervisee had been given a room next door to her usual one because of a radiator flooding. Not wishing to burden her patient with irrelevant information, and as the new room was right next door, she just said, 'We're in here today.' No apology, no explanation. On the coffee table were women's magazines with a how-to-keep-your-man quiz advertised on the cover of the top one – shades of the girlie magazine. And though it was true the room was stuffy, Gwendoline's remarks sounded to me very like the complaint about the smell of drugs in the car. The therapist that day was being experienced no longer as a helpful referee but as a heartless and morally suspect sister.

## Function 5: Working With the Transference

It could be argued that part of all experience is transference. Human beings learn to survive and adapt through transferring lessons previously learned to present, untested situations and working out how much 'fit' there is, whether the lessons as they stand or in some adapted version might work once again, or whether the terror of facing something quite strange must be faced in order that new lessons can be added to the repertoire.

The human animal will find ways of making new situations familiar and therefore manageable, by nudging them wherever possible into the same shape as past experiences. When this is achieved with almost total disregard for any new and different elements in the situation then we are in the area of transference. It amounts to a distortion of the new situation/person, to force it into a semblance of the old that any observer could identify but to which the transferrer is blind. How many times have I heard from sage colleagues: 'So-and-so's got a new bloke, but she can't see that under the charm he's the same as all her others.'

Given that transference is one of the mightiest pillars supporting the edifice of psychoanalysis, it is hardly surprising that working with it is set down here as one of the psychotherapist's main functions. Despite its centrality – or perhaps because of it – trainees go earnestly prospecting for transference like gold and often miss what is under their nose. I recall vividly my trainee days when it was my turn to present a case to the seminar and I had been unable to detect any transference – I felt as if I were about to face a firing squad.

An awful lot of mystical nonsense is talked and written about transference. It is neither mysterious nor holy, but a perfectly ordinary aspect of human functioning that becomes highlighted in the therapeutic setting because unlike social exchanges when two people meet, one person is deliberately unrevealing about herself, thus driving the other to test and test the therapist's personality to find out if he, the patient, is welcome, and if this is a safe place. The patient therefore projects onto her assumptions, expectations, hopes and fears from previous encounters in an attempt to put himself in some kind of manageable relation to this important person on whom he is relying to get well.

All that he transfers, to the therapist and other key people in his current life, should assist the therapist in understanding him. It isn't *finding* the transference that can be helpful for patients,

31

but the sensitive manner of *working with* the transference when it pops up of its own accord.

A quick test for transference is to wait till something feels awry in the session, the material continuing to make little sense. Now think: what if you were to replay what the patient is telling you and feeling about you (or some other central person in his life – boss, girlfriend, bank manager) in a completely different setting much earlier in his life while his identity was still forming? If you can only find the right setting or situation then what he is doing and saying will make perfect sense. If you are stuck you might even ask him to help you in this exercise – he has all the data after all.

Transference then, might be said to be the right reaction in the wrong situation.

I gather the above-mentioned technique, stumbled over in dire necessity by most therapists, now has a technical term attached to it: recontextualizing. For example, should the patient complain that the therapist doesn't care about him really, it's just a job to her, he's just one more statistic, when in fact the therapist is so concerned about him she has just agreed to extra sessions even though officially she has no vacancies, one has to assume he is transferring these negative qualities to her. But where from? He's just been telling her about his gallstones and the dreadful opera-tion where he felt like a slab of meat carved up by unfeeling butchers. He is transferring from the surgeon to the therapist. But who came before the surgeon and before that person? And how, when, where and why was this belief in the malevolence of others reinforced rather than disconfirmed or modified? To answer this you will need to trace or reconstruct all his early contexts, when such complaints would have been as appropriate as they were accurate.

Good therapists have mastered the art of working with cueing and transference simultaneously. Reciprocal cues, sent and received accurately, be they verbal or non-verbal, conscious or unconscious, keep the reality-based communicational bridges open; they nourish, maintain and strengthen the therapeutic alliance so that transferen-tial interpretations can be borne. Readers will know from their own experiences as patients just how threatening to one's self-image and confidence such interpretations can be. It is essential the patient feels the therapist to be on his side.

There is a fuller exploration of transference and some of its less common (or less talked about) manifestations in Chapter 10.

*Function 6: Making Interventions*

Chapter 8 looks in some detail at the whole business of making interventions, the how rather than the what or why of therapy.

An intervention, be it a question, a prompt, a nod or grunt, or a fully-fledged interpretation, may be technically correct but the mode and timing of its delivery can make or mar the patient's acceptance and consideration of it. Albeit with the best will in the world, I have said some pretty foolish things to patients in my time, and I am amazed how often my errors have been overlooked or even gratefully received because the patient detected the goodwill behind them. Of course on occasion this is a bit of transference, the patient experiencing the therapist as a god who can do no wrong, but all the same I am constantly surprised and gratified by those patients who regard me as anything but a deity yet are willing to draw a veil over clumsy interventions and struggle on with the therapeutic endeavour in spite of them.

These comments serve as an introduction only. The subject is elaborated on in Chapter 8.

*Function 7: Making the Assessment*

Psychotherapy is such a complicated proceeding it is tempting to try and simplify it by putting its many aspects into some kind of hierarchy of importance. In practice this is impossible, for where transference interpretation is the keynote of one person's treatment, catharsis and cueing may characterize another's with virtually all the transference manifestations linked to some person outside the therapy. Some patients use a therapist one way, some another; that is their right. All therapies are different, even if they share common but differently arranged features.

If I were pressed to name the cornerstone of the kind of therapy that is feasible and desirable in the public sector (or that part of the private sector used by patients unwilling to have or unable to afford psychoanalysis) I would say it must surely be the Assessment. I use a capital letter here to distinguish it from the largely administrative and usually cursory assessment that is made of patients to see who is available to treat them, when and how, given current staffing restraints, medical rotas and existing caseloads.

Neither do I mean the purely clinical assessment that comes up with a psychiatric diagnosis through which suitability for that institution's or that team's methods or ideological approach can be measured. I refer rather to an Assessment conducted *with* the patient, not done to him or about him in his absence. Properly done, this Assessment can be seen as a miniature version of the therapy to come. The Assessment is to therapy what the single human cell is to the whole organism; it carries all the genetic material required for successful growth and specialization. It is the template, the foundation, the compressed potential for the complete treatment process.

So important is this Assessment in my view that I have devoted two chapters to it later in the book. Under the rubric of Assessment will be found also the intimately related issues of making a therapeutic alliance, building a dynamic formulation and making a proper contract.

## Function 8: Getting Supervised

This is one topic that sends me straight to my soapbox. No therapist should be let loose on patients without supervision facilities. Many employers regard supervision as a luxury and fail to see why someone who is qualified should need to discuss her cases with anyone else. Such people need educating, help to see that it is as unethical and irresponsible as it is dangerous to meddle in someone's deeply private feelings, hurts, memories and thoughts without adequate recourse to the second opinion of a more experienced practitioner.

Giving and receiving supervision will be examined in depth in my forthcoming book, *The Supervisory Couple in Broad Spectrum Psychotherapy*, Free Association Books.

CHAPTER 3

# Reassessing the Therapist's Functions: Functions 9 and 10

## Function 9: Operating as GP to the Mind

Understandably, most new professions ally themselves with older but similar professions as a route to credibility and respect. The renaming and upgrading of training for ambulance staff – now called paramedics – is a case in point, the very word *medic*, not to mention the apparatus and electronic gadgetry they carry, showing where their allegiance lies.

In the same way, people that used to be condescendingly referred to as 'only counsellors' (implying they would not recognize the Unconscious if it got up and hit them with a mallet) have redesignated themselves (with some exceptions, many of whom wish to disassociate themselves from the psychodynamic tradition) as psychotherapists. The justification for this is that the monopoly of psychoanalytic training and practice by two or three hallowed organizations (all of them in London; heaven help aspiring Glaswegian therapists!) has at last been broken. New institutes and associations have and still are proliferating, many excellent, some strange and experimental, and some downright awful.

Naturally the new psychotherapists wanted a home, and senior 'relatives' for professional protection. They have turned their eyes, mistakenly I believe, toward their sister discipline of psychoanalysis, itself relatively new, and because of its professional insecurity still largely wedded to medicine. It was not until the 1970s that non-medically qualified people, however experienced and/or qualified in related helping professions, could expect, save in the most exceptional of circumstances, to be taken on for psychotherapy training. Hence the appellation 'counsellor' – if training is not allowed in through the front door, it will surely creep in the back. Still, every non-medical but well-trained counsellor I met in those early days felt tolerated rather than welcomed by the psychoanalytic establishment. This tension and suspicion between the 'true heirs' and the 'adopted children' persists to this day.

The result of this attempt to shelter beneath psychoanalysis was that the few established psychotherapy training bodies – who might be expected to sympathize with and welcome the newcomers, for had not these bodies too waged a long fight to be properly accredited? – simply tightened up their entry requirements, leaning closer than ever to the psychoanalytic church for fear of contamination by the counselling heresy. A hierarchy of training bodies then developed, the most exclusive, expensive and with the lengthiest courses becoming arguably more psychoanalytic than the Institute of Psychoanalysis or the Tavistock Institute, when what they ought to have been doing was promoting a broader church, or even a separate, if fraternal one.

This purist philosophy still exists today. Those unfortunates who live outside London and/or cannot acquire funding, never mind leave from work several hours a week for years on end, have to satisfy themselves with less prestige-conscious trainings and often end up feeling inferior to those who have done 'proper' (that is, more psychoanalytically orthodox) training. There has to be a better way of preparing our future psychotherapists than this.

A pyramid of priestliness exists, though it is rarely admitted openly. Doctors-cum-psychoanalysts are at the apex, then graduates of the oldest, lengthiest and costliest London-based courses, next graduates of 'other' courses (by this far down the details scarcely matter), and then the Untouchables, those who really are inadequately trained, their courses not requiring them to be a patient or have ongoing supervision. Such is the demand for psychological help that many such people still find employment.

While impossible to prove, it is an open secret that some educational and NHS establishments often turn a blind eye to inadequate training so as to be able to save money by paying a low salary no properly qualified therapist would accept. Tragically, many gifted, highly qualified therapists are thus driven into private practice when they could perform a vital role, especially in recruitment and training, within the public sector.

In an attempt to avoid accusations of quackery by the public, maintain their position in the hierarchy and maybe even assuage their feelings of inadequacy, most therapists scoot about for postgraduate courses and workshops or write arcane (and often unintelligible) texts so as to get a leg up the said pyramid of priestliness beyond which stretches the bare blue heaven of psychoanalysis – not an angel of broad spectrum therapy in sight, nowhere a bird of institutional dynamics, no rainbow of group, family, couple therapy.

Let me make very clear that I am not anti-psychoanalysis. In fact I am rather conservative about it. I do not believe in trying to dismember it and then reconstitute it in some quicker, cheaper form, so the therapy world and his brother can practise the discipline at the drop of a hat. Its uniqueness must be protected and aided to grow. Its most eminent personalities should go on writing their books and giving their lectures and we Broad Spectrum Clinical Therapists working daily 'at the face' need to go on reading and hearing the latest ideas. But who ever writes or talks about our idiosyncratic work, the parts of it with which psychoanalysts never have to deal? There is more, much more to psychotherapy than psychoanalysis.

Psychoanalysis is not just a grander form of psychotherapy; it is significantly different in its adherence to strict technique and constant attention to the workings of the unconscious. Applied at the wrong time, to a fragile patient, this can be positively harmful, as any competent analyst would agree, whereas Broad Spectrum Therapists in the public, voluntary, charity and church sectors, or those in private practice taking on a wide range of patients rather than just a few for 'pure' analysis, can vary their approach while still remaining psychodynamically oriented. Analysts' and therapists' psychological terrain and many techniques are similar, but the Broad Spectrum Psychotherapist will handle her caseload and deploy these techniques (and others not in the analytic repertoire) very differently to the psychoanalyst. Her pacing is different as is her Assessment (see Part Two). She will offer therapeutic services tailored for each particular patient rather than selecting the 'right' patient for just one, albeit rigorous, method of working.

In short, the Broad Spectrum Psychotherapist functions more like a GP than the analyst, who functions as a specialist. Specialists only see selected patients: what's the point of taking one's ingrowing toenails to a brain surgeon, or asking the brain surgeon to run the doctor's surgeries in the hope of finding one brain tumour? From a *clinical* point of view analysis and therapy have a complementary not a competitive relationship, while *functionally* the Broad Spectrum Therapist is much more like the GP except she is a general treater of the mind rather than the body (even though it is well recognized that these are not so separate as once supposed).

Increasingly, GP practices offer a small psychotherapy service so that many emotionally upset patients, acute and chronic, are kept 'within the family', seen in familiar surgery surroundings so they do not have to brave the local mental hospital to visit a stranger who turns out to be a busy consultant psychiatrist who soon passes them on to someone lower down the hierarchy, who might well be on rotation and abandon them within a few weeks.

But whatever her actual setting, the Broad Spectrum Therapist operates similarly to the GP in that from the outset she will see anyone who wishes to consult her, and knows a range of referral

37

sources if it turns out she cannot help. She accepts that different patients will need different kinds of treatment and trims her wick accordingly.

This is not the way a psychoanalyst works (unless he is trained as an analyst but practises as an NHS psychiatrist, which by definition means broad spectrum work). His private setting is much more isolated from other agencies: ordinarily, if at all, he would not participate in a team 'treatment package', attend case conferences or review medication with colleagues, psychiatric medication on the whole being frowned upon as the agent of resistance. Whereas, depending on the case, a GP to the Mind therapist might sit with a patient for weeks, patiently waiting for medication to render a psychotic or profoundly depressed person accessible and motivated, before tapering off drugs and increasing the pace and depth of the joint work, with the advantage of what by now is a rock-solid Therapeutic Alliance.

On occasion other family members may need to be interviewed or referred to other therapeutic agencies. It is very rare for an analyst to do this.

In summary then, we might say the Broad Spectrum Psychotherapist's treatments, unlike the psychoanalyst's, are blended affairs; the main ingredients, along with her and the analyst's shared preoccupation with the unconscious, are those of the modern GP – prevention (this subsumes support, it being supportive to prevent illness and preventive to support healthy functioning), containment, education, management, crisis intervention, and letting herself be used. I will try to illustrate these ingredients by use of abbreviated case material, though it has to be recognized that several of them mix and mingle within one case. I will begin at the end: letting herself be used.

BEING USED

If you wanted to make friends with a certain child you had not met before, say a colleague's shy or anxious toddler, how would you go about it? Like most sensitive and sensible grown ups you would probably refrain from forcing your presence onto her, but would allow her to size you up, look you over and work out how she might use you once contact had been satisfactorily established and you had passed all her security procedures. You might end up as the dragon in her play, the narrator of her story or admirer of her teddy, after which there is a basis on which to build a closer relationship. This is your reward for having had the sense to 'ignore' her and allow her to take the lead.

Seeing a new patient for therapy can be just like this. Some patients welcome the structured opening similar to the doctor's 'Where does it hurt?', but others, more frightened or suspicious, like to inch their way forward, cueing and re-cueing (like the child's security tests) before deciding what to make of the therapist and in what way to use her.

At this early stage her psychological stillness along with her unspoken observations on the patient's behaviour and attitude toward her will prove far more valuable than linking and interpreting at him, which so soon in the endeavour usually represents an attempt to cope with the therapist's own anxiety, not only in a new situation, but one where she rightly senses she, not the patient, is the object of assessment.

It is imperative that a patient needing to conduct the first session this way be allowed to proceed unhindered by questions and elaborations from the therapist, who must learn not to be in charge all the time. The session is for the patient's use, not the therapist's performance.

Guy was a thirty-five-year-old American doctoral student at London University, unable to finish his thesis despite two extensions. He wanted 'very private' therapy and his GP gave him my name.

He was a huge, muscular man possessed of a series of peaked caps and lumberjack-style checked shirts, yet he was always excessively careful with my furniture and fabrics, crossing my carpet on tiptoe. I nicknamed him at once 'my gentle giant'.

In our first meeting he sat on his hat, squirming with what looked like fear and embarrassment. I was rather perturbed by his agitation, his gasping for air every few seconds, and his profuse perspiring. I waited, as he hummed and hawed, starting a sentence then stopping, finally announcing he had a terrible family and really serious problems. Did I deal with that kind of thing? I read this as, 'Can you stand it, as I can't?', but I said simply that yes, I did.

He then launched into a horrendous account of repeated rape at the age of six by an uncle, and a savagely puritanical British public school father who, on being told of the rape, reminded him the uncle was rising fast in the armed forces and in a man's world you have to expect that kind of thing, before refusing to discuss it ever again.

This material (the above is but the briefest summary) came out in a torrent, the gap between gasps for air getting longer and longer, his squirming becoming less as the poison (so it felt to me) was discharged.

During the remaining two-and-a-half years of therapy, after which his money ran out and he had to go home, alas without his doctorate, he never once permitted me to mention 'those things' again, hoping like his father that they might just go away.

The agitation vanished. I saw bouts of suicidal melancholia in the consulting room, wild hopes and plans for the future, hopeless yearnings for a partner that made him weep silently, week after week. I listened to long lectures on artillery and American politics, detailed and regular accounts of his efforts at reducing noise pollution in his rented accommodation, lessons on the finer points of baseball – but never ever again did I witness that panic. I came to feel that preventing that panic was the only service I managed to do him, for if ever I hinted at 'those things' he would say: 'You are right, I know what you're getting at, but not now Wyn, please.' The rest of the session would be spent on his analysis of the weather forecast or the pros and cons of giving up sugar in his coffee.

A few times I felt he might break down, or attempt suicide, and twice or thrice I thought him unhealthily euphoric. All of the time I believed him to be hovering in some twilight world between sanity and madness. Sometimes he asked me to teach him how to talk to girls and again, if I so much as hinted it might be worth investigating what frightened him about them, he would grit his teeth and say with forced politeness: 'Now don't tell me I am changing the subject Wyn, but did you see the ice hockey last night?'

Guy used me like a safe deposit box for his darkest conflicts, fears and fantasies about sex and violence, but when even I failed to contain them all, he would go 'European walkabout', as he described it. This involved trips to Second World War sites: mass graves, concentration camps and such. Then it was the poorest parts of Hungary, Poland, and finally he must walk the most dangerous streets of Belfast. He understood 'the Troubles' better than most English people and rehearsed with me the kind of tactful things he might say should he get involved in political debate. As ever, I was impressed by his survival skills, but oh how I longed for him to announce a quiet sojourn in the Lake District!

I had to accept though, that these places of ravagement and despair represented his internal world and to visit and survive them with nothing but a phrase book and a backpack was deeply necessary for him. On his return he would always tell me in great detail about these places, but would only discuss their history and politics, never their deeper meaning for him.

This case illustrates how various are the GP to the Mind's approaches. She may well treat one patient much as a psychoanalyst would, but with another, like Guy, she eschews too much interpretation as dangerous and instead adopts a mainly support-ive role, buttressing reality for him when it wavers, containing catharsis and/or despair when it erupts, and perhaps plying a little insight now and then when she judges he might possibly use it without ill effect. But always he is in charge: if he says stop it is unequivocally stop.

Some patients have to regulate how much and how often they can accept therapy. To some, concentrated attention from a thera-pist is seen as undeserved luxury or wicked self-indulgence, to others evidence of no backbone, a weakness; while a few see it as punishment, atonement, or as the confessional. Therapists can be forgiven for believing therapy to be 'a good thing' and for assum-ing its purpose is healing, but it is only by letting themselves be used that they learn how it is experienced by, and what it means to, their patient.

Mrs Bloxham, called 'Sugar' by her vast family, was sixty-four, with chronic irritable bowel syndrome which worsened when she was depressed, and violent mood swings in both directions. The GP in whose surgery I ran a weekly clinic was worried about the amount of mood controlling drugs on which he had unsuccessfully tried her, and asked me to assess her.

At first she clearly distrusted me yet seemed at the same time hungry – no, *starving* – for contact. Talking very fast and without pause for breath she twirled before me to show me her new rinse, then sat down to show me pictures of her dog that she had just collected from the chemist, telling me about every plant in the garden as she pointed it out in the prints.

I showed polite but not excessive interest and continued to let her 'walk round me'. Gradually her talk came to centre on herself, assuring me she'd be fit as a fiddle and happy as a sandgirl if it wasn't for these black moods when nothing seemed worth while. But she cooked and sewed and painted and knitted; why look, every-thing she was wearing she had made herself. (True, she dressed beautifully in bright but tasteful style, and never wore the same outfit twice to come and see me.)

Long before I was able to contribute any worthwhile utterance I had learned from her circling of me that she was deeply ashamed of her depression and feared I would see it the same way. Throughout our work together she would never take as much as I offered, and pointing this out to her she would grin and say, 'You can't have everything in this world, can you?', before racing off on some safe, chatty topic.

As her trust grew I risked a few shots in the dark. '*Why* can't you have everything? D'you fear somebody might take it away again or something?' Her eyes filled with tears and her body sagged. 'See, just like that, fine one minute ...'

She was bewildered by her symptoms, but further gentle prompting helped her put feelings and memories to these particular tears. She had been brought up in the war, the only child of an adored mother. While Dad was away fighting and the winters grew cold ('no central heating in them days, no duvets neither') Sugar and mum cuddled up at night in the marital bed, warm and secure.

Just before she was fourteen, her father returned and she was banished to her old bedroom, made to endure the sounds of their lovemaking, feeling terribly left out.

This pattern of apparently euphoric chatter followed by sudden sad dips into her past continued through our five sessions (the maximum allowed by practice policy). By the second session I still had not felt the maternal transference I had expected to feel. Then, when she was fitting old feelings to another bout of tears, I suddenly realized who I did represent – the sibling she longed and begged her mother for, but never came. The gossipy intimate tone, the girl talk of clothes and nail polish, the jokes about the awfulness of men and in-laws, was her way of getting some part of what she had missed as a teenager and young adult, through me.

Sugar declined private therapy with me, on the grounds that she could not spend her husband's money; but really, I think, because she had problems in taking anything for herself. She was a compulsive, but unconsciously resentful, caregiver. (She had three children, plus one adopted, several fostered who still regard her as mum, a dependent husband and hordes of grandchildren and honorary nephews and nieces, all of whom regarded Sugar as 'a dear' and abused her generosity, hospitality and domestic talents while assuring themselves and each other that she loved having demands made of her, it had always given her a meaning in life.) How very (sadly) true.

But in our second lot of five sessions, some months later, as we planned a Christmas trip to Capri for herself and her husband alone, she quipped that she was considering changing her name from Sugar to Vinegar!

By now she had much more insight into her depression and at home had started standing up for herself more. She still insisted on taking care of me by forcing herself to cheer up after every sad bit in the session, so I wouldn't be 'put upon' as she called it. It became safe though, to look at her need to bring me things; recipes, clothes patterns and such. She accepted this took time away from helping her with her depression but she convinced me she was getting a lot out of being able to talk to me as a sister, so we developed a half conscious cueing system where each session we did a bit of sistering, then, eye on the clock, I would discreetly call a halt.

I never got her to accept the need for regular therapy, and as I write she waits patiently for the months to go by till it is permissible for her to get on my practice waiting list again. She has been off all medication for eighteen months.

I allowed myself to be used in her chatty, some would say anti-therapeutic, way for a good while before discussing it with her, in order to gain her trust. Imagine my saying straight off: 'Mrs Bloxham, we are not here to admire your hair' or worse, 'I think you are showing me your dog because it really represents you and you want me to love it as you do.' I can hear her riposte: 'You're off your trolley dear,' and that would have been the last I saw of her.

Regarding my standing for the sister she never had, I chose to supply, rather than interpret, her emotional needs just enough for her to want to stay in therapy, which she clearly saw both as deliciously tempting and terribly wicked.

Rather than have no therapy at all, for the moment I am letting her decide when and how much she can bear to take.


CRISIS INTERVENTION

When a sudden external event such as bereavement, desertion by a partner, discovery of a spouse's adultery or loss of job strikes an already stressed or distressed person who has no coping reserves on which to draw, he can be said to be in crisis.

This distinction from ordinary symptomatology is important, because the reaction of people in crisis is not measurable by the same standards applied to routine patients. In crisis people can behave totally out of character, smashing furniture in rage, weeping morosely, attempting suicide, losing their memory, or going temporarily mad. Alarming though this may be, it is an attempt by the person's mind to absorb the shock, and often (though not always) dramatic symptoms subside quickly into a numb misery that the GP to the Mind therapist can speedily get to grips with, often circumventing hospitalization or medication that keeps the patient quiet but fails to address his need to come to terms with his trauma.

Bill, fifty, ran a small popular nightclub in the city, his wife Martha helping him in the business. In recent years she had become alcoholic, which Bill seemed to have dealt with by trying not to notice, in spite of friends' warnings, her frequent disappearances, and her drinking, swearing and fighting binges at the club when she was supposed to be working. Everyone agreed she was a lovely woman when sober but shook their heads at Bill's eternally blind eye. He paid her debts, cleared up the mess, did their two jobs and forgave her each time she vowed to get treatment, only to find her paralytic a few days later, often with another man.

This had been going on some years, when suddenly Bill was sued for divorce, Martha's affidavit containing lies about his beating her up and cheating her out of large amounts of money. His friends rallied round, but a few weeks later he was summoned to court, and when he learned that she was claiming their house and club as hers in a proposed once-and-for-all settlement, he collapsed, crying over and over that he couldn't face her in court. His heart was broken, how could she do this?

The night before the hearing his friends put him to bed and went home. One of the club's cleaning women arrived in the early hours, realized the dog was howling to be let out of the bedroom and found Bill asleep with an empty bottle of paracetamol at his side. Medical help was fetched at once.

Bill's GP, at whose practice I had a clinic and who had dealt with the emergency a couple of nights before, asked me to make an assessment before deciding on medication and management.

Bill was a sturdy, masculine, down-to-earth sort of chap, who grinned bravely at me when I met him in the waiting room, but broke down in tears as soon as he was in the consulting room. He said it had been a daft thing to do but he'd been desperate. He was ashamed he hadn't had the sense to crush the pills first, so he'd puked most of them up and made a right old mess of the carpet.

He was still greatly shocked so I just attended while he talked on and on, going over and over his story as if to try and get it straight in his own head. He was consumed with self-contempt for not being able to face Martha in court, for letting his pals down, for this endless weeping that had forced him to stop work and hand over the club to a friend for a bit.

He was most apologetic to me for his 'rambling on' and 'crying like a baby', but he jumped at my offer of another session next week. I judged him contrite rather than suicidal, but badly shocked as a result of having to face years worth of denied misery and pain all at once. I felt he needed more catharsis in a safe environment, not pills, and this view was confirmed the next time I saw him.

He cancelled our third session. It appeared the woman looking after the club, who had had her eye on him for ages, was taking him to America to visit his grown son who he had not seen for two years!

The relationship blossomed, but he was still very much in love with his wife. On his return home, he came to see me a few more times, then, wretched but under control, he said he wanted to soldier on alone, it was now all a question of time.

Despite the brevity of the intervention, the practice did Bill a good turn at a time when life was not worth living. Psychoanalysis is not designed to deal with such emergencies, and without a broad spectrum psychotherapist to assist, Bill could easily have ended up in hospital 'to be on the safe side', which would have injured his self esteem even more (if that were possible) and would certainly have resulted in numbing medication and a long convalescence.

MANAGEMENT

Sometimes the essence of a treatment turns out to have been its management. Along with containment and permitting the patient to use the therapist in his own way rather than the textbook's, good outcomes can be achieved for the right patient with only the most meagre interpretive work or attention to the transference.

Tony, thirty-nine, was an engineer referred to me privately by his GP, an old colleague of mine. His helpful letter summarized Tony's life to date. From a 'good' airforce family, he had been an able child but always in trouble at school. As a teenager he had been sent to psychologists who could do nothing with him because he was uncooperative. As a young man he engaged in petty crime and a bit of drug-pushing that necessitated a sudden 'holiday' in the Far East where he worked for a while on a freelance basis. Returning home he married and divorced in quick succession. There followed a quieter period of some ten years when he lived with a woman and their child, now six.

Last year Tony suddenly fell in love with a much younger woman, married her, moved her in and got her pregnant, while the other woman moved down the road and the child divided her time between the two households. Tony was a devoted father and maintained the child financially. After three months of marriage, violent quarrels broke out, culminating in Tony hitting his wife and threatening the unborn baby's life. His wife walked out, swearing never to return. Could I please help Tony stop his violence so he could get her back again?

It sounded a bit of a tall order, but I arranged to see him at once, only to find he had made four other appointments: one with another private therapist, one at Alcoholics Anonymous (he'd never had a drink problem), Relate, and an NHS community mental health scheme that hadn't got off the ground yet.

He arrived unshaven, trembling and very agitated, weighed down with DIY therapy books which he proceeded to lay out across my floor so I could recommend the best. Then he opened a manila folder and unscrewed his pen in a nervous but businesslike manner, ready to take down my every word.

I invited him to tell me what had been happening to him and he related the same facts as the GP, including the admission of many previous bouts of hitting women, of which he had always been ashamed afterwards, but had assumed it was incurable and no one would want to take on such a bastard for treatment in any case.

The poor man was in absolute panic, writing long daily letters to his wife begging her forgiveness, waylaying her at work (but she wouldn't talk to him), sending her flowers, promising he'd go for treatment, take any pills necessary, no matter what the side effects. He begged her to come and talk, bringing bodyguards with her if she wanted; but it was clear she would have nothing to do with him. His plan now was to get treatment fast and prove to her he could change. Could I cure him? Could I guarantee a cure? If not, where else might he go?

I explained that in order to assess whether I could help, I would need to hear a lot more from him about his childhood and background. However, this could prove too disturbing when he was already feeling so out of control and frightened. First we must aim for a bit more calm and accept that no miracle was going to bring back his wife overnight.

At this he buttoned his jacket, straightened his hair and made heroic efforts to sit still. We looked then at all his appointments. On balance I thought it wise not to discourage him from keeping them, providing he let them know he was seeing me for Assessment. He was so badly shaken I felt it was critical he still felt in charge of *something* or he may make an impulsive suicide bid.

He was impressed by the structured approach of the AA ('I just substitute "life force" for "God" and I can buy the rest'), so had pretended to be an alcoholic and signed up, there and then. I would rather he had talked to me first, but not wanting to undermine him I wished him well of it and got him to agree to keep me abreast of developments at AA in our sessions. He didn't like the other therapist, and Relate sensibly suggested he stick with one therapist at a time. The NHS project put him on their waiting list for a psychodrama group, but he agreed he had quite enough drama in his life already, so we let that one lie.

The next bit of management then, was a clear contract: (1) No other therapist allowed without discussing with me first; (2) I could contact his GP at any time; (3) If he hit me, therapy stopped then and there, no second chance; (4) I could guarantee nothing but I would undertake to help us both understand where and how this violence developed, once his life outside had quietened down. Until it had, I would see him once a week on a supportive basis. He spat on both palms and held out a hand: 'You've got yourself a deal.'

During the next year we managed only one conventional therapy session unclouded by external events. There was a new crisis each week. First the wild grief and protest at the court order stopping him pestering his wife. Then the shutting down of all communication from his in-laws. He was dreadfully hurt. I got lost in the maze of writs, reports, court hearings and unaccountable deferments to do with his wife's demands for personal maintenance. I tried to work out why Tony was hiding behind trees to avoid having writs served on him if the man only left them on the mat, but he seemed quite certain it was the right thing so I didn't argue. He got information from the public library and Citizens Advice Bureau, and conducted his own case, including correspondence with his wife's extremely unpleasant solicitor. Given something practical to do he rose to the occasion, but the euphoria was short-lived and despair rushed back. Such was the risk and the serious disturbance of sleep as the months went by, antidepressants were prescribed by his GP, but they seemed to make little difference.

Then his wife went to the police with accusations of marital rape (nine months after the alleged event) and the affidavits started again, rapidly followed by a run-in with the Child Support Agency. He was outraged that he was expected to support the new baby but not allowed to see her, not even have a photograph of her. He would not accept he was the 'absent parent' as the wife had done the absenting, albeit with reasonable cause, but here he was getting professional help and longing to make amends.

As the pair had only been married a few weeks when they parted, the wife had to wait till a year was up before suing for divorce. He lived in dread and terror of the postman. He swore that all her submissions to the court were wildly exaggerated and with regard to this was eventually allowed to cross-examine her in court. Beforehand he released his fury, misery and sense of injustice in the therapeutic session, then treated me to a dress rehearsal of the proposed cross-examination. Perry Mason could have done no better. This dry run was essential management, but I longed for a chance to do some 'real therapy'.

There was just one quiet week when he felt strong enough to

look at his miserable childhood. His father had been a pilot and a great sportsman, but was tragically paralysed from the waist down in a car crash when Tony was six. His frustration was vented on Tony, whom he would throw across the room and force to crawl back on his knees, before repeating the whole process over and over again. As Tony grew up he could better protect himself but not fight back. You don't hit a man in a wheelchair, especially one you once admired and loved. His mother was timid, placatory and always on his father's side.

At some point in this session I found myself greatly moved, heard myself trying to show him the link between his past, his present inability to stand rejection from a sexual partner, and his father's sadism. Looking into his face as I spoke I saw hundreds of jigsaw pieces fall, nay cascade, into place. From that day he became quieter, more thoughtful and, praise be, more hopeful about the possibility of a 'cure'. A curse had been lifted.

The crises continued and I was drawn into management again when the judge ordered a welfare report on Tony over the question of access to the now three-month-old baby.

I knew Tony had changed but worried that there had been no working through of the material about his family. Would his new gentleness stand the test? We didn't have to wait long. The mother of his first child was in the picture again. She and his daughter had practically moved back in, but the mother was bitter about her previous rejection by Tony and did not want to be hurt again. She teased and provoked and undermined, gave and withheld sex at whim; in short, all the tried and tested ways of making him resort to violence. There were furious rows but he did not strike her and on each occasion was able to discuss it all calmly with her the next day.

Tony is now very sad rather than agitatedly depressed as before. When the agitation was at its height, he could not bear to even think of his original family. Just the mention of his parents would cause his body to jerk, his eyes to fill, and his chest pains to start. However, he completed his AA 'Ten Steps' programme and became something of a guru to his group, egging them all on to look at their childhoods! Those meetings were a great source of self-esteem to him when his confidence was zero, and they reduced a little of the terrible loneliness he suffered. He accepts now that the marriage is over, but goes on fighting for access, even supervised access. As there is no longer any point in placating his wife yet there have been no further violent incidents, perhaps I can assume the AA and I haven't done such a bad management job between us.

I would have liked more time, but Tony has been too distraught to work, so will not be able to pay me much longer. Meanwhile the

NHS has offered him a place in a psychodrama group after a year on their waiting list. I suspect this is a bit soon, but we have agreed the best policy is probably to suck it and see. I trust his judgement.

This treatment was far from ideal and far from complete, but it does illustrate some patients' drive to self-healing, which if contained and rechannelled rather than brought into line with an orthodox treatment plan that sometimes infantilizes and controls, the patient can mature, grow in wisdom and develop self-worth, as well as simply 'get better'.


EDUCATION

Having made a plea for certain patients to be allowed to use the therapist in their own way, I wish to emphasize now the need for others to be educated, prepared and/or trained to use her beneficially. Many patients will meet the therapy situation head-on in a way that for them is characteristic of all new situations, and much can be learned from simple observation of this; whereas others are cautious and reserved until time and a non-threatening interactional space, maintained by the therapist, makes it possible for them to proceed warily. Yet others are confused, anxious, prejudiced and appreciate being shown the ropes.

Mr Friedman was a senior civil servant in a dark city-suit who sat facing me as if strapped to a broomstick, under threat but on his dignity. All I knew from his colleague, an ex-patient, was that he was fifty, educated at a well known public school, married, and depressed for some years without knowing why.

My memory of our opening minutes of the first session goes something like this:

Mr F: (After an uncomfortable silence in response to my smile and lifting of enquiring eyebrows) 'I don't know what to say. What should I say?'

WB: 'You could say whatever is on your mind at the moment.'

Mr F: 'Word association, eh? I know about all that.' (Pause) 'Anything?'

WB: 'Mmm.'

Mr F: 'That's daft. I might want to start with what I had for breakfast.'

WB: 'It's as good a place as any.'

Mr F: (Disbelief, then challenge) 'Right, you're on. Let me think.

Muesli. With kiwi fruit and banana. Egg and bacon – lean, grilled tomato. Toast. Two cups of coffee. Look, this is stupid.'

WB: 'You seem to take a lot of trouble with breakfast.'

Mr F: 'What's wrong with that?'

WB: 'Nothing's wrong with it. I just wondered why.'

Mr F: 'You're supposed to be the one with the answers.'

WB: 'I'm supposed to provide breakfast?'

Mr F: 'Well, yes, I suppose so, in a way. I mean, well, I'm paying for this ... ' (embarrassed)

WB: (Raising of interested eyebrow, little smile)

Mr F: 'I made all the damn breakfasts when I was a kid. Every day. No one paid me.' (Stops, fidgets with tie)

WB: (Cueing him to continue) 'You made all the breakfasts?'

Mr F: 'Yes I did. I may be your typical civil servant now, nice car and house and everything. But my family were always hard up. There were five of us. Me, I'm the oldest. Dad was on night shift. I always made the breakfasts. Got to go to school with something in your stomach of a morning, get through the day ... ' (fidgets)

WB: 'And Mum?'

Mr F: 'Oh. Hypochondriac. Never up before midday. Always had a migraine. Couldn't be a headache like anybody else. Always ill. Aches and pains. "Rex darling, fetch the doctor." "Rex, darling, a little something on a tray for mummy."' (Silence) 'So I got to be quite an expert on breakfast. My wife does ours, I never go near a cornflakes packet if I can help it.'

WB: 'Because it brings back the feelings?'

Mr F: 'What feelings? Look, what has this got to do with anything? Time is money you know. What about this damn depression?'

WB: '"Where's my breakfast"?'

Mr F: 'I beg your pardon?'

WB: 'You come here, pay out good money and still have to get your own breakfast.'

Mr F: 'Well, you're sure as hell not going to give me any. A body could starve round here.'

WB: 'Indeed.' (Sympathetic)

Mr F: (Disconcerted) '"Indeed". What is that supposed to mean?'

WB: 'It means you want me to help you but you fear I'll let you down like your mother, so you put up this prickly exterior to protect yourself.'

Mr F: 'Prickly ... ? Well, you didn't help me get going. You just sat there smirking. I, well I – '

BOTH TOGETHER : '– had to get my own breakfast!' (Two big grins)

Mr Friedman had mugged up on psychotherapy but had only cognitively understood what he had read. His requirement that I explain myself was perfectly fair and his suspicions about my motives were based on genuine ignorance of the psychotherapeutic experience, not on paranoia or malice.

When I made another interpretive remark later in the session, he asked in some excitement: 'Oh, was that another bit of transference then?' I smiled assent *so as to send him to school with something in his stomach*, rather than destroying his optimistic mood by further interpreting his now 'eager pupil' transference, which was to colour our dealings for some time.

As a very unhappy and lonely child his solace was in learning; he loved school, as he came to love therapy once I had helped him get the hang of it. Therapists should not be too clever, feeling obliged to comment on everything they see. Rewarding the 'pupil' rather than interpreting at him, thus verbally smacking him over the wrists for being a pupil, helped build his self-esteem in relation to me, when in relation to his bored and ill mother he'd found none.

Another example of the Educative function:

Derek, forty-five, had three sportsgear shops and was the proud owner of two 1950s Jaguar cars and a collection of very expensive leather coats. His social and sex life was busy to say the least, but all his hectic activities did not prevent his sleep problems and panic attacks, when he would hide in the lavatory till it was over, terrified his secretary might find out and 'blab', thus destroying his man-about-town reputation. As it was a point of principle to have affairs with his secretaries, this made discovery of his symptoms even more threatening.

By the third session I had learned that Derek was the child of a single mother who died when he was less than a year old. He had a series of foster mothers, then went to a children's home, and then out of the blue a distant relative died leaving money in trust for his private education and he was sent to a minor, but very sadistic, public school, where at fifteen he got himself expelled. He took a job as a shop assistant, vowing to build up a successful business or bust.

At eighteen he traced his history, to discover that his mother, far from being the innocent maid whose babe had been cruelly ripped from her arms, had been a heroin addict too ill to care for him. She had dumped him at his grandmother's house and disappeared. The grandmother, who he could not remember, died soon after. This knowledge badly shocked him and he rushed into marriage with his

51

first proper girlfriend. The relationship was disastrous and they divorced two years later.

At twenty-six he owned his first shop. From then on he became ruthlessly self-interested and the business went from strength to strength.

He recounted all this 'boring ancient history' dutifully, saying he supposed I had to take a history, but the real trouble was getting these panic attacks under control. When could we start on that?

In the third session, he talked endlessly about the holidays he took, the first-class travel he always insisted on, the women he had 'pulled'. We, or rather I, had already talked about his need to impress me, but this had been dismissed outright. Today it was his sexual conquests. He'd had sex with his cleaner before leaving for the office this morning. He was taking his secretary to lunch, and had made a note to ring two other women for assignations as soon as he got home. Then he had an all night date with the wife of a friend.

This was a man so afraid of solitude, pitching him as it did into earlier experiences of abandonment, he compulsively phoned his women friends and then went out, usually with another woman, so that there would be return calls on his answer machine to listen to when he got home. He flatly refused to accept that he was lonely, or that there was anything unusual in his promiscuity.

'Come on Wyn, old love,' he said. 'Just because you're a bit past your sell-by date you don't have to spoil it for everybody else. I bet you were quite a goer in your time.'

I was very glad I was behind the couch ('Might as well have the works while I'm here') and not opposite him so he could witness my reaction! But I think I must admit it was this remark that decided me to take a more educative line with him. He was going abroad for six months shortly and I was sure he would not return to me if he hadn't made an alliance with me in the meantime. He launched into another anecdote about another seduction, and I wondered aloud why he felt it so important to squander his sexuality on women for whom he later felt little but contempt?

The response was predictable. 'Wha'd'ya mean, "contempt"? I *love* women. Hey, you're not going to do the loony lesbian feminist bit on me are you?'

'When you were a little boy and couldn't control anything, you never had a mum. Now that you're a powerful and sexy business-man and can control things, you go out searching for one, but because you distrust the lot of us, you abuse us as a way of getting your own back. That's what I mean by contempt.' Oh dear, I thought, was I lecturing him? Was *I* getting my own back?

'Whoa – wait a minute!' cried Derek, sitting bolt upright on the couch, then, remembering where he was, lying down again. 'Which hat did you pull that out of?'

'My therapist's hat,' I said. 'It's my job to help you look and see beneath the surface of things.' At least he was engaged now, rather than performing for and seducing me, after which I, too, would become an object of contempt.

'Well would you mind spelling out what you are talking about in words of one syllable so a poor shopkeeper can understand?'

Without being conscious of it till later, I lowered my voice, adopting the tone I used when my son was little and I'd sit behind his bed, as I now sat behind the couch, explaining the world and the things in it that frightened him.

'Let's say there are two Dereks: the grown up, intelligent, smartly dressed man of business, and the lonely motherless little boy inside him that lives on even though the grown up Derek locks him away. When the grown up Derek sees a good-looking woman he wants what grown men want, but the orphan child within sees the chance of some warmth, cuddles, home. Big Derek tells himself he's pulling crumpet, doing them a favour with his credit card and swish cars, but really it is he who desperately needs the favour. And when the woman is safely captured, phoning every night, little Derek's hatred of the mum – all the mums – that never shaped up, can come to the surface. She is thrown aside as worthless. Then the search, *little Derek's search*, for his missing mum starts all over again, with exactly the same outcome.'

There was a long silence. Derek had not moved a muscle. Then: 'Jee*zus!*' Therapy had started.

I am not normally given to long interventions, but here was an intelligent and able man determined to put me in the same category as the rest of my sex, and as a result of so doing could not take anything useful from me (desired or loathed women may be, but never *useful*). Every conventional therapeutic intervention was greeted with derision, after which he would try to tempt me again with tales of all that could be mine, should I play my cards right. (He had already seduced one therapist, and I have to confess that over the years with me he provided me with the names of some of the best restaurants in the region.)

Derek needed help to *actually* use me rather than an interpretation as to why he *couldn't* use me. Grown up, leather-coated, Jaguar-driving Derek could not hear my professional observations, but the lonely little boy he carried within was very susceptible to a story – his story – coming from a soothing source just behind his head.

CONTAINMENT

Metaphorically speaking, this is where a very distressed patient spills his guts onto the therapist's carpet, quite unable to contain them himself. The therapist scoops them up onto her lap, sorts through them with no show of distaste, stirs them about a bit, identifying which bit is what and where very roughly it belongs. Once crudely sorted, she either holds them out to their owner with the promise that they will be further sorted each time he comes, or she leaves them on the table for safe keeping until the next time when the patient might be ready to at least look at them, or some of them, with her support and attention.

Daphne was referred privately by a medical colleague, who assured her I did not bite, but when I went to collect her from my waiting room, expecting to find her on the sofa, she was standing rigidly to attention but trembling, as if her coat, hat and scarf were the only things that held her body together. When I invited her to come through to the consulting room, and led the way, she bolted out of the front door. I ran after her. She had stopped again at the gate, still rigid, still trembling. I thought of a rabbit paralysed by head-lights. I knew I mustn't touch her. I made soothing noises: 'Would you like to come in, just sit and talk?' That kind of thing.

She fixed my face with robotic stare lasting a full minute, then followed me in. I sat down and she remained standing. Then she wobbled on her feet, collapsed into the chair, and burst into tears. She wept throughout the session so I only heard about a quarter of what she was saying. Even that made little sense, as she jumped about in time and place and person, very confusedly. I gave up trying to follow and sat quietly till she got it all out bar the weeping, which sounded as if it would go on for ever.

Over the next four months, twice a week, we sifted and sorted this spillage, Daphne reliving before me all the trauma she had undergone but not been able to process, because the Self that should have done the processing was itself too fearful and doubting to even start. I made no interventions to speak of, but mainly listened and watched, as the story and re-enactment of her recent troubled years unfolded. (She was now thirty-eight.)

The first major trauma was her adored father's death, she and her mother having nursed him devotedly through a long illness. Her sister, who had always hated her venomously, was a doctor, and when the last days were to hand she took over, arranged admission to hospital and made sure all manner of drug treatments and undignified medical procedures, which Daphne knew her father would have hated, were administered. She also made sure the staff saw Daphne as eccentric, if not downright crazy, so Daphne was callously ignored throughout her father's last hours, her protests about his treatment falling on deaf ears.

There were pressing demands from her new teaching job at a boarding school. The anguished guilt about letting her father down was becoming unbearable, so the unfinished mourning for him along with the impotent rage at the sister was efficiently but unconsciously sealed in some deep chamber of her mind.

For the first time in her life she fell deeply in love, with a fellow teacher who she felt treated her with the same gentle affection as her father. She was blissfully happy. A few weeks after their engagement his mother interfered, there was a row and he ended the relationship in a cold formal letter refusing to discuss it further.

To her amazement he had already arranged for her possessions to be removed. Distraught, she left the school at once and for months after tried to get anyone there to give her information about her ex-fiance, but no one would answer letters or calls. He had worked there many years and the staff were a very tightly-knit group. She felt socially ostracized as well as rejected.

She began to be excitable, restless, tearful; then excruciating headaches started. Her doctor wondered about brain tumours and had tests done which were equivocal. Two of his colleagues disagreed over the diagnosis, one confident this was something rare and sinister, the other, a specialist, insisting this was a psychiatric matter: Daphne was 'an immature, over-emotional personality'. This difference of opinion confused and frightened her. She felt especially attacked by the suggestion she was a psychiatric case: hadn't she had this attitude from her doctor sister all her life, and especially recently over her father's death? The uncertainty over diagnosis continued, Daphne becoming more and more 'nervy' all the time, her fear and suspicion of doctors increasing.

Following further acute episodes of agitation which sometimes coincided with her period, she was dispatched to a well known hospital unit specializing in premenstrual tension. Here she was put on large doses of hormones and became even more agitated ('I felt like a guinea pig: I was indoctrinated: I felt I had no choice').

There was another round of medical consultations in which she felt infantilized and labelled as a malingerer, and in reaction to this would fly off the handle, give the medics a blistering telling-off, four letter words and all, before walking out. She was getting herself quite a reputation for aggression, whereas her internal experience was one of increasing terror.

By now terrified to trust anyone, but seriously doubting her own judgement too, Daphne became behaviourally disruptive, exhibiting panic then rage whenever anyone crossed her. Broken crockery and slashed tyres were the order of the day. Yet hearing it all from Daphne's point of view, the degree to which she felt abused by all around her though powerless to stop it, this behaviour made complete sense. Undoubtedly her emotions were in a vulnerable state after her father's death, but it was equally clear (I spent a whole evening poring over her copious medical file) she was the victim of inexcusable mismanagement by the medical and psychiatric profession.

Inevitably her mother and sister became involved. There followed a series of disasters, including attempts by her sister to have her sectioned. She was admitted to and ran away from various psychiatric hospitals after insensitive handling of her distress by the staff, who constantly threatened withdrawal of 'privileges' and an increase in medication. Her notes confirm that she was perceived as 'immature', 'a hysteric', 'personality disordered' and quite unmanageable without large doses of drugs that she didn't want. No one thought to ask her what the matter was, or how she felt.

Eventually she moved to be nearer her mother and put herself on the list of the colleague who subsequently referred her to me. All she could manage professionally were odd childminding jobs. She was deeply unhappy, having lost all confidence in herself and in the world. Her mother was supportive in practical ways but could never bear to see distress or anger in anybody, so that whenever Daphne tried to talk to her she told her to get a job and pull herself together. On several occasions she made Daphne leave her house at once, her behaviour was just too upsetting. The loneliness became intolerable. My colleague, by now her only friend in the world, persuaded her, though it took weeks, to come and see me.

After four months of sustained catharsis she believes now that I believe her. She believes she has never been mad, and that her aggressive actions were based on extreme frustration and a distrust born of actual experience; nothing was, as her sister insisted 'just imagination'. Having got all that straight in both our heads it is time to move on from containment to something approaching conventional therapy.

Only now is she strong enough to begin facing, bit by bit, her disillusion with her mother, whom she had all her life idealized and pacified, never developing a will of her own. The repressed fury with her and with her sister, vented upon those members of the medical profession who treated her in the same callous way, is now emerging in the consulting room. Originally she had described her early years to me as 'an idyllic childhood with darling Mummy': she had been utterly sincere. Now she recognizes the self-deception. This frees her but brings great sorrow and loneliness in its wake. A proper mourning for her father has commenced. There is much work still to do.

During a period of containment rules of good practice are necessarily (but never carelessly) broken. This patient was one of four in my whole working life to whom I have sent a holiday postcard. On all four occasions I felt their sanity, maybe even their lives, depended on it. I was prepared to grant emergency sessions and I accepted her gifts of home-made jam as sincere expressions of gratitude without any hidden agenda. After our first session, she was so relieved she threw her arms round me and kissed me soundly on the cheek, before running out of the room. She has never done so again, nor abused any of the 'allowances' I have made for her special case.

PREVENTION

I have always felt the job of therapy is unfinished if the patient has simply lost his symptoms and been restored to his former mental state. My hope is that in offering him a new way to understand his interior and interpersonal world, the therapeutic approach might be assimilated into his other ways of viewing life, so strengthening his capacity to reflect on and care for himself that new symptoms are unlikely to appear even in times of real external crisis. Therapy is not only disinterring the past, but also finding or making new tools out of the rubble with which to tackle the future.

Mrs Goldstein, sixty-two, was going for a cataract operation in a few weeks. She knew it was a safe procedure and she trusted her doctor implicitly, but found herself more sleepless and more anxious with every night that passed. A senior secretary in a busy school, she was horrified to find herself weeping into her hankie for no reason. She passed it off to her colleagues as part of her eye problem. Her GP, in whose practice I worked, asked her to see me, explaining the maximum I could offer would be five sessions.

Mrs Goldstein was originally from New York, but had travelled the world and most of its universities with her author/academic husband. He had died four years ago after a forty-year marriage and she still could not believe he was gone. She had found herself a job, forced herself to make an acquaintance or two, went to the library a lot and cooked for her mentally-disabled grown up daughter who shared her flat.

As she talked, I felt she had led a full and fascinating life that, without fully realizing it, she now believed was over. It was as if she counted the days to when she could join her husband, but as an atheist was certain no such joy awaited her. She was a well read, sophisticated woman and told me frankly that she had not been able to mourn properly, and had just kept going on 'automatic pilot'. She'd be glad if I could make her cry.

We had already discussed the possibility that the very necessity for the eye operation might spell degeneration to her, rather than the hope her doctor held out. As an avid reader of modern novels she was bound to be especially sensitive to any threat to her eyes. We ran out of steam on this and, conscious of the shortage of time and feeling this might be a mourning problem, I asked her would she like to tell me a bit about the marriage.

She recalled many happy, funny, tender times she had shared with Frank, and began to cry, saying what a wonderful person he was and how empty her life was without him.

She arrived next time, smartly dressed and a bit more cheerful, saying she'd been weeping at home about Frank and this seemed to have reduced the anxiety attacks at night. Feeling we had made good contact quickly, and she was the kind of woman perfectly able to tell me to mind my own business if she chose, I asked her about her personal relationship with Frank, rather than the globe-hopping history of the previous week. No one could be so marvellous as Frank had allegedly been, so my aim was to enable her to get a more balanced retrospective view of him, so as to let his memory go a bit, and perhaps start to live again.

She was an excellent raconteuse, producing sometimes hilarious accounts of Frank's notorious moodiness and antisocial behaviour, yet devastating charm and persuasiveness on other occasions. He was often childish, especially over competition. A fanatical bridge player, she asked him to teach her one night and got so hooked on it she eventually joined his circle of players. When it looked as if she was going to do better than him he left the group in a sulk. She found this funny rather than insulting. She went on to say how much she had willingly given up for him, his demanding career and restless personality stopping her from getting a qualification of her own; how possessive he had been so that she had no friends; how rude and churlish he could be. However, it had all been voluntary and she didn't regret a minute.

Now I had my focus for the remaining three sessions. Unless she raised them again I would ignore the hints at a lonely childhood, continuing problems with the disabled daughter, some difficulties in her thirties that had led to a brief spell in therapy, because she reported these topics in a flat voice as if just filling me in on her history. They lacked 'heat'; she had already come to terms with them. But what she had not even started coming to terms with yet was the independent, single life that now awaited her.

I encouraged her to continue counting her blessings in having had a long and happy marriage, but to look back also with a view to what she missed, especially in the social and professional area. Yes, of course she was out of practice now and felt shy, but without Frank she now had a chance to do and be all those things she gave up before. Rather than eke out her remaining days being the Mrs Goldstein she had always been, willing shadow to her husband, she might become more herself, or at least discover who that self was.

'You mean take up bridge again?' she said drily.

'At the very least,' I replied.

She claimed it was stupid to think you could start a new life at her age, she wouldn't know where to begin. She never went to the theatre, or watched TV. She knew nothing about the latest crazes and didn't want to know. Oh it was all too late ... wasn't it?

'I suppose that is up to you.'

'But I've not given a dinner party in years, decades. Frank hated them. And I don't know how to behave in a social situation without Frank. Either I faded into the background if it was going well, or I came forward to smooth ruffled feathers if he was playing up. I *understood* him.'

'Who understands you?'

And so it went on, for what remained of our brief contact. Part of the time she used for grieving, part of the time for toying with ideas for an independent future. She shied away from this at first, as if she were considering an act of infidelity. She gave a guilty laugh when I suggested this, but then seemed easier about pressing on.

I never did discover the precise relevance of her eye operation in all this, for I don't think it was just a presenting symptom. However, by the time we made our farewell she was quite looking forward to it and I trusted this to be a good sign.

This patient needed help to de-idealize her partner before mourning his loss and letting the marriage go, while of course keeping the treasured memories. I had to strike a careful balance, reminding her of the loneliness and pain he often caused her as well as the happiness he provided, while trying to avoid directly criticizing him. If I had concentrated only on the loss itself I think she would have experienced the relief of emotional discharge but would have been no more prepared for the future than she was when she first arrived, outwardly living in the present, privately living in a glowing past.

## Function 10: Getting Rest

All competent psychotherapists have at least one personal quality in common. They are good at suffering. This is a double-edged talent, however. It stands them in good stead when they have to bear extreme pain in their patients rather than rushing to mop it up with empty reassurances and useless advice, but the capacity to bear great psychological weight is discernable by others and weight will always be placed where it can best be borne. If they are to be of real and continuing use, therapists must decline the role of Atlas, holding up the world despite fatigue and stress. This often means standing up to family and pointing out resource problems and bad management practice to the employer.

Clinical supervision and the therapist's willingness to top up her own therapy in times of need are the two most recognized and respected ways of dealing with suffering overload. Unfortunately, in the rush to be accepted for accreditation and eventually legal registration, most courses now demand simultaneous therapy and supervision while the trainee is still undergoing the theoretical training (and probably holding down a full-time job as well). This defeats the whole object of the enterprise, causing more not less stress in the trainee.

Supervision and therapy should provide not only golden opportunities for learning the art, craft and science of psychodynamic therapy, but are supposed to operate as a personal support and anxiety reduction service too. All too often they are experienced as persecutory, one more time-consuming and expensive appointment in an already overcrowded diary.

Personally, I prefer the old-fashioned idea of apprenticeship – a leisurely basic training with plenty of time allowed to digest it, read round it, question and debate it, then having the trainee come in her own time, when she feels she is ready, for the actual clinical experience that necessitates personal therapy and supervision. In both instances, as she gets more confident and able, she can progress to more senior and experienced therapists and supervisors. This way the learning and personal development is spread throughout the therapist's entire working life. Training becomes a never-ending journey, not the acquisition of a hoop-jumping certificate.

Men and women in mid-life career change, or mothers embarking on a therapeutic career once their children have grown up are especially vulnerable to unwitting abuse by an employing organization where therapy is not the primary function of the institution. Colleges and schools are good examples. There is an appreciation that pupils and students need some kind of helping service, but money is scarce and no one is quite sure what psychotherapy is really about. Experienced therapists shake their head on reading the advert and leave well alone, whereas grateful newcomers to the profession accept the role gladly, not realizing the caseload is way beyond any one person's capacity to carry it, and essential clinical support and medical backing is entirely lacking. The therapist appointed is confirmed in her self-doubt when she fails to cope, and all too often tries harder to do an undo-able job till she reaches breaking point.

What is a reasonable working day like? What should therapists seriously concerned with maintaining their mental health be aiming for? Assuming treatment sessions to be the traditional 'fifty-minute hour', I would say that five patients per day ought to be the maximum, if high quality therapy is the goal, rather than impressive statistics. This allows three hours for something to eat, staff meetings, case conferences, supervision, casenotes, consultation with colleagues and correspondence. A varied day is best, patient appointments being interspersed with these other activities, and where feasible the patients themselves being varied: new mixed with old; easy with difficult; a mixture of individuals, families, groups. Of course such a carefully designed day is easier to organize in private practice, but the principle still holds: a change can be as good as a rest. Heroic, stressed-out therapists may be dealing with some inner masochistic problem of their own: they are certainly not doing their patients much good, and their apparent devotion serves only to perpetuate management failure and inadequate organizational provision.

A case exists for getting rest in the session itself, though this can be so easily abused, it is rarely admitted to. There is a kind of patient with particular bees in his bonnet that the therapist nonetheless appreciates have to be allowed to buzz about a while, till the patient's anxiety is reduced enough to attempt some work. The therapist might sit back, with one ear – the third – open and the others just lazily flapping, ready to be opened should anything unusual happen; but grab a bit of restorative peace in the meantime.

Obsessional patients obviously come into this category, as do non-obsessional patients, who, like the rest of us, have work crises, for example, or problems with their children that feel as eternal as they are unsolvable. These problems may have little to do with the central conflict that brought the patient for therapy but the patient is terribly preoccupied with them and feels the need, each session, to have what one of my patients calls a 'scrub out' – an off-loading of the week's accumulated stress – before settling down to what he calls 'the deeper stuff'. Getting things off one's chest is important for us all and does not necessarily reflect neurosis; during such times the therapist can relax the intensity of concentration a little, saving what this same patient calls her 'laser beam' for later in the session.

However, when a patient who has no such pattern of emotional discharge suddenly adopts it, the third ear on sentry duty should wake up the other two at once. This patient might for the moment be experiencing a strong transference reaction, or engaging in projective mechanisms, or identifying with his earlier aggressor. This shift in the pattern of the session could hail the arrival of a critical new stage in the therapy and a snoozing therapist just will not do.

I realize it is stating the obvious, but from what I observe in my colleagues, my supervisees, and (more often than I am happy with) in myself, it cannot be stated too often. Social recreation, hobbies and solitude ('space' as current fashion would have it) on a regular basis is essential for proper professional functioning. Each of the other nine functions of the therapist laid out here depend upon this foundation of rest for their effectiveness. It is useless knowing about such functions if the therapist is too exhausted or stale with overwork to fulfil them.

PART TWO

# Making the Assessment

## CHAPTER 4

# Making the Therapeutic Alliance

Assessment, with a capital 'A', is the linchpin of what I have come to call Broad Spectrum Psychotherapy, this treatment being conducted by what I have come to call a GP to the Mind. This Assessment is a joint enterprise, a partnership, something that is done with rather than to or for the patient as though he were as helpless to shape events in the consulting room as is the anaesthetized patient on the operating table. He may need help and encouragement to participate in Assessment, however, if tradition has taught him to see himself as the passive and grateful recipient of treatment.

The Assessment constitutes a therapy in miniature, such that were the therapist unfortunate enough to fall under a bus after its conclusion but before the therapy's completion, the patient would already have a template in his mind, a working model of what needs to be done.

To use a different metaphor: another therapist taking over would find all the ingredients for a successful therapy ready and waiting in her new patient to be mixed and baked by both. I have read in cookbooks that a dish is only as good as the quality of its ingredients, but I have also read that ingredients, no matter how pure, make a dish that is only as good as the cook (or cooks!) who blends them. With regard to post-Assessment Broad Spectrum Psychotherapy, both statements are true. Assessment finds and prepares the ingredients: post-Assessment therapy should cook them to perfection.

The process of Assessment can be broken down into sections for descriptive purposes, and though generally speaking they operate in sequence, nothing in psychotherapy is as predictable and orderly as one might like it to be, so readers should be cautioned against squeezing the patient into the scheme I present here. A good therapist is always willing to abandon theory temporarily, in favour of the patient's need to express something utterly incomprehensible to her. Mapless and lost she may feel, but if the patient feels heard, the Therapeutic Alliance has already begun to form without the aid of anyone's supposedly helpful guidelines.

This chapter concentrates on the therapist's efforts in bringing about the best Alliance that is possible with that particular patient. Both patient and therapist have only so much potential for bonding and will bond better with one partner than another, depending on their respective personalities, though it has to be said that the more experienced the therapist, the more extensive should be her Alliance-making capacities. Young therapists begin their careers with the limited set of bonding capacities they have used in their personal life so far. Later in their career they find themselves still preferring one sort of person over another for the purposes of friendship, colleagueship or love, but for professional purposes they are able to make a genuine Alliance with all manner of unfamiliar, remote, weird or even downright uncongenial patients. Chapter 5 will deal with the second part of Assessment: making the Dynamic Formulation. Chapter 7 will explore the last phase of Assessment: Contracting and making the transition to longer-term work.

Although therapists working with a broad spectrum of patients and problems make their Assessment with a view to treating the patient themselves, not all therapists operate this way. A few private therapists specialize in Assessment (usually one, two- to two-and-a-half-hour session) prior to referral to a suitable therapist. Some consultant psychotherapists in the NHS also do this before allocating the patient to a member of the team. The principles of Assessment are the same with one or two notable exceptions.

It is vital *not* to make an Alliance if the patient is to be referred, since feelings of disappointment will ensure the patient finds making a second Alliance that much harder. Any early transference may need interpreting to avoid the Assessor being taken into post-Assessment therapy as an additional problem to the one already suffered by the patient.

Assessors of this type are always very senior so tend to be revered or idealized by the patient who is in danger of seeing his permanent therapist as a much lesser mortal. The Alliance is thus jeopardized, or at best there is much comparing and contrasting of the two practitioners – a difficult situation for the trainee or newly-qualified therapist to handle.

On the whole I prefer that therapists do their own Assessment, but it has to be recognized that where there may be psychiatric illness, the possibility of suicide or a confusing and complex clinical picture, an Assessment and allocation by someone of senior status provides protection for a junior therapist and assurance for the patient that he is not being used as a guinea pig.

*The Therapeutic Alliance*

In a continuous therapy, then, the making of the Therapeutic Alliance comes first, consciously worked at by the therapist but not to the exclusion of other developments. However, if the patient is producing lots of exciting material and process from the very start, the therapist may have to prioritize, concentrating initially on factors conducive to the Therapeutic Alliance and banking most of the other information for future use – by which time much interest may have accrued! A therapist trying to do everything at once becomes confused and is then tempted to overstructure the session, forcing it to fit a familiar pattern and so relieve her anxiety. *She* may feel, indeed be, more in control, but the patient correspondingly has less control, so for him self-expression is restricted.

Like the so-called chemistry in sexual attraction, the Alliance is sometimes automatic and instantaneous for both parties. Other Alliances must be heroically struggled for against huge odds, patiently waited for (though the seeds of the alliance have been sown in Assessment, the harvest is sometimes reaped only months afterwards), or built piece by laboured piece over several weeks. Whichever way the Alliance comes about, the therapist needs at all times to be aware of its current state. In some treatments the Alliance is present but weak, in others it waxes and wanes, yet others are rock-solid always, while some therapeutic couples never achieve it at all, and a wise therapist arranges a 'constructive' divorce rather than drag her patient through a dead marriage with no reward at the end for his endurance.

It is never a good idea to rush into divorce however. Some patients have only a limited capacity to make an Alliance (that is, get on with folk as opposed to get *by* with them) with anybody, so shifting them from therapist to therapist only confirms their feelings of failure. Better they are helped to stay put and make the best of it. Such a patient can be extremely frustrating but represents a real challenge for the seasoned practitioner confident enough to work without quick rewards.

On the other hand, often through inadequate or careless referral procedures, some patients have simply joined up with the wrong therapist and could quite easily make an Alliance with another one. Therapy is as intimate as marriage, and people with any sense do not commit themselves to the first person they meet, or the one everyone else seems so sure is right for them. Naturally, they want to see how they feel about the person first, watch them in action, establish what wavelength they are on.

Alas, all too many vulnerable, over-trusting, dependent patients believe their therapist infallible and in their neediness cannot discriminate between the good and the bad ones. It is such patients that our profession must protect at all costs, even to the awful point of having to 'tell' on a colleague. Where there is a conflict of interests the patient comes first.

I shall take the reader through Assessment in some detail, assuming the therapist I am describing is in the most favourable of clinical positions: that is, she can take as many sessions as she needs for Assessment and is able to offer the patient ongoing therapy once or twice a week afterwards should they decide this to be the best way forward.

But I am conscious that many therapists in the public sector are restricted from the outset in the number of sessions they can give. I appreciate that their Assessment has to be swift and accurate, if not so detailed as here set out, if there is to be any opportunity of working through the material chosen at Assessment as being the prime focus.

In many cases the Assessment *is* the treatment. If there is no other agency in the area and the patient cannot afford private help, he is left to struggle on alone, at least knowing what it is he has to tackle (in other words, he understands the Dynamic Formulation: see Chapter 5), rather than continuing to experience himself as the helpless victim of meaningless symptoms. He may not be better yet, but does now possess some tools with which to attack his problems.

It is quite useless, and sometimes damaging, to give a patient six sessions of 'reassurance and support' on the grounds there is no time for 'deeper work', and then withdraw that support without the patient being any the wiser about himself and how he operates than he was when he started. No therapy is preferable to pseudo-therapy that only leads to further disappointment.

The argument rages on as to whether it is better to spread resources thinly so that all patients get a sniff of therapy at least, or whether resources should be concentrated on just a few, for whom the job is done properly. When the reigning policy dictates only six sessions per patient, an Assessment still needs to be done, so that after one or two sessions the therapist, if not the patient as well, has a clear idea of how the remaining precious time is to be spent.

In short-term work, time may not permit a clear division between Assessment and therapy proper, the more interventionist Assessment approach of necessity continuing throughout the few appointments available. Such an approach includes a higher than usual therapist transparency (showing her own personality) and the short cut tactics of asking questions and putting forward clinical hypotheses before the therapist has had time to feel reasonably confident about them. However, this does carry the advantage of involving the patient much more in his own treatment; having the therapist ask him to check out her hypotheses can be very flattering and raises self-esteem.

Where longer-term help is possible the Assessment is quite separate from the remaining therapy. The patient is told that the early sessions are exploratory and appreciates that when post-Assessment therapy starts, the therapist will take much more of a back seat – literally so if the patient changes from chair to couch.

Where the therapist is free to take her time, an Assessment can take anything from one to six sessions, occasionally longer, depending on the experience and skill of the therapist, the degree of psychopathology in the patient and his ability to communicate it, and the speed and sureness with which the Alliance is mutually forged. A solid Alliance makes for faster work.

The term 'Therapeutic Alliance' refers to an authentic relationship between two human beings (as opposed to 'therapist' and 'patient'). It does not have to be based on liking and is not the same as friendship. It does have to be based on mutual trust and respect, which have in turn to be worked at: these qualities do not appear by themselves. Practising therapy as if they were present, when they are not, is but a feeble imitation of what psychotherapy is all about. At best it is a convincing bit of cheating, at worst the patient eventually recognizes the inauthenticity and blames himself for failing at yet another relationship.

The Alliance represents a joint commitment to the therapeutic endeavour that is much more than the mere linking of the patient's longing for wholeness to the therapist's wish to heal. The Alliance is nurtured within the favourable climate provided by the consulting room and the therapist's professionalism, but is quite distinct from it. The couple have *met*, rather than merely occupied the same room and talked: the couple have touched one another's central self, built a bridge between.

Though hardly ever referred to by either party, the Alliance is personal and intimate and cannot be faked. When the therapy gets stuck, is too painful to bear or the transference is momentarily so strong it threatens to wreck the peace of mind of both, it is the Alliance that will see them through. When the therapist makes a technical blunder, or the patient acts out cruel impulses toward her, it is the Alliance that makes forgiveness possible. When an established therapy is suddenly intruded upon by bereavement, job loss, a stressful move or marital separation, the preoccupation with the patient's past and with his unconscious mind may have to be put to one side for the duration of the crisis. No easy solution presents itself but the Therapeutic Alliance will enable both parties to weather the crisis until 'normal' work can be resumed. It is frequently the Alliance that stops a patient attempting suicide, when all the interpretations of which the exhausted therapist is capable have failed to do so.

The Therapeutic Alliance is approached by the therapist from four angles: Opening the First Session; Using Silence; Finding a Common Language; and Separating out the Transference.

*Opening the First Session*

Sometimes the patient is in crisis, and/or in ignorance of what therapy is about. It may be that the 'Operating as a GP' function has to be deployed before anything else. Containment, education, management and letting a highly anxious or suspicious patient use her, as discussed in the last chapter, may have to be brought to bear before both parties can settle into an exploration of what has brought the patient for help, and hopefully through this begin to build the Alliance.

All therapists know from their training about 'free floating attention', how important it is to give the patient time and psychological space to say whatever is on his mind, especially at the outset when anxiety is bound to be high.

Accordingly, most have developed, deliberately or through habit, a characteristic way of opening the session. Some announce one or more boundaries straight away, to induce a sense of security. For example: 'Well, Mrs Jones, we have fifty minutes at our disposal, and of course we can arrange to meet again ... '. Or, laying down the hope the patient will master the art of free association right away, 'Would you like to tell me, Mr Green, in your own way, in any order, what has been troubling you? Take your time.'

Some therapists sit very still and show no hint of emotion or curiosity, in the hope their new patient will intuit he must meditate aloud *à la* psychoanalysis, forgetting that he has not yet been schooled in such matters and could be frightened or angered by what he construes as lack of interest. (I once treated a mediaeval military strategist who had struggled with then abandoned his former therapist. In the opening minutes of our first session he described this therapist as looking 'just like those mediaeval battle commanders who, though killed in the mêlée, had their corpses strapped upright in their saddle, eyes wedged open, and their horses goaded back into the field so the ordinary soldiers would not realize they were dead and lose morale or desert.' I couldn't have had a clearer cue!)

There is no one ideal format for opening first sessions, but all other things being equal, I normally smile after we are seated, cock my head a bit to one side and raise my brows expectantly. But if the patient is not behaving in a run-of-the-mill fashion I try to respond sensitively to the situation in front of me. For instance, a patient might admire the pictures in the consulting room. 'Is that a photo of Florence?' he might say. I would murmur an assent so as not to make him feel snubbed, but I would certainly not answer a whole string of questions or regale him with accounts of my holiday. Usually such preamble is just boundary-crossing behaviour, in other words a way of making the transition from the known world outside to the unknown and probably scary new world of the consulting room inside, that bit easier. The behaviour is usually given up when the patient has had a few sessions and is feeling less tense about being new.

I wince when I hear over-zealous supervisees telling me (and the incredulous patient) the alleged unconscious meaning of behaviour that is plainly and legitimately simple comfort behaviour. Wrongly translated to the patient, this can wreck the beginnings of an Alliance.

However, if such behaviour persists it becomes material for analysis, but this can be done lightly at such an early stage, almost playfully, thus demonstrating that therapy does not always have to be the earnest and solemn business the patient might fear.

Mr Harding's first session took place on a muddy November Monday at my home, the ground floor of which I try to keep clean and tidy as a mark of respect to my patients. At the door to the consulting room he hesitated, nervous. 'Shall I take my shoes off?' he asked.

'That's considerate of you,' I replied.

However, the next week was cold but sunny and dry. He still took his shoes off. I let this go unremarked till later in session, when he was telling me about his boss's meanness.

'If I need so much as a new pencil to do my work, her office rules, pinned to the noticeboard, say I have to take the stub of the old one to the stores depot as proof I'm not nicking her precious property. Worse than my mum, she is.'

'Mmm?'

'Well, she used to pin things up. Take the bathroom: "LEAVE THIS ROOM AS YOU WOULD WISH TO FIND IT." Got on my nerves it did.

Always obeyed her notes, but secretly I rebelled, imagined myself squirting toothpaste all over the mirror, wiping my bottom on her clean towels.'

'Perhaps you'd quite like to trample mud all over my carpet too?' I asked, but with a conspiratorial smile.

He blushed, then grinned. 'Well, it is a bit posh in here. Like the front room she kept spotless for visitors, weddings and funerals.'

After that *he* decided, without consultation, whether or not it was muddy enough to warrant removal of shoes. Each time he did remove them, he initiated a shared joke about my being mum. The fourth or fifth time he just winked at me as he bent down, and after that neither of us ever commented: we were too involved in and wanting to get down to the work.

My humour offset what might have been heard by a new patient, unfamiliar with my technique, as a rebuke or criticism that could in turn have jeopardized the beginning of any Alliance. Yet in making the observation at all, I was demonstrating in a non-threatening way what therapy and transference were about, giving him a sample to see how he would react to the taste. If he didn't throw up I knew I would be able to offer him more solid food still, without destroying his as yet embryonic trust.

Many patients just starting therapy react to premature or clumsy interpretations as if they had been poisoned; it is important to go carefully. Others sweep aside gentle efforts to make an Alliance, insisting on getting down to 'the real issues' straight away.

Gordon was a studious-looking thirty-five-year-old about whom I knew nothing except that he wanted help but would not tell the doctor who referred him what it was about.

He strode purposefully into the GP's consulting room where I was doing my weekly clinic and sat down squarely upon the chair. I waited while he stared at the floor in concentration, as if summoning the power to speak. Then he raised his head and stared at me.

'Do you believe in God?' he demanded.

A bit taken aback, I said: 'Goodness, that must be a terribly vital question to you if you bring it up first thing like that.'

'Don't hedge with me. Do you or don't you?'

A pulse beat swiftly in his temple and his forehead was beaded with sweat. He was in deadly earnest. If he was ever to trust me only the truth would do.

'No,' I said. 'But I do believe there is a spiritual side to our lives which it is folly to ignore.'

'So what is your greatest moral obligation as a human being?'

Oh dear, I thought, how long should I let him interview me? Yet his intensity was such I decided to meet his need to use me this way, bearing in mind the Alliance for the moment was the important thing.

'Well, er, I don't really go in for obligation much, moral or otherwise. I do what I do voluntarily not because I am obliged. I try to help people in distress and balance that with sharing some of my joy in the world with my fellows, because, well, that's the only sense I can make of everything really.' It sounded pretty lame, but it was true.

'So that's the meaning of the universe for you, is it?'

'I guess it must be.'

'And no one, no system, no religion, no form of therapy tells you that's how you should behave?'

'No,' I said, deciding to keep it simple or we might be here all day.

He stared right into my eyes for a minute, then suddenly slumped back in his chair, seemingly at ease.

'That'll do,' he said, folding his arms and smiling. 'Now you can ask the questions. Go ahead, feel free.'

'Only one question for the moment,' I said. 'What the hell was all that about?'

Our subsequent discussion was very open and genial. An introverted, intellectual boy, he had become engrossed in religion but worried about the 'True Path', comparing all the different sorts of Catholicism, including the heresies, throughout history, never sure which group might have got it right, their persecution perhaps being a cover up by the orthodox church. At seventeen he met and developed an intense relationship with a much older lay preacher, who insisted that physicality was part of brotherhood, and had Gordon doing all night vigils with him in lonely chapels, their arms around one another till dawn.

Gordon broke off the relationship as the man became more possessive and frightening. He felt used and betrayed yet never quite sure that the man hadn't been right. After all, there had been no overt sex: could it be that Gordon was homosexual and blaming the man for his own sin?

On completing university, he arranged to lose his virginity to a woman so as to disconfirm this hypothesis, but as she was a prostitute his shame did not permit him to keep his erection, though he was reassured that at least he did have one.

For the next few years Gordon wandered about the East, trying to find himself, but always failing. On his return, a fellow student, now a priest, recommended him a therapist priest but Gordon felt the

73

man was too Freudian and he was once again in the grip of a 'cult'. As a last resort he went to his GP.

The reason he had interviewed me so vigorously, and been so quickly reassured, was that I had made plain no sect, not even a therapeutic sect, could claim my loyalty so I had no 'religion' in which to cloak my devious designs. He knew that in treatment my only loyalty would be to him. I made clear in this our first session just how keenly aware I was of his terror of being exploited again.

I sensed Gordon was cueing me to respond with a directness equal to his own if I expected to be trusted.

It is true that another patient with a different history might have turned me down, because only a Christian therapist would do. But a patient has a right to choose his own therapist and I would not have been offended.

In the first session issues of the therapist's professional 'religion' are common. How many times have I heard: 'You are not one of those Kleinians/Jungians/Freudians are you?' The patient has a right to have his questions answered truthfully, but it is equally important to get at the fears, hopes and fantasies that lie behind the question. When I have explained that I am 'psychodynamic' and what that broadly entails, I usually say something like: 'But what would it have meant to you if I had said – oh, that I was a rabid Freudian, for instance?' The answers are very revealing of the patient's underlying preoccupations. At the same time the therapist's willingness to discuss such things as her qualifications non-defensively assists in the making of the Therapeutic Alliance.

## Using Silence

How can silence contribute to the Therapeutic Alliance (called 'Working Alliance' in some textbooks)? Certainly not the way a first-year trainee answered this question when I raised it in a seminar: 'Well, if the therapist refuses to speak, the patient has got to say something eventually hasn't he? You can't lose.' Sadly, the trainee had got hold of that old stereotype of the dynamic therapist as a stern, poker-faced, mute figure forcing the patient to fill the silent void between them with 'confessions'. This is not the way to build bridges with patients.

Some patients take advantage of the silence put there for their use straight away. Others are intimidated by it. 'Why aren't you asking me questions?' they say. The therapist might explain she is leaving space for him to express things his own way. 'Well my doctor says I should tell you about my boarding school.' The therapist might reply: 'But what do *you* want to talk about? That's why I didn't fire questions at you, I want to hear what *you* have to say.' The patient may be flustered, unused to being granted such importance, but is beginning already to get the hang of this therapy business.

The therapist is here functioning as an educator, enabling the patient to learn how to use silence. She explains the purpose of it rather than seeing his nervousness about it in transference terms and then either attacking him (as he might see it) with 'wild' interpretation or maintaining the silence in the hope of further revelations. This just leads him to flounder further in anxiety, embarrassment and feelings that he has again failed. Both premature interpretation and punitive silence prevent rather than contribute to an Alliance.

What the therapist aims to achieve with these early silences is a balance of sufficient feelings of anxiety in the patient that he will want to unburden himself, with sufficient relaxation of his usual and necessary inhibitions that he feels free to talk. Too much anxiety paralyses, and the patient may leave therapy, whereas handing over the peanuts and gin would turn the meeting into a social one and banish discussion of the very problems with which he has come for help. I think the seminar trainee was giving us a distorted view of this balancing principle, but did at least realize that dynamic therapy is not about lulling patients into a false sense of security, making them feel cosseted and at ease. What he missed, though, was the other side of the equation, the fact that misery and pain can only be shared by the patient where the purpose of the space and silence provided for him to show that unhappiness is properly understood.

Far too many patients recall their first session as an ordeal, the experience of a mute, therefore sinister stranger waiting for them to admit things, especially if the consulting room is bare and clinical, reminding them of a wartime interrogation experience. Where there is reality in this perception, the excuse that 'it is all transference' just will not do.

Transference does occur in the first silences, however, and should not be missed. The successful managing of it helps the Alliance develop.

I had been taught in my training that the setting was most important, especially in the first session. The room should be warm and the level of lighting low, making a confiding atmosphere.

Still in my twenties then, and keen to do things properly, I brought a young male lecturer into my Student Counselling room, invited him to take a comfortable chair carefully angled toward my own – not directly opposite and confrontational, not too slanted so we couldn't look at each other – and with the requisite coffee table between. The gas fire glowed before us. I waited quietly for him to speak.

It was a dark winter afternoon in London, the lights low and the curtains pulled against traffic noise so he could talk in peace. I prided myself on how cosy it all was.

The lecturer began to fidget terribly, until his anxiety was so great I thought he would leave the room, and how was I going to explain *that* in my supervision seminar? So I asked him what the matter was.

'It's like a night club in here,' he growled. 'Do you realize the whole polytechnic has strip lighting, while you have that orange fringed lampshade thing, and curtains – *velvet* curtains – instead of blinds like anybody else? I'm surprised you don't have whisky and cigars on the table. You running a brothel here, or what?'

A bit shocked, I pulled my miniskirt (this was 1970) over my knees and said: 'If you feel that way about my room, you must be very worried about me.'

'Eh?'

'That I won't behave professionally with you.'

He scowled. 'Depends on your profession I suppose.'

'Look,' I said, 'my room is like this to put people at their ease, help them talk about difficult things. I may have overdone it a bit, but I promise you I am a therapist and not a prostitute. You are quite safe.'

He seemed surprised by my direct speech, but clearly relieved that I had set the record straight. We got along a lot easier after that.

I could have just pursued the transference line, his experiencing me (like all women? like his mother?) as a predatory harlot, as indeed I did to great effect in later sessions. But at this nascent stage with no Alliance yet arrived at, reassurance and plain speaking proved a better way to bring us together in some degree of trust.

Needless to say, sex and guilt were the main themes of this short therapy. But the point of the illustration is to show that however careful one is about the setting and about silence, each patient will react differently.

It is no use keeping silence simply because some imagined rule says one must. But denying a patient his entitlement to silence from the therapist can also prevent critical material, such as this lecturer's intense suspicion of women, from surfacing. Again it is a question of balance. Too much silence can become persecutory or just barren: too little can turn a golden opportunity for joint psychological exploration into a tea-and-sympathy session. The job of the dynamic therapist is not to console and comfort the patient's distress, but to help him face and understand it.

What might actually be occurring in the kind of silence that paves the way to an Alliance? (For there are all too many dead, unproductive silences in some treatments.)

The patient may feel he is drowning in uncertainty and in need of a lifeline, which the observant therapist throws. He may be experiencing a peace and freedom he never gets at home or work and only the foolish therapist interrupts. He may be weighing up the therapist in the silence, the way most of us do on meeting a stranger, yet fantasizing about her at the same time. If he is enabled to speak these fantasies, as did my lecturer (comments about the setting are virtually always about the therapist) the therapist is presented with the choice of making a transference observation, an 'educational' reassuring explanation, to make him more at home with the therapeutic approach, or ideally a mixture of both, as I tried to do on that occasion.

Often in the first silence, as it dawns on the patient he is not going to be bombarded with questions, he becomes aware of feelings welling up inside that are normally kept at bay by the busyness of his working day. He finds himself weeping, or overwhelmed with sadness, or becomes unaccountably tense and agitated. This is understandably hard for the therapist who has just met him and may have no idea what the behaviour means. Should she ask, comfort, pass the tissues? Almost always her body posture (attentive but not rigid), facial expression (calm concern), her alert stillness is sufficient to convey a sense of safety to the patient, gives permission for him to continue, lay down his burden for a while. A fussy, overly concerned response can shut the patient up in seconds, terrified *the therapist* might cry, or panic, deducing from the tissues being rammed under his nose that he should 'dry his eyes'. Farewell to any Alliance.

In the silence, the therapist for her part may simply be *attending*. It took me years to learn how to do this, and I think I am learning still. Rather than going *to* the patient for 'information', she lets the patient and his actions, or inaction, *impinge* on her sensibilities. She is in a state of receptivity, like a well tuned lute waiting to be played. The music brought forth from her by the patient and the results of her meditation on these sounds – her

77

understanding of the music – is what she uses to guide the patient to a fresh way of meditating on himself and his problems.

In the silence the therapist might also be busy trial-identifying, scanning the session so far, hypothesizing about the transference, classifying process, deciphering or sending a cue, linking bits of disparate material into a pattern, examining her own reactions to her patient, preparing an intervention, *thinking*. One thing she must certainly not do while the delicate business of building the Alliance is under way, is take a rest. Yet because of the exhausting nature of this early work it is the time she most often wants to.

Some patients seem intractably silent yet are patently ill at ease with it and not deriving any discernible benefit. Trying to avoid implied criticism while encouraging such a person to speak is a daunting task, for if the obstacle is unknown, how can the path be made easier? It is at such a point that the silence can become chronic, the therapist fatalistically accepting, the patient despairing. There are dead silences and living ones, so that the dying ones in need of rescue must be distinguished from silences that though protracted are still eloquent, and if tolerated for long enough without the therapist losing her nerve, will yield up their secret for analysis at last.

A patient's silence can be respected with reciprocal companionable silence; for another patient, the therapist's silence amounts to neglect or surrender. A patient can be invited out of silence or assaulted out of it. Mutual silence can be creative and necessary and conducive to the Alliance, or boring and empty and anathema to the Alliance. Every silence needs to be understood in its own context. In some therapies silence is an active but never mentioned feature; in others silence is and should be discussed exhaustively by the pair producing it.

For one patient the therapist's early silences, designed for his benefit, are experienced as extremely hostile. Perhaps his parents 'sent him to Coventry' when he misbehaved and so he takes the same message from the therapist's silence. Perhaps it reminds a boarding school child hiding in the cloakrooms of the sheer loneliness of his childhood years. The patient may assume the silence means he is boring. Perhaps the exuberant patient is running away from the silence he could not bear between his parents, which will be replicated in the consulting room if he doesn't keep up his constant stream of gags which the wretched woman refuses even to laugh at.

One of my rules of thumb is: 'When in doubt, ask the patient.' I have often got results from such naive techniques as: 'I don't know what to make of this silence, Jack, do you?' or, 'Is it too embarrassing, or shaming perhaps, to speak? Might I not approve or something?' or the very direct, 'Look I'm in a pickle here, Joan. I want to be of help but because I don't know anything about you I find I don't know the right things to say. I mean I wouldn't want to put my foot in it or anything. Yet to find out about you I'd have to question you and that feels intrusive. How do you think we might proceed?' Such efforts should never be seen as first resorts. Most patients will pipe up in their own time without such heavy prompting.

Silence for some patients is the only self-protection they feel they have and should be respected until they are ready to lay it down. Some use it as a challenge, a gauntlet: 'Go on, *make* me speak.' Some are too depressed to speak or believe no one would want to hear what they have to say, or that life is so grey that there is nothing *to* say. Some are so intimidated by authority they are afraid to speak and are often much reassured by hearing their therapist speak not in strange, learned tongues, but in plain English.

For others silence is indelibly associated in their mind with personal trauma. Often such a person cannot bear to remain in therapy unless that trauma comes into the open.

Alison managed to say hello and tell me she could see no point in living, but for the sake of her children had pledged to keep alive. After that, all I could get was yes, no and maybe, and often not even that. She was always tense, her arms crossed, hugging herself as if she was cold.

As each session during early Assessment progressed she became more, not less tense and in the last minutes of our meetings seemed to be inching her way toward the door, begging with her eyes to be let out. I fed this and other similar observations back to her, without response.

Half-way through our third session, after a long silence she suddenly said: 'Please, please would you mind putting your clock in the drawer?'

I did so. I waited. Then I asked: 'Does that feel any better?'

She burst into sobs that felt to me like relief, and eventually helped herself to tissues, rubbed at her eyes and explained.

There had been a grandfather clock at the foot of the stairs when she was ten. It was very old and needed winding every couple of days. This job was frequently neglected so the ticking fell silent, often for days, sometimes weeks at a time, Alison always knew when her father was coming to sexually abuse her, because late at night he would stop to wind the clock. He was very quiet on the stairs so no one would hear (her ill mother slept on the ground floor), but she knew he was coming when she heard the ticking of the clock break the silence. For three and a half sessions she had sat listening to my clock ticking and reliving those horrific experiences.

Silence, on both the patient's and the therapist's part, can be pregnant with meaning. To avoid silence, then, is to miss rich pickings indeed. But even so, many experienced therapists still talk far too much, especially in the mutually nerve-racking first session.

At the other extreme, silence inflicted on a new and anxious patient in a deliberate attempt to force him to speak is as inexcusable as it is unethical.

The successful negotiation of silence such that both can be comfortable with it, or feel free to comment when it is uncomfortable, is one of the chief indicators that the Therapeutic or Working Alliance is under way.

### Finding a Common Language

Finding a way to communicate comfortably with each other goes on at a latent level while overtly appointments are being made, a history is being gathered, a life story (much censored till the common language is found) is being told, symptoms described, mental aches and pains revealed.

The therapist tries to facilitate the patient's self-exploration, inspire hope that he can do much more of the work himself than he ever thought possible, while at the same time he is trying to adjust to the strange and new business of really being heard, wondering if it is safe to speak so freely or might it be some sort of trap? Two languages are being broadcast at once, one of encouragement, one of reservation.

Both parties are understandably anxious. The therapist knows that unless she can put her patient at his ease sufficiently to enable his self-reflection she will be prevented from understanding his problems except in the crudest psychiatric terms. Unless she is fluent enough in his language he will not trust her with feelings about his problems, how they affect his most intimate relationships, where they fit in his developmental history. The Dynamic Formulation (see Chapter 5) will be held up, and in short-term work especially this can be critical. Yet she knows that in her haste to adopt his language she must not abandon her own, for both are vital to the enterprise: she must assist the patient in learning her language too.

To make himself feel safe the patient needs literally a shared language, confidence that both parties mean the same thing when certain words or phrases are used; that colloquialisms and jokes have a joint referential frame, that a shorthand exists between them, that soon they will be able to finish each other's sentences, that he can be certain the therapist will never use specialist language to humiliate or mock him. (I once had a patient who conducted his first few sessions almost entirely in Latin phrases, such that I had to deduce his meaning from the English bits that joined them together. When he referred repeatedly to his 'senescent pater' I could scarcely resist replying, 'you mean, "me old dad?"' but managed to restrain myself. Happily the Latin subsided as he grew more confident that I was not going to hurl psychoanalytic jargon about. When we joked at our success in finding a mutual 'modus operandi', I recognized our Alliance had arrived.)

For her part, the therapist knows that if this relationship is to be more than a mutual admiration society she needs the patient to speak many other languages than his own. There is the language of free association, of transference; she has to introduce him carefully to the language of his unconscious, the messages his symptoms are sending him and the world, of which till now he has been unaware. The language of dreams is to be opened up for him and, though exciting, she appreciates this can be frightening too.

Because of her years of practice the therapist can generally be expected to learn the patient's language before he learns hers. She should give him time to catch up, realize that what might be bread-and-butter concepts to her can be revolutionary breakthroughs to the patient – a coalman, say, or a farmer – who needs time to ponder on, wonder at and apply the concepts she has taught, without being rushed.

As a young nursing sister in a psychoanalytically-oriented therapeutic community in the sixties, I can remember feeling quite dazed by the implications of dream symbols, mechanisms of defence and transference, and I was allowed to digest these ideas in my own time. A refresher course in wonderment and a little less patronizing of patients might help older, more jaded therapists learn a bit of patience. I find that participating in a patient's sense of wonder, and feeling I helped make it possible is one of the greatest rewards of the job. When I am tired it is such experiences that revive me and help me carry on.

However, many therapists are under a lot of pressure to treat patients in a conveyor-belt fashion and it is hardly surprising that such a factory-like mentality at the workplace has knocked most of the wonder out of them, or in the rush to increase patient turnover they must save it for high days and holidays. They are being deprived of the job satisfaction that would make them more, not less, efficient therapists.

The issue about patients learning the language of psychotherapy leads us to the vexed question of 'psychological mindedness'. It is true some non-trained patients take to the interpretive side of psychotherapy like a duck to water and that others never seem to 'get the hang' however skilled the teacher/therapist is. But between these two extremes lie the majority of patients, willing and eager to learn, though it may take special expertise and patience to help some understand. This can only be achieved after the patient feels the therapist speaks *his* particular language, the one he feels at home with, has spoken all his life.

This highlights another significant difference between classical psychoanalysis and Broad Spectrum Psychotherapy. The analyst selects people or has them selected for him, who are already defined as psychologically minded, so work with transference, dreams and so forth can go ahead immediately; whereas the GP to the Mind has an educative function on top of the interpretive one. Moreover, in the public sector she will have less time at her disposal to fulfil that and the therapeutic function as well.

Psychological mindedness should not be confused with intelligence. Many patients who do not seem especially bright are able to master psychodynamic principles if they are explained in plain English: for example, 'Perhaps you missed the vital train that was to take you to your interview because although you wanted the job for the money it would bring the wife and kids, you feared *underneath* that you weren't up to it, so if you missed your train because the alarm clock failed, you couldn't be held responsible.'

Equally, university professors can have brilliance stamped all over them yet be so invested in a rational, intellectual view of the universe that getting them within a light year of any emotion feels like a miracle. These people, too, can be helped to see their rationality as a massive lifelong defence that has cost them dear in terms of relationships, but there has to be that bedrock of psychological mindedness present in the personality for this to be possible. It may be a long, long way down, in both geniuses and dunces, but if it is there at all, then with skill and persistence it can be mined by the therapeutic pair and hauled to the surface.

There are degrees of psychological mindedness of course. Deciding on the extent to which a patient can be expected to use dynamic concepts is part of early Assessment and helps the practitioner design the subsequent treatment approach. To put it crudely, the therapist must recognize when it is impossible to fashion a silk purse out of a sow's ear, yet still find a way to make some other purse, just as durable, just as worth while.

It should be remembered, too, how differently constructed we human beings can be. Therapists should not play holier-than-thou. They do not have a monopoly on mental health; indeed, their job could not be carried out by overly integrated people. It seems hard for some therapists to accept that many worthwhile, able people, even some very great people who have made mammoth contributions to the human race are, or were, totally unpsychologically minded. The point is not that psychologically-minded people are 'better', but that from a clinical perspective, underestimating a patient's capacity to learn to work dynamically, or conversely trying to force him into areas he cannot understand, high IQ or no, can have a most adverse effect on the building of any Alliance.

From the earliest stages, a readiness to play with speech and encouraging the patient to play likewise helps therapist and patient develop a lexicon of their own. A supervisee provides this simple but potent example:

Rosemary is nineteen and fat and loves her Dad.

'I think the world of him, but what's the point? He ruffles my hair and calls me "My fat girl". I hate it, hate it.'

The supervisee said: '"My *fat* girl", or *"my* fat girl"?'

The patient stopped in her tearful tracks. She had never looked at it that way. Afterwards she began studying all her family's utterances in a different light.

Another supervisee has a nurse patient who is also fat, and who needs regularly to have a good gripe about her shape before settling down to more intense work in the session. On this occasion the patient was reviewing all the well researched causes for fatness, complaining that all her professional knowledge did nought to help her condition.

'So much for aetiology,' she grumbled. 'Hey, I have to write a paper next week. How do you spell that word?'

The therapist had a bash, spelt it E-A-T-iology, though ordinarily she knew perfectly well how to spell it. They both laughed, speculating about what this slip might mean.

Such moments of play, in firming up and maintaining the Alliance, really do widen and deepen the common language and prevent it going stale.

My own patient, Gemma, had mood swings that disturbed her greatly. When 'high' she felt she was flying like a swallow, and when depressed she felt like a hedgehog looking for a pile of leaves to burrow and hide in.

By the third session we both referred quite freely to her 'swallow self' thinking such and such, while her 'burrowing hedgehog' felt something quite different at the same time. She worked out via this imagery that her school work and relations with her sixth form teachers would go much better if she could work towards just a 'jumping rabbit self' rather than a 'flying-too-high swallow self', and be an 'out on the pavement hedgehog' – still prickly but not having to bury herself.

She began using animal imagery for her mum, dad and siblings too, and gradually the buried family conflicts that she had been containing for them came to the surface. She could not accuse people directly, but was able to describe the hurts and joys the family produced in her by bringing a veritable zoo into the consulting room, having hedgehogs talk with lions and skunks, while screeching parrots and an elegant cheetah with silver claws also played their part. Outsiders overhearing would think us completely mad, though we two knew exactly what our conversations meant.

At the end of Gemma's short therapy we joked about getting Walt Disney to make an animated film of our proceedings but agreed folk would find it too fantastical. The language and the Alliance had been ours alone: it was incommunicable to anyone else.

## Separating Out the Transference

There are exceptions to every rule, but it is generally true that the transference and the Therapeutic Alliance are never more intertwined than during early Assessment. Later they gradually or suddenly unplait, and by post-Assessment the therapist is working predominantly with one or the other. In early Assessment both are emergent, so it is not yet clear to the therapist which is strongest and where she should put most of her energies; at this stage it is watch and wait.

If a lot of transference emerges quickly of its own accord and at the same time it becomes apparent that the patient is very psychologically-minded, then already a medium- to long-term treatment plan is taking shape in the therapist's mind, one in which the clinical work is going to be very similar to psychoanalysis and will therefore require an experienced therapist with advanced training to carry it out. Will this be herself or should she refer? Will the referral process itself impede work with another therapist? Will that therapist's seniority of expertise outweigh this disadvantage?

If the Alliance is robust, the patient not so psychologically-minded but able to learn, the transference weak or located elsewhere (in a marital partner or boss, for example) then the therapist begins to envisage a different treatment. This might be a medium-term contract to allow for 'teaching time' and the drawing out of any latent transference, but because of the good Alliance that allows speedy work, and the fact that transference will not be exhaustively mined, it should not warrant a lengthy commitment (depending of course on the degree, depth and accessibility of the problems). She appreciates from the outset that this will be a therapy with a psycho-analytic flavour but not a psychoanalytic essence. This is neither better nor worse than the former treatment plan: *it is right for the patient.* As it is she who has developed the Alliance with the patient, it is almost certainly she who should treat him, Alliances are not transferable and solid clinical work in the building of an Alliance should not be wasted.

A strong Alliance combined with strong transference manifestations in a very insightful patient is every psychodynamic therapist's dream. Here is the patient who, if he has no alternative, can make use of intensive, fast short-term work and benefit. With a longer time available for treatment he will do even better.

However, few patients are so ideal and ways must be found to help the others without seeing them as second-class candidates. Sadly, many patients are blamed for their symptoms, especially if they are arrogant, ungrateful, bitter, whining, hostile or unconsciously determined to stay ill. This is a great pity and is about as helpful as complaining that someone with measles has spots. The spots are the sign of what ails him as surely as arrogance indicates the psychotherapy patient's underlying conflicts sorely requiring help.

As sister of the adolescent unit in a therapeutic community, I had managed to get the youngsters to do some playreading. They were nervous and self-conscious at first, then began enjoying it, getting really involved. We were reading Jean Anouilh's *Antigone*, our leading lady a shy trainee hairdresser who rose magnificently to the occasion, amazing us all with her passionate denunciation of Authority.

At this point Lawrence, a nineteen-year-old Greek scholar at Cambridge, wafted through the Community room, nose in the air, making for the door opposite. He heard but a couple of *Antigone*'s sentences, and with a pained expression drawled: 'My dear, surely you're not doing that speech in *English?*' Then, carrying on from where she left off, in perfect French, he sauntered out of the other door, leaving the hairdresser in tears.

My immediate task was to prevent a lynching when I felt like leading it. Yet I knew from many conversations I had had with Lawrence, especially when on night duty and no one was around to see his 'weakness', that he longed more than anything in the world to be accepted by his peers. His superior attitude and overdone public school accent were defences against feelings of vulnerability: if he must be unpopular with his fellows he would be spectacularly unpopular; he would give them something to hate him *for*.

The Broad Spectrum Psychotherapist, then, uses the Assessment to determine where on the non-interpretive to very-interpretive scale the patient currently sits and how far along that scale it might be possible to move him, given the right therapist and the best 'education'. She also judges how strong the Alliance is and if it might be strengthened in post-Assessment work. Then, when post-Assessment therapy commences, she knows where to start and where realistically she is likely to finish, as well as knowing what the Alliance can and cannot withstand.

The classical analyst can always start at more or less the same place and use more or less the same techniques with each patient because the Assessment has already been done, usually by an outside Assessor, and the patient deemed suitable for that type of work. Because of this suitability, which includes high motivation, the analyst can afford to hotly pursue the transference, leaving the Alliance to develop, whereas the Broad Spectrum Psychotherapist has to forge an Alliance as top priority, attending to transference later (unless it is so strong it intrudes of its own accord). She works for this Alliance not least because without it she will not be allowed *inside* the patient sufficiently to make the clinical judgements necessary for design of the best treatment plan.

All the same, the wise therapist does not cultivate the Alliance to the extent of dampening an emergent transference. Working creatively with unconscious negative transferential distortions is as valuable a contribution to the Alliance as working with conscious positive feelings about the therapist. When the patient understands his negative attributions as transference from the past, he makes room for 'corrective' perceptions: in other words he starts to see the therapist as she is, a professional person genuinely concerned for his well-being. If he is not enabled to see that, there can be no hope of a true Alliance.

On the other hand, what might appear to be conscious, good

'allied' feelings on the part of the patient toward his therapist, can themselves turn out to be transference. Distorted positive feelings – idealization of the therapist – need exploration by the couple no less than negative ones. It is a mistake to assume the patient must be making an Alliance if he has good feelings about his therapist, and must be exhibiting transference if he expresses bad feelings about her. Expressing good feelings can be a cover for the opposite *unconscious* feeling. Showing bad or critical feelings can mean the patient *is* allied: he trusts his therapist enough to be honest with her.

Just to complicate matters during early Assessment, the burgeoning transference and the emerging Alliance can occur at the same time. Ideally both should be addressed by whatever intervention is made, so neither is lost or discouraged.

Darryl, a married thirty-three-year-old cab driver, came to seem me privately, via his GP, after he failed to get on with a previous counsellor. He left her after the first consultation. She was an experienced Rogerian counsellor who I knew slightly professionally, but neither he nor his GP knew that.

He had a blunt manner and opened the session by announcing his hope that I wasn't going to be like her. 'Money for old rope,' he muttered, then stopped to inspect my face for a reaction.

'What was wrong with her?' I enquired mildly, responding to his bluntness in equal coin, though avoiding any hint of confrontation.

(I have found that blunt patients seldom trust evasion or understatement in a therapist, especially in the early sessions, though they don't always enjoy the bluntness they may receive in return. A discussion of this helps them realize the effect of their bluntness on others, and marks the start of implicit negotiations as to just how therapist and patient are going to confer. This in turn results in a softening of the exchanges between them, a 'frankness-with-tact' compromise. The Alliance is growing.)

'One o' them blue rinsed do-gooding types, she was. Meant well, I dare say, but talked bloody funny, 'scuse my French.' He peered at me again from under his bushy brows.

'Yes, go on. I'm listening.'

'Well, she folded her hands like she was praying and kept saying "What I'm hearing is this," and "What I'm hearing is that," till I thought I was in a ruddy echo chamber. Kept repeating back to me what I'd just said. When I complained she said: "I just want to get *alongside* you." Honest to God she did. She said it again half an hour later. I'd 'ad enough. "Listen 'ere," I said, "the only woman as gets alongside me is my missus," and it was then I decided I wasn't doin' business with her. No way.'

I was trying to suppress a smile – his caricature of the reflecting-back Rogerian was so evocative. He must have caught – or perhaps I *let* him catch? – a flicker at the corner of my mouth, for he said: 'You *do* know what I'm talking about, don't you?'

'I recognize the style,' I said, cueing him that though I accepted the truth of what he had reported there was no way I was going to 'slag off' (to use one of his favourite terms) a colleague. He took the cue and began to tell me about his problems.

Among other things, he told me his mother, a loving woman who he could just remember, had died when he was seven. His dutiful devout paternal grandmother brought him up, and he hated her. He was bursting to say more, but clamped his mouth shut.

'Would you like to say more about her?' I asked. 'I don't mind the French.'

Permission granted, he swore plenty. Surprise surprise, gran had blue hair (the counsellor didn't: he only imagined she did). Gran was always at church and held prayer meetings at home – hence his sensitivity to the counsellor's hands. She made him visit the old people's home with her, and the inmates frightened him. He was told he was wicked and unchristian for refusing. Gran, then, was a do-gooder, like the counsellor.

By the end of the session, I saw that an Alliance had been steadily forming. He had been immensely relieved by my believing his account, by my hint of humour and by my non-Rogerian manner – though I was careful not to do the 'blank screen' psychoanalytic presentation either; heaven knows what he would have made of that. However, we were also deep into positive transference. He couldn't wait for his next session. No wonder: I had become for him the reconstitution of the loving mother he had lost.

He was to deny this observation for many weeks, insisting I was just being modest, that I really was a lovely, kind lady. His session time was 8 a.m. and one day, though everything in my home was ready for the first patient's arrival, I had forgotten to unlock the front door. (Patients need not ring; they can just walk straight into the waiting room.)

I dashed to let him in and apologized. In the session he was very quiet and I asked if he were still thinking about the door. He became very distressed indeed.

'Look, it could 'appen to anybody. You said you were sorry. You've never done it before. The door was shut that's all. The door was just bloody shut. It's not a hanging offence is it?'

'But you'd like to hang me all the same?'

To his great shame he broke into sobs: 'This is sodding ridiculous. Big bloke like me bawling.'

'No, not ridiculous, Darryl. Your mother just locked you out.'

When the tears subsided we talked at some length about what had happened. Darryl was not the most psychologically-minded of men, but by the time the session ended he fully appreciated how much he had idealized me, how much of what had looked to him like a miracle cure was actually due to his joy at finding his mum again. He was now bitterly disappointed and angry to discover I wasn't perfect like her at all. Yet our Alliance was strong enough – just – for us to weather this necessary disillusion, and eventually find a more realistic basis for our work together.

A cautionary note needs to be sounded here. Occasionally a very fragile patient needs the positive transference very badly in the early stages and it is unwise to bring about a disillusion that he is not yet strong enough to accept. Transference interpretations can be frank but must never be brutal. Timing is critical. I have one patient with no family at all, who has adopted myself and her male GP as her parents. She attributes almost magical powers to us and relies on our loyalty and our care absolutely. It is a terrifying responsibility.

Interestingly, despite the power of this attachment to us, she never asks for more than we can give, nor contacts us outside appointments. It may be she is frightened of alienating us with what she sees as her greed, losing us as she has lost everyone else in her life that mattered, but I am tempted to hope that deep down she knows this is an emergency measure, that one day when she is stronger she will be able to withdraw her idealization and convert the transference into a firm Alliance with two real people without a smidgen of magic between them.

If the therapist is uncertain whether positive feelings from the patient are here-and-now 'real' Alliance feelings or transference feelings, it's a good idea to find out whether she might have a split transference on her hands. So she is experienced as good; that much is clear: is she half of a whole though? Is there a corresponding 'baddie' somewhere? If the (good) therapist is experienced as everything the (bad) parent was not, she is in the area of split transference. Wait till she has the effrontery to take a holiday, or forgets a session or cancels because a conference is more important. The rage or depressive disappointment that follows in the patient confirms this as transference.

Often in the early stages, the therapist breathes a sigh of relief believing she has achieved a good Alliance and that all the transference is safely sealed in some other person, so the way forward is clear. But during the first few sessions the material can change very quickly and such hypotheses have to be jettisoned. It is important not to hang on to first impressions just because they are comfortable and starting again is so humbling.

Donald was a trainee therapist who came to me because he had to be in receipt of therapy as part of his course. My name had been suggested by his female tutor for whom he now had a high regard, but with whom there had been personal conflict during the course.

We had one Assessment session, at the end of which I gave him my written Contract. Next time he got onto the couch as agreed, and proceeded to talk about the difficult time he had had with the female tutor. I wondered if he might be warning me that I, too, would soon be experienced in the same way, or maybe there was going to be some split transference, my colleague being the bad one, and me being the goodie.

However, Don came regularly and on time, bringing dreams, associations and reflections of immense richness. He would then meditate aloud on them and come to very insightful conclusions. In short, he was the ideal patient. It was all very puzzling.

My Contract stipulates among other things that fees are payable monthly in advance. Don had done everything impeccably so far, but by week three no fee was forthcoming. Perhaps he just hadn't settled down yet, got into the routine: I'd leave it one more week.

Still he did not pay. Still he brought interesting material and worked hard on it. As a trainee he knew all about transference and when I tried to subtly probe his feelings toward me so far, he assured me there was no transference blocking things. The problems with his tutor had been transference but all that was cleared up now and he was happy at the way things were progressing between the two of us.

I was certain then that the unpaid fees held the key to the mystery, though I could not for the life of me see how. I had to find an unambiguous but non-critical way of saying *he* might be happy but *I* was not: I hadn't been paid. I was still in the dark but decided the time had come for a non-aggressive confrontation over the fees, so we could enter the muddle and the mire, the 'ers' and the 'ums' of real therapy, rather than continue indefinitely with Don's virtuoso performance on the couch while I sat about with nothing to do, because he was doing it all himself. Why would he not let me in?

At first he assured me he was happy to pay, had just been waiting for me to bring it up as he wasn't sure how or when to go about it. I pointed out how meticulous he had been over every other item in the Contract, and what a perfect patient he had been so far. In the light of all that it seemed curious he should fail to have read the requirements over fees, which were the first item on the document.

He acknowledged then that there had to be some unconscious process at work and our hunt was on! I said my only clues were: (a) that in Assessment I had found myself a bit unconvinced by his assurances that he really wanted therapy for himself and not just to fulfil the requirements of the course; and (b) he'd had some fights with a powerful-sounding woman on the course who I might stand for in some way.

Don associated round this for me while I asked for the odd clarification and eventually we had it sorted. Though he had not realized it himself till now, his real feelings about me were: 'I don't like the woman and I am damned if I am going to pay her. She can sing for it.' Like the tutor and the female head of the course who required him to have his own therapy whether he needed it or not, here was another woman trying to run his life. He knew it was useless to resist; he was stuck with me for the next year at least, so, as with his mother, he was trying to make the best of a bad job by being a 'good boy', maybe even picking up a bit of love and attention along the way, if the hard-hearted so-and-so had any to spare.

Underneath his flawlessly presented material (which was really pseudo-material) he was furious with me and the power he felt I wielded. Yet, as with his mother (who had died recently), he still yearned for warmth and recognition. How better to obtain that from me than by being the best trainee and the best patient?

The immediate but denied negative maternal transference was now in the open. Some real therapy had taken place. Much elaboration remained to be done but we had made a start on the transference and in so doing had created the beginnings of an Alliance. The confirmatory evidence was that my fees from then on were paid promptly and in full.

In early Assessment, if the therapist can be receptive and passive in the best sense, rather than calling out the lifeboats, she will see the Therapeutic Alliance and the transference develop before her eyes into a 'plait', two strands running above and below each other as the plait as a whole twists and turns. To see and use this movement (dynamism) requires a certain distance on the part of the therapist, yet at the commencement of treatment the patient is likely to be at the height of his anxiety (because he has no sense of Alliance yet to calm him) and needs to feel the therapist is emotionally close to him. How can she be close and distant simultaneously? How can she callously stand by while the patient screams out for a word of consolation, reassurance? There is no easy answer, but seeing the importance of the question is a start. It is such professional conundrums that prompt me to say a too-healthy person could not possibly do the therapist's job. Someone who is used to and unafraid of being torn in half is required.

Later on the patient can tolerate and often actually appreciates the therapist's carefully measured distance from him: for then he too is extricated from overly intense feeling involvement in the other person and can for once think, not just emote and then react, knee-jerk style.

To see the Alliance/transference double helix forming before her very eyes, the therapist must be in a calm and receptive frame of mind and this is not possible if the patient is exhibiting a high level of distress or disturbance. So I emphasize again, as I did at the start of this chapter, the importance of bringing to bear the GP to the Mind subfunctions, so as to bring a chaotic clinical situation under control. Sensible boundaries must be provided, within which both parties can get to know one another before even dreaming of engaging in the delicate, detailed process that constitutes interpretive psychotherapy.

## CHAPTER 5

# Making the Dynamic Formulation

Just as an accurate and comprehensive weather forecast can help one make the most of a precious holiday period and sometimes even avoid out and out disaster, a skilled Dynamic Formulation is immeasurably useful in aiding the therapist to design and execute the treatment plan without calamity.

True, some weather forecasts are more reliable than others, owing to the complexity of prevailing conditions combined perhaps with a less experienced forecaster. There is no guarantee a Dynamic Formulation made in Assessment will solve, or even alert the therapist to, *all* future clinical difficulties; but without it the therapist has nothing but luck and her wits to rely on. Considering a patient's mental health, relationships and his attitude toward the rest of his life, is in the balance, let alone extremely tight NHS or other therapeutic resources, then luck without prediction of and preparation for all therapeutic weathers just will not do.

As with the weather, a Formulation sometimes has to be made on the basis of unusual, gradually shifting or very unstable data, depending on the patient's mental and emotional state. Formulations are not once-and-for-all affairs but may need to be modified or even overhauled completely in the light of new events in the Assessment. In rare cases the Dynamic Formulation remains unclear until post-Assessment therapy is well under way.

The Dynamic Formulation is a neat encapsulation in words of what is really 'up' with the patient, as opposed to a psychiatric diagnosis, a case summary or life history. It must give some indication of the patient's unconscious conflict(s) to qualify, and in the light of these should predict future clinical needs and problems.

'Conflict' is not synonymous with 'problem'. Shortage of cash can be a problem but that does not mean one is in conflict over money. One simply wants it and hasn't got it. A conflict over money would mean wanting and not wanting it with equal intensity.

The term 'conflict', then, specifically refers to simultaneous opposite wishes/needs that are irreconcilable; the conflicted person is torn in two. The symptoms presented in therapy represent an inadequate attempt at compromise, resolution or avoidance of conflict that is too psychologically or interpersonally expensive and/or painful to maintain. The solution has become as unbearable as the conflict itself.

93

A full Dynamic Formulation should also contain comment where possible on the unconscious aims of the patient with regard to his key relationships (for these are likely to be repeated in the transference), noting the significant points in his history where these have been frustrated with resulting stress and/or illness. Major trauma (where it exists) associated with the start of such patterns needs also to be mentioned, along with any symptoms and behaviour that in Assessment have been decoded as defences against the central conflict. An evaluation of the degree of entrenchment and budgeability of these defences is always helpful in predicting how long treatment might take.

The therapist should always write her Dynamic Formulation in the notes so that in the event of her illness, leaving, or having to refer the patient on, the completed or near completed work of Assessment can be passed on to future therapists.

In supervision, too, the Dynamic Formulation can speed up presentation as well as aid the supervisor and fellow supervisees understand the case and feel better able to offer help (unless of course the making of the Dynamic Formulation is itself the problem being brought to supervision).

At the conclusion of therapy it is most illuminating to review the first Dynamic Formulation made, see how far the therapeutic couple have come since then and how much or little the Formulation altered throughout the course of treatment. Looking back over completed treatments is as valuable a learning endeavour as the anticipatory approach taken in most supervisions.

Despite the busyness of the working day, note-taking is still very important, for one's own professional learning, one's memory – especially in times of stress – and for clarifying one's thoughts, as well as communicating with the rest of the team. Once the Dynamic Formulation is made it takes only moments to write down, saving pages and pages of cluttered and often irrelevant or indecipherable bits of information. There is no point in making notes unless they are going to be useful.

In the next chapter I shall give some brief illustrations of how a number of Dynamic Formulations came to be made and what exactly was written down in the notes. No Dynamic Formulation is absolutely complete or perfect but readers will see, I hope, that so far as was possible at the time, the above criteria for a Dynamic Formulation were taken into account.

When teaching trainees about Dynamic Formulation I am always concerned to impress upon them that they are not in the business of writing great literature: elegant, succinct phraseology is a bonus rather than a necessity. What counts is whether or not the unconscious essence of what is troubling a patient, and some tracing of that problem's development and defences against it, is expressed in the Formulation. It need not be pure poetry but it should be a concentrated, brief statement of the therapist's unique understanding of the patient, so that, contrary to so many trainee's fears, it cannot be marked like an exam paper as categorically right or wrong.

Apart from five or six lines constituting the Dynamic Formulation (perhaps ten or twelve if a fuller Formulation is requested, or the patient very complicated), what else should appear in the Assessment notes? I would suggest that following the Dynamic Formulation itself (in italics or highlighted in some other way), the therapist should note: (1) What this proposed therapy might realistically achieve and what kind of therapist should carry it out; (2) How any psychiatric background may be relevant; (3) What the future holds in terms of patient response to being 'churned up'; that is, what internal and environmental resources he can draw on; (4) How he has responded to trial interpretation in Assessment; (5) Where psychological exploration has been deliberately restricted during Assessment and whether such restriction should be kept up post Assessment; (6) What anxieties and questions the patient remains concerned about with regard to his treatment.

*Setting Achievement Goals*

Setting realistic goals in the light of the Dynamic Formulation and the patient's capacity to tolerate the uncovering nature of psychotherapy is important both to prevent possible patient breakdown and to preserve meagre treatment vacancies, especially the long-term ones which are always the scarcest. Similarly, patients must be allocated to therapists with an appropriate level of experience. It is not sensible to squander senior clinicians on straightforward patients or wreck the confidence of trainees by giving them the most complicated.

Four goal categories of therapy exist, into or between which most patients fit. First, there is the patient for whom there are no short cuts. The ailment, as with a tenacious devouring weed, must be completely rooted out to prevent regrowth. The damage is deep and pervasive. Providing he can cope with it, analysis is the treatment of choice and it is unfair on him and his therapist to be referred to a trainee or inexperienced person, who might well do more harm, and certainly very little good. Alas, such treatment is not available on the NHS.

Second, there is the patient who will thrive if only the main root and stem of the problem is cut away (the so-called 'focal therapy' approach). The ailment feels largely 'of a piece', rather than scattered throughout the psyche, virulently reproducing itself. Because there is no longer any food supply from the main root source, once therapy is completed, the peripheral bits of pathology just wither with time or are not sufficiently troublesome to seriously disrupt the patient's life.

It is my belief that more people than previously imagined could make use of this approach if therapists were more willing to extend the time available from a few weeks to a few months and if they were willing to operate as educators as well as interpreters.

Third, there is the in-between patient who will also go some significant way to health by having the main stem and root of his problem treated, but the root system has been found in Assessment to be a hybrid of numbers one and two above. This means that new pathological roots will develop slowly over time, once therapy is over, but by then the patient may have saved up for more long-term private help, or he may have been absent from the public sector services long enough to qualify for a second chance.

Even better, he may have been fortunate enough to have worked with a therapist who taught him how to deploy his unproblematic areas ('ego strengths') and his new-found insight into himself to combat new root growth. He might identify and treat *himself* as soon as new symptoms appear.

Fourth, there are patients for whom any attempt, partial or whole, at uprooting problems will result in destruction of the whole plant. As the medical GP must sadly accept he cannot cure everyone, so must the GP to the Mind deal in psychological palliatives, make the patient as comfortable as possible, recruit the help of family and friends, then wait and hope.

Only the Assessing therapist knows into which category her particular patient fits, and writing it down saves the patient and the helping agency the time and expense of doing it all again. For the patient, repeated unnecessary Assessment can be extremely demoralizing as well as threatening to any Therapeutic Alliance with a future clinician.

I remember one initial private interview when a woman sat down wearily opposite me, held out her hand and said: 'How do you do? I am a parcel.' It transpired she had been assessed four times in twelve weeks: once by her GP; once at her church; and twice by NHS agencies. In desperation she had cashed in an insurance policy that was for her old age and decided to 'go private' so she wouldn't have to be passed on again. I had to deal with her fury before any Assessment of my own could begin.

To collect data that helps the therapist decide in which of the four categories she is going to place her patient, she must think about technique. It is a mistake to over-structure the Assessment sessions, because the way the patient presents his material is as revealing as the content of his story. On the other hand, once the Alliance is cemented, he won't mind too much if he is occasionally asked for clarification, or direct questions are put to him to fill gaps in the therapist's knowledge.

When trying to find this middle way between structuring and free association, the therapist must remember that allowing a patient to ramble too freely so soon in the treatment can prevent the therapist from being able to organize salient material into a Dynamic Formulation while encouraging him to make an attachment and commitment before the Contract (see Chapter 7) has been made, a Contract that, depending on the outcome of Assessment, might not include lengthy work with this particular therapist.

## Using the Psychiatric Background

It is a great pity that most psychotherapy and counselling trainings do not include the teaching of clinical psychiatry. Antipathy for the 'medical model' of viewing psychic distress abounds still, associated as it is with the labelling process so many psychotherapeutic patients rightly detest. But as a consequence, many otherwise well trained senior therapists have no idea what a borderline personality might really be, or what the term schizoid means, or how variform can be 'the Depressions' – blithely assuming there is only one.

Many are ideologically opposed to the notion of illness, insist on seeing breakdown as *only* the result of inadequate social, family and political structures. Such extreme views are as dangerous as the ultra-conservative ones they are designed to challenge. I would have more respect for such views if they had been arrived at after some months spent with hospitalized, acutely ill psychiatric patients who have not yet been prescribed drugs.

As a staff nurse in the early 1960s I remember admitting a manic patient from an ambulance, who, despite an elephantine intramuscular dose of Largactil, emerged tearing off her clothes and frenziedly dancing down the ward, while her husband wept and begged her to stop. She foamed at the mouth, singing nonsense words in a voice strained and cracked from over-use, her hair caked with soil, berries and leaves. This had been going on for three days: neither she nor her husband had slept in that time.

To deprive her of medication and in-patient privacy (when she recovered she remembered it all and was suicidal with shame); to deprive her husband of relief from 100 per cent care; to force 'the community' to deal with such disruptive symptomatology (that would inevitably draw care staff away from others and drive many recovering ex-patients over the edge) was unthinkable.

We still need asylums, in the most humane sense of that word – a place of refuge, a place where the normal social rules do not apply and there is space, time and meditation enough to come to terms with demons that need not or cannot be hidden, a place where others will care for, protect – and, yes, control you if that is what is needed to keep you integrated. Yes, in-patient psychiatric units have been vastly abused. That does not mean they should not exist.

My next hospital after that was a pioneering and controversial Therapeutic Community. The 'Movement' (for in those days it was a heady, exciting anti-Establishment, anti-psychiatry crusade; there could be no deviation, no revisionism) was reaching its apotheosis. Innocent and idealistic, no one welcomed or praised it more than I. I felt privileged to have been selected as a nursing sister at the tender age of twenty-four. Based on belief in in-patient community support combined with interpretative psychotherapy, drugs and electric shocks were banished as outlandish evils. Humane psychiatry had arrived at last.

Or so I thought. A woman suffering postnatal depression was admitted with husband, new baby and second son. The family worked hard to become part of the community, took their full share of cooking and cleaning responsibilities and were generally popular.

Mum deteriorated rapidly, though, her self-reproach, feelings of unworthiness and guilt at not loving the baby mounting until she was suicidal. Other mums on the family unit helped her to wash and feed baby and 'sat' for her whenever she couldn't cope. She was grateful, apologetic, increasingly self-blaming, hating the child and hating herself for feeling that way.

Her wretchedness was worst at night. She paced restlessly, wringing her hands and weeping, never sleeping. Her husband had a full-time job so had to sleep. The community organized a 24-hour rota to sit with her and stop her killing herself. Her doctor gave her daily therapeutic sessions instead of the usual two a week. Nurses spent hours of their shift with her at the expense of other patients, which only made her feel worse. Her older son was being neglected, showing signs of disturbance. She begged to be allowed to die.

Meanwhile the staff were deep in discord. Many of the nurses wanted her put on Phenothiazines at once, having seen women with this diagnosis respond quickly. Some advocated ECT in a nearby hospital, so she could return to the community and other women's support at night. Some doctors had to sadly agree while others defended the community ethic to the end, saying if we failed with this patient then all our psychiatric beliefs were just hot air; we must carry on and have faith in the therapeutic ideology which had brought us all to work here. Definitely no drugs. Certainly no ECT.

This argument produced massive guilt in some and fury in others (including me), who felt the hospital's reputation was being put before the patient's needs. (There were many powerful political forces at work trying to shut us down: it wasn't me who would have to defend our right to exist, so it was easy for me to be virtuous!)

Psychological interpretations were lobbed between the let-her-go and let-her-stay staff factions like angry missiles. Sending her away, ran one let-her-stay interpretation, was just to protect the other patients and ourselves from our pain at seeing her in such a pitiful state; we needed to be tougher and have more faith in our approach: her suffering was terrible but would be vindicated in the end.

Drugging her was not to help her but to shut her up, complained the anti-drug lobby, because we were unconsciously angry at her for failing to respond to our powerful therapeutic community ideals. We must acknowledge and manage our anger better then there'd be no need for drugs.

Another argument from the let-her-stay people claimed that the opposition only wanted rid of her because they couldn't stand the doubt and exhaustion in the rest of the patient community, as well as their criticism. By now patients were holding their own meetings, some of them demanding the staff transfer her, and others feeling horribly guilty at not being able to cope, asking why the staff, who were after all the professionals, had not come up with some other solution.

The staff could not provide the miracle, so a new cry went up. Discharge her, admit defeat to save staff and patients from corporate depression and an ideological split that could demoralize the community for months. The staff who had always claimed she should go denounced these turncoats, angrily insisting that sacrificing the one for the many was morally unacceptable. If she were to be discharged the only legitimate reason, which we should openly admit to, would be so that she could receive the treatment she really needed in a medically-oriented hospital. To some this was heresy indeed!

Most of the in-patient members were by now questioning 'the Faith'. What was so terrible about drugs and ECT if they worked when nothing else had? Why should this woman be allowed to go on suffering so?

These patients had been taught that communal support and psychotherapy could overcome anything. Now they were disenchanted and angry. Weren't we all? This led all of us to consider the most fearsome interpretation of all. Were we making her much worse? Was she introjecting the underlying hatred of those staff and patients who saw her, albeit unconsciously, as a witchlike figure undermining our most sacred beliefs? If so, should we not redouble our efforts to accept her, not cast her out?

The meetings – staff's and patients'; staff *with* patients – went on, more and more acrimonious, guilt-ridden, always divided, while the patient herself got steadily worse.

The atmosphere was funereal on the day she made her suicide bid and had to be transferred for her own safety to the local mental hospital.

While day after day the whole community met to consider its depression, the patient, by now too far gone for medication, was given several ECTs, followed by careful conventional nursing and no responsibilities. She gradually recovered, despite all we had done to her.

A quarter of a century later I can see she was badly assessed, possibly by a young inexperienced psychiatrist who thought all depressions looked the same. She should never have been admitted to our kind of unit.

But how many non-psychiatrically trained psychotherapists today can truthfully say that in his place they would have recognized at once that this was no ordinary depression, but the early stages of a psychotic breakdown totally unsuited to a psychotherapeutic approach – at least one in which medication was banned? How many of these therapists might have seen 'baby blues' when what they were faced with was incipient madness?

Surely it is time some psychiatric work experience and some lectures on psychiatric disorders were included in therapy training courses?

Hostility and envy between medically and non-medically qualified therapists should not be allowed to prevent the appropriate use of psychiatric knowledge. Where a psychotherapist not possessed of psychiatric experience is working with a persistently unclear picture, which an Assessment has failed to sort out, she may well require an additional psychiatric evaluation. This frequently provides the missing link.

Alas, many therapists feel that to work with a psychiatrist in this way is to 'sell out' on dynamic principles (admit that psychiatry is, in the end, superior), that such a consultation is evidence of professional submission. Interdisciplinary teamwork is alive and well on paper, but has a very long way to go in practice. It is not only patients who have severe problems with trust!

When Assessing a patient for psychotherapy it is essential to know before making a Contract, whether there have been any breakdowns or hospital admissions and the circumstances surrounding these. How old was the patient and what else was going on in his life at the time that might have been precipitating factors? Are such factors likely to recur in the course of the psychotherapy now being considered? How often were the psychiatric episodes and was there a recognizable pre-illness pattern that could be identified again in the future? How life-threatening were suicidal attempts, as opposed to being 'cries for help'? Has the patient ever been out of touch with reality (psychotic) and are there particular relationships or situations which appear to induce or exacerbate such periods? What medication has the patient been on, and with what result?

A psychiatric history in itself does not debar a patient from being able to use psychotherapy, but his susceptibility to further breakdown must be carefully gauged because dynamic psychotherapy can and usually should (for a time) make the patient as disturbed as he has ever been. If his current distress is such that the risk of another breakdown is worth taking, rather than depriving him of treatment and prolonging his misery, then it is essential the Assessor make recommendations for proper psychiatric cover.

For example, a colleague of mine felt unhappy about the fate of one of her patients and asked to chew it over with me. The patient was a cheerful young woman the therapist had been asked to see for 'late adolescent relationship difficulties'. The patient had been quite open about a brief breakdown in her late teens, including anti-depressant medication. Assuming she had now been told the worst, my colleague made a contract and the work started immediately.

At first all went well. Nine months into therapy the woman became uncharacteristically depressed, agitated and unable to think clearly. This continued for some weeks, alarming the therapist who finally asked if these feelings might be like the pre-breakdown ones.

'Oh no,' came the reply. 'These ones are for my brother.'

Surprised, the therapist said: 'I didn't know you had a brother.'

After a long silence, in which the patient kept shaking her head as if clearing cobwebs, she finally replied: 'I don't any more. He was my twin. He shot himself on our fifteenth birthday. My birthday is tomorrow.'

The therapist had dutifully collected the psychiatric *fact* of the breakdown, but not explored its contributory factors, which were critical to the whole therapeutic enterprise. The facility to hive off unwanted pain into a separate mental compartment (dissociation) was beginning to wane in therapy, hence the patient's headshaking confusion as the birthday approached. This year the brother was not going to stay away.

The capacity to dissociate had been completely missed in a routine, preliminary interview, the therapist completely beguiled by the smiling exterior of the patient, who turned out to be far more disturbed than anyone had realized. She broke down again, while everyone panicked, trying to find a hospital she would accept. In the end she was sectioned and admitted to a depressing unit she hated, full of much older people and miles from her home and friends. The mental health team concerned had been totally unprepared for this predictable emergency, and everyone felt badly about the outcome.

Just because the patient looks and/or sounds well (or ill) in the first few meetings, does not mean they necessarily are. In proper Assessment the Assessor finds out how much of what she is seeing is the outward expression of constant inner disturbance and how much is the patient's emotional reaction to being in the early and middle stage of Assessment, or to other work, family or social pressures outside the session. She needs and takes time to appreciate what is *not* reported as well as what is, and whether omissions are significant. More than one Assessment session gives opportunity for the display of a variety of behaviours and feelings so that the therapist can work out what the patient's mental state is like *overall*.

A grounding in psychiatric medicine might have helped this colleague avoid the error of taking what she observed at face value. She had never seen such classic dissociation before so was not on the look-out for it.

*Forecasting the Future and Measuring Resources*

The case vignettes above readily demonstrate how important the prediction of future breakdown can be, and the serious consequences of missing critical data in Assessment. By the time a Contract is made, the therapist should be able to make informed guesses about whether this person might for a period become mentally or psychosomatically ill in treatment, or so depressed he

102

loses his job, or his wife might leave him, his acting out might lead him to prison, promiscuity, violence, or the stress of therapy drive him back to drink.

Is it better to leave well alone? Will the relief of one kind of suffering induce another? Could one apprise the patient of these possibilities and let *him* choose? Does the therapist encourage the committedly gay schoolmaster to 'come out', knowing the threat to his work and the possible effect on his children? What does she do about the talented, emotionally fragile woman determined to leave her dull but dependable husband, whose lack of psychological resources might suggest she is safer staying put? (that is, the therapist is pretty sure the strains and responsibilities of freedom without protection would lead to a breakdown).

Who are we to judge? But if our opinion is sought and paid for, can we withhold that judgement? Is it possible to do therapy and expect no side-effects in the patient's life? Are we not obliged to warn them that, as with psychotropic drugs, 'no side-effect, no therapy'?

The myth of the value-free, non judgemental therapist has to go. What is needed is responsible judgement, not no judgement. Therapists are judging every minute of Assessment, trying to put their knowledge and experience at the disposal of the patient, while at the same time deciding what it is and isn't fair to offer him in the light of what that therapeutic offering might do to the rest of his life.

I have heard two therapists of equal stature argue equally cogently in a supervision group for assisting a given patient to keep her marriage together till the kids grow up, while the other one argued for an early break while the kids were young enough to adjust, not know what they had missed: single parenthood would feel normal to them. Meanwhile the mother would be prevented from having a depressive breakdown attributable to the marriage and unhelpful for the children. The first therapist countered that with therapeutic help a breakdown was not inevitable.

Naturally, everyone in the group including the presenter agreed it had to be up to the patient herself, who was pulled equally in both directions. But the frank and heated level of discussion among therapists who knew one another well proved beyond doubt that therapists cannot be truly value-free, any more than a parent can be expected to be without bias concerning his or her own child. We concluded that what was important was that therapists become more conscious of their private values and how and why they are using them in the consulting room, rather than trying to get rid of them, which only results in unhelpful repression.

Part of Assessment is to make another judgement: what inner and outer resources does the patient possess to deal with any side-effects of psychotherapy? What extra resources, if any, can the therapist or health team provide? If he is hospitalized, can he still see his therapist? If marital problems develop, can his wife be seen? If problems occur at work will supportive psychological reports be written to his employer?

Internally, how much resilience to pain does this patient have? How much has he borne before, and is today's situation better or worse for pain-bearing? How much insight can he take? Is he so self-regarding that any 'criticism' will be experienced as a terrible blow to his self-esteem and he may leave therapy? If his repressed anger or grief is contacted, will he be able to contain it? And if it is not contacted, then what is the point of treatment? How many sessions a week can be spared to ensure containment? If there is only a once a week vacancy available, is this the right patient for that vacancy?

## Making Trial Interpretations

The best way to make a trial interpretation is cautiously. Some patients feel criticized by interpretations, offended by any suggestion (as they see it) that they don't know their own minds. They feel angry and defensive at being told what they 'really' think or mean. An angry reaction to a trial interpretation can denote a paranoid element in the patient's personality or can be a perfectly reasonable reaction to an unconscious attack or put-down by the therapist disguised as a helpful interpretation. This often happens when a therapist feels threatened by a challenging or psychologically sophisticated patient.

Many patients have to be educated so that they understand the function of an interpretation as well as its content. Most people do not come up against psychotherapy in their daily lives and need help to see what it is all about. Like demonstrating a new car, they need to be shown the controls and properties of the car, compared with what they are used to. Expecting them to drive smoothly without this preparation and then calling them rotten drivers is unfair and inaccurate.

Once they are familiar with all the therapeutic 'gadgets' – silence, transference, free association, dreamwork, linking and the like – then and only then is it safe to decide whether or not their response to interpretation is positive or negative.

Those who respond to the first cautious interpretation with a blank look may be unsuitable, but it may also be that the inter-pretation was clumsy, premature, or plain wrong and so made no sense to the patient.

If the latter, then another attempt at gentle interpretation needs to be made at an appropriate time. If the patient responds with interest, asks for help to understand what has just been said, or immediately produces material that confirms the hypothesis tenta-tively offered, then the therapist can go on to make firmer or deeper observations, to see how much insight the patient can comfortably take, and whether he might even collaborate in making interpretations, once he has got the idea.

Some take to interpretation quicker than others. Responses to these early interpretations give an indication as to how fast and deep the prospective post-Assessment therapy might go and so ensures allocation of an appropriate vacancy, in terms of time and therapeutic expertise available. Such a factor is vital in a unit under pressure to be cost effective.

A patient's reaction to early interpretative attempts often gives away much about his hidden motivation. While on the surface he seems keen to get well and produces information very readily, he might balk at the interpretation, for its very utterance places on him the responsibility for thinking about himself more deeply, facing uncomfortable possibilities that might lead to further even less palatable revelations. What seemed a fast-stream patient at first can turn out to be a very slow one.

Many patients are thoroughly Assessed except for the making of trial interpretations, on the grounds that it is too soon and too disturbing to put them in touch with their unconscious. However, if interpretation is not tried out for its effect the patient takes on treatment without knowing what he is letting himself in for and this is unfair and dishonest.

It can also be time-, cost- and expertise-wasting. I know of many patients who appeared highly motivated and co-operative until required to consider interpretations in post-Assessment therapy when the mutual commitment was already made. It turned out the patient wanted not understanding, enlightenment, growth, but an eternal friend to lean on who would listen and accept unconditionally the patient's own view of the world. Some very self-absorbed patients love to hear themselves talk but cannot bear to consider an alternative view of the world. For them the role of the therapist is that of appreciative audience.

Some want a perfect parent who will magically cure without the patient having to go through any self-exploratory suffering. A variation on this theme is the belief many patients have that therapists are possessed of arcane mysteries and can do things to the patient to make him better. A middle-aged man once got very fed up with my efforts at trial interpretation and said shortly: 'Never mind all these flipping guessing games. When are you going to put the heebie-jeebies on me?' I tried to help him see what the guessing games were really about, but he concluded that as I had no bag of tricks I must be a con artist, and never came back.

There is a kind of patient who often gets through Assessment successfully because he appears to react well to interpretations. The depth of his resistance to therapy is only uncovered much later on. Sometimes, but not always, the situation can be rescued if the practitioner is sufficiently experienced.

Doctor Mason, a writer of popular scientific books, was in his early forties and came to see me because of a repeated pattern of failed relationships with women, including three marriages. There was a complex family history that gave many clues as to why he was compelled to repeat this pattern of charming seduction, fierce jealousy and possessiveness, and finally contempt, followed by break-up and then depression. Each idea I offered was gratefully taken up and elaborated on. We got on like a house on fire.

Doctor Mason had been analysed in Paris, Prague and New York. He explained that he travelled to a new country to research each book and so each analysis tended to last about a year. He then returned to his house in England for the write up where he had a regular resident therapist who had unfortunately died some while back and he had been given my name as a possible substitute.

I observed out loud how addicted he seemed to therapy. He responded insightfully, saying yes, and furthermore there was always a pattern in his therapies not dissimilar to that of his relations with girlfriends and wives: his Prague female therapist had worked all year with him on that theme.

He almost convinced me that the change in therapists was really unavoidable because of his work, and after all, didn't he always come back to the English one in the end? Still suspicious, I asked about any improvements in his six years or so of analysis. His rather hurt reply intrigued me: 'Can't you *see* the improvement?' I had expected him to report a change in the way he dealt with relationships outside the session.

The Assessment continued, his understanding of his early family life seeming complete in every respect, each analyst having gone over the same or similar ground, Doctor Mason having learned that little bit more with every one. I was curious, puzzled and cautious, while he was eager to start work. We made a Contract, and began the following week.

After three months it became clear to me that Doctor Mason did not want to change. He derived great pleasure from becoming as expert on psychoanalysis as he was on science. His very damaging childhood had become an endless source of fascination for him. He knew he intrigued therapists (I was no exception) and enjoyed playing psychological and verbal chess with them. It turned out there had been several other short-term therapists whom he had found unworthy of his talents and had sacked them. Therapy, at which he was an immense success, was more interesting and rewarding than real life, at which, in relationship terms at any rate, he was a dismal failure.

I had to find a clear but tactful way of conveying this to him. He ignored or deflected my remarks for a long time, but when I finally got through he was very angry and nearly left. The only thing that kept him coming was that I had produced a new angle for him to analyse, that had not come up before. He couldn't resist it. He set out to prove me wrong and a long struggle between us began.

I refused to work on the juicy titbits of his past, which he kept offering me. He knew his childhood backwards already and was using it to justify his inability (fear) to tackle the present. He had not been near a woman in six years – claimed he was waiting till he was better – and instead conducted a much safer and longer-lasting love affair with therapy.

To his great annoyance I kept pointing out that I was a woman as well as a therapist, and how long was he proposing to go on desexualizing me? I was getting cheesed off with walks up the intellectual garden path: when could we face his fear of the present and start some real work?

It took four years, but in the end he grumpily admitted he had met his match and we settled down to getting him out of rather than into therapy. He relates better to women now, but will always be scarred to some extent. These scars he is still coming to terms with, rather than using them like before as currency with which to purchase a pseudo-life in one consulting room after another.

In Assessment this patient seemed the ideal candidate, but his 'good' response to trial interpretation was in fact part of his symptomatology.

Trial interpretation, then, might be regarded as the suck-it-and-see technique. Having been very careful to establish an Alliance, having taken due regard of the psychiatric history, having evaluated the patient's external and internal resources, the time has come to take necessary risks. There is no point in having a Dynamic Formulation that has not been confirmed, at least in its spirit if not its letter, by the patient. The only way to see if he agrees is to present him with the full or partial Formulation in the shape of a carefully couched interpretation that is not so hesitant he can't make sense of it, but not so bold or confident that he dare not play with it, amend it, and where needful, bin it.

## Restricting Exploration

Where part of the evolving Formulation includes suspicion of psychotic or borderline processes, exploration of the material may need deliberate restriction. The therapist notes the material and its implications but refrains from interpreting it to the patient for fear of disturbing deep layers of experience that, having once contacted in the session, the patient is reluctant or unable to put away again.

Grant, twenty-five, worked in church administration. He came from a strictly religious, rule-bound family, with a severely ailing but authoritarian father he could neither respectfully obey nor rebel against, due to guilt about the illness and guilt about the biblical Commandment to honour parents. He had been talked into early marriage by a slightly older woman, by whom he had a child he loved yet seemed in rivalry with.

When my supervisee did her Assessment, she found his main preoccupations to be those of late adolescence. He was hungry for sexual experience and had many bizarre sexual fantasies about which he felt very guilty. Psychologically he related to his wife as if she were his restrictive mother, yet in behaviour at least, honoured and obeyed her. Due to the lack of any satisfactory male models in his life he could not accept his aggression or hate, having repressed them and channelled them into at times fervent religious preoccupation. Women were worshipped from afar or seen as harlots and temptresses, neither category affording him any satisfaction: the one not permitting sex, the other producing guilt.

So far so typical. But the supervisee was properly concerned with his religious fantasies which came into play (she posited) whenever there was intolerable guilt resulting from illicit sexual and, she suspected, sadistic desires. He would turn away from these conflicts and resort to strange mental states in which he saw himself as the Saviour in the desert, suffering terribly for his people, yet in a state of high exaltation. Or there would be lurid Sodom and Gomorrah scenes in which he heroically fought temptation and again won out for his people, after which he would appear to them in all his transcendental glory.

These fantasies, featuring very primitive bodily symbols and some-times sadistic colourations, were not in themselves that unusual or hard to understand, given Grant's internal conflicts. It was not so much the content of these prolonged waking dreams, as the quality with which he reported them, that alerted the therapist to include them strongly in her Dynamic Formulation. They made the therapist feel odd, out of touch with a patient she had five minutes earlier felt very close to. She felt the fantasies were but the tip of an iceberg, in that he had created a whole mythology, symbol language, an alternative world to live in when ordinary life got too difficult. He seemed almost to believe that this other world was more real, than the day-to-day one, and tried often to change the sessions into discussions of mysticism and supernatural possibilities.

The supervisee was an experienced practitioner and so contracted to treat Grant, but because of his borderline state decided she would avoid entering this part of his inner life. Instead she would work on his relations with self, wife and early family to assist him legitimize and accept his aggression and sexuality. When he daydreamed aloud, she would hear him out then take up his fantasizing with him as an escape route from intolerable conflict – the role of ecstatically suffer-ing martyr far more appealing than wicked sinner no one would want to sin with anyway, his being only half a man.

Care had to be exercised not to offend his religious sensibilities: he had to be helped to see the difference between usual religious feeling and his religious fantasies which in their own way were as exciting as his denied forbidden pictures.

This vignette shows that a correct Dynamic Formulation can make work with 'unsuitable' patients possible. The supervisee concen-trated on helping Grant come to terms with the real world of sexual and social relations, as well as finding ways of seeing his parents, especially his father, more objectively and without guilt.

As he improved in this regard, the inner life of martyrdom that had so fascinated him beckoned less. He was enabled to see his child as a separate being and not as an amalgamation of the two of them. He came to accept, even though he could not eradicate it, his rivalry with and envy of the child in relation to his wife/mother. He stood up to bullies at work, felt more of a man.

Grant was discharged much improved with an invitation to return should he need to.

I am sure the supervisee was right in her Dynamic Formulation: it clearly stated that for once the therapist should not act in the conventional way, pursuing the deepest recesses of the patient's fantasy life, but should aim to rebuild with him a relationship with everyday reality so rewarding that he might lose interest in the fantasy world she chose to largely ignore.

Here is a patient I lost precisely because I did not sufficiently restrict exploration while I was trying to find a Dynamic Formulation.

Melville, fifty-one, was a rich entrepreneurial businessman who sat on a charity board with a professor at the university where I ran the counselling service, and who gave him my name for private treatment.

My immediate impression was of an incorrigible rogue with a monstrously narcissistic personality, but I couldn't help warming to him. He was always impeccably dressed and groomed – hand-made shirts, silk cravats, perfectly coiffured silver hair, silver-headed walking cane, fresh flower in his button hole. He lectured me on the whys and wherefores of his symptoms (problems with women and ex-wives, and sudden dips into despair), while simultaneously flattering and flirting, retracting apologetically, charmingly, each time he saw he had gone too far.

His family and relationship history was not hard to understand dynamically speaking, and he responded enthusiastically to my trial interpretations about it. I was struck by the relish with which he approached therapy, as if we were settling down to a good game of cards, or a Christmas dinner. He often said things like: 'You're good at this aren't you?' These comments made me very uneasy.

The Assessment was protracted as I felt I had not yet got the measure of Melville. He was quite happy to talk about his despairing moods so long as it was clinical, descriptive and in the past. But such conversation was always fleeting and followed by a joke and change of subject.

When manic defences seemed to be coming down and he had stopped telling me how to do my job, I decided to try and move the work on. He was showing off as usual and I was supposed to chuckle appreciatively. Instead I linked his hours spent in the gym, at the hairdresser, the health farm, and on extreme diets (interspersed with gourmet blow-outs), with a fear of decay and dying. He flew into a rage, his face puce, and ordered me never to mention the word death again. I was astonished at his anger, never having seen a hint of it before.

There were no significant deaths in his history but it was clear to me he was terrified of his own demise. Each time I tried to approach the subject – and I did so very obliquely and only when the material strongly suggested it – he would interrupt, bang his fist on the table and demand silence. I suggested we talk not about death itself then, but about why he was so angry with me for mentioning it. His crafty gambler's grin came back and he said: 'Ha, you don't catch me that way.' He was all charm once more, changing the subject to his latest girlfriend.

I bore with this for a while, but it became increasingly clear that Melville enjoyed his therapy only so long as it involved a battle he could win. He accepted interpretations so long as they did not touch on anything to do with his despair (that is, so long as they were useless), and he fed me all manner of interesting anecdotes so I would continue making them. When finally I pointed this process out to him he grinned, saying how much he liked 'plucky little women'. I felt condescended to and furious. I tried to use these feelings to help me understand how he had related to other women. When I made interpretations about that he also agreed with me.

By the fifth session I must have looked thoroughly defeated, for he turned very serious and said he fully realized that I felt he was a condescending bastard ('All my women do, but they love me just the same ... '), but I should realize that I had really helped him. He did take notice of what I said about women and things were improving in that department.

It was then I made my fatal mistake. I think I must have made it because I was angry and determined to recover my ground, though at the time I told myself I would lose the Alliance if he saw me as weak (he had tremendous contempt for traditionally feminine women).

'But your women are not the main point. They seem to function only as consolation, temporary protection from your fear of ... depression,' I said (I dared not mention death).

His face darkened. 'You may be right, but I have *told* you you are never to broach that subject. If you can't stick to the rules woman, you'll have to go.'

I spoke quietly and seriously. 'Melville, if I go on sticking to your rules you'll never be able to get any help from me. It's the same with your women. You find and admire the gutsy ones, get tremendous satisfaction from conquering them with your charm and influence, then you sack them when they rebel and won't play it your way any more. Can't you and I do it differently?'

He understood me perfectly. 'Your way means talking about ... *that*,' he said sulkily.

'Eventually, when you are ready.'

He roared away in his Porsche as usual, then wrote me a note saying he was not coming any more. I wrote back but he did not reply.

Had I rushed Melville? If I saw him now, with fifteen years' more experience, would I do any better? Would I be able to restrict exploration until he could cope with it? Would he ever be ready to look at death or would he endlessly repeat his defiance of it by subjugating me to his will, diverting himself with our 'games', as he subjugated and played games with all his other women (who clearly represented his powerful mother – he was in total agreement with that)? I do not know.

## Attending to Patients' Questions and Anxieties

Patients tend to go on being anxious even after their Assessor has invited then replied to their queries about post-Assessment therapy. It is important to write down these worries in the Assessment notes, especially if a therapist other than the Assessor might conduct the treatment.

Where marital therapy is being proposed, for example, the patient may ask if treatment could break up the marriage, especially if he or she suspects that is what the other partner wants. There is no simple answer to this, but the question itself may need to be brought out early in the conjoint sessions.

Assessing for a group I am almost invariably asked: 'Won't I be sort of infected by all the other people's problems? I have enough difficulty trying to cope with my own.' I find an answer of sorts, but the worry goes on – the issue needs to be aired in the group itself, after Assessment is finished. Answering the question shows the therapist has heard, and that matters; but it does not take away the anxiety behind the question. Subsequent therapy should do that, providing the therapist is not so foolish as to believe her original answer had been sufficient.

There are the eternal questions: How long will it take? Will I get better? Will I be given a senior or a trainee? Will my symptoms come back? Many Assessors do not invite questions from their patient precisely because they do not know how to answer them without having to truthfully say: 'I don't actually know' or resorting to cliches and phrases like, 'It all depends,' or, 'How long is a piece of string?'

Many patients pick up the therapist's unspoken cue not to ask too many questions, or are simply too overawed or fearful of retribution to ask. The therapist may feel relieved but is colluding in a conspiracy of silence that effectively reinforces the patient's lack of confidence and does nothing for the Therapeutic Alliance. Already the patient is learning that he must not presume to participate in his own healing. Even the 'piece of string' answer is preferable to that.

CHAPTER 6

# Making the Dynamic Formulation: Short Examples

The Dynamic Formulation represents the condensed meaning of all that the patient brings to Assessment and is based upon his central conflict. Some Formulations take longer than others, being more complex, or the patient less forthcoming; but there is little doubt that the therapist's speed and accuracy in finding Formulations increases with practice.

I have been asked if there can be more than one Formulation. Certainly there are different ways of couching the same Formulation: reading the notes it is often easy to guess which school of psychotherapy the Assessor trained in, especially if she is recently qualified and so still rather reliant on 'proper language'. A Neo-Freudian, Jungian, Kleinian and Winnicottian can arrive at the same Formulation based on totally different reportage from the patient and using different concepts to articulate that Formulation. Providing the person reading the notes is a good translator there is no problem with this, though I always advise supervisees to use plain English whenever possible.

Where a patient complains of several apparently dissimilar problems these are usually linked by a single Formulation. What the Assessor is seeing/hearing is the same Formulation, or one of its offspring, working itself out in a different setting or developmental period. In other words, the Dynamic Formulation will spawn mini versions of itself throughout the patient's life-experience, adapting and disguising these 'babies' to suit new conditions. The job of Assessment is to pursue and identify the mother Formulation from which all others spring, albeit in various specialized forms. Sometimes the therapist finds the mother by following the children; at other times knowing the mother enables the therapist to understand the children. Thus are they all grouped together, one family, one Formulation.

To make a confident Dynamic Formulation four areas of clinical material need to be studied: textual, subtextual, contextual (past and present), and conflictual areas. If the reader will bear with me for just a few short paragraphs of theory I will then illustrate that theory with some clear clinical examples.

The textual area includes all hard information gleaned from and

114

about the patient: what he says and does; how he behaves, dresses, treats the therapist; the contents of the referral letter; the way in which the referral came about; any pre-appointment communications between the patient/referrer/therapist; any previous history available to the therapist. Like starting a book, the patient 'falls open' for the therapist to inspect. His 'text' is laid out before her; she can read it at face value or attempt to 'read between the lines', that is, look for the subtext.

But the text itself is vitally important, otherwise wild guesses can be made about the subtext. The therapist's imagination can be kept in order by constant reversion to the actual text. As I often demand of trainees who produce colourful descriptions of the subtext: 'Where is your evidence? Where in the text is such a thing suggested, and where in the context is it corroborated?'

The subtextual area, then, refers to the patient's inner world of constructions, what special meanings he gives to things as opposed to the commonly-held meaning. (In a training workshop I once asked trainees what a chair meant. For one member it meant peace and quiet, for another a senior university appointment, and for another a place of execution; that is, the electric chair.)

If a patient says he is depressed the Assessor needs to know what he *personally* is experiencing when he makes such a claim, how he arrived at that special meaning for the term. Was his mother depressed so he gauges his feelings against hers? Is he labelling his sexual impotence as a 'stress disorder'? Is he so angry at his wife that he unconsciously believes himself wicked, lapsing into self-punitive melancholy which he sees as 'fatigue' or 'ME'? If the therapist cannot understand the patient's private lexicon she is in danger of imposing her own, or ascribing a mere academic meaning to what he brings.

When it feels hard to gain entry into the patient's world of personal constructions, the Assessor might gear her interventions to finding the contextual frame in which all he is communicating to her is set. Acquiring some background to a problem often puts that problem in a clearer light, and the subtext is suddenly accessible.

Similarly, when a patient seems reluctant to give any context but is quite happy to discuss what a word, or image, or thing actually means to him, this amiable discussion of the subtext can provide the therapist with vital clues as to what the context might once have been, to give rise to such constructions.

The rule of thumb, after getting the text, is to go first into the area – be it subtext or context – where the patient feels most able to communicate. Almost invariably, providing the therapist is skilled and sensitive, one thing will lead to another and what started off as simple text will develop into subtext and context and the central conflict will stand revealed.

In working toward a Dynamic Formulation, though, it must be remembered that what is being sought is an *unconscious* conflict that has grown, been elaborated upon, retreated, maybe even lost for a time, then found and refined, perhaps redirected for a period, then eventually buried or abandoned, only to return again in full force leading to this consultation. The therapist, therefore, might have to consider not one but many, many contexts, past and present, before feeling sure she has got the Formulation right. New therapists properly check their findings in one context with several others, at different periods of the patient's life, before they feel they have sufficient evidence for a Formulation.

For an experienced therapist working with a relatively straight-forward patient, hearing material from only two contexts, one past and one present, then making a link between (facilitated by her appreciation of the subtext) is sufficient to bring about the Formulation. The remaining contexts will be worked through in post Assessment therapy.

In more complex cases, if one context does not bear fruit, it is useful to invite the patient for a walk round other contexts, at other periods of his life. ('And how was it when you became a teenager?' or: 'Becoming a father ... ?' or: 'And getting married ... ?') If enough historical contexts are explored, guided by the map of the patient's personal world of meaning (an understanding of the subtext), the central conflict will sooner or later emerge. This can then be offered for confirmation or modification to the patient in the form of a trial interpretation.

I am grateful to a trainee GP who offered this case in a workshop on Dynamic Formulation.

Mr Biggin, a fifty-two-year-old insurance broker, came to see Dr X in Saturday surgery, reserved for emergencies. He was clutching himself in the region of his solar plexus and was sweating heavily. He'd been up all night with 'heart pains' and was terrified of imminent collapse. He'd not dared disturb his wife who slept next door, for she had a busy charity day ahead, important committee meetings and such. But he'd got here as soon as surgery opened.

It was clear to Dr X that this was no heart seizure; the symptoms were all wrong. It looked like a prolonged panic attack to him. What he wanted to know was why?

The workshop group and Dr X covered the four areas above using material from the two sessions he'd so far had with the patient. We

116

gleaned enough data (here sifted and sorted to make accessible reading) to make a reasonably confident Dynamic Formulation, which would become the kernel of any subsequent psychotherapy, providing the patient were judged able to use such an approach.

TEXT

Mr Biggin clearly communicated a state of high anxiety, fear of death, and physical pains that on examination suggested no medical condition. Scanning previous notes, Dr X found no recent serious illnesses or psychiatric history.

SUBTEXT

When Dr X asked Mr Biggin why he was convinced it was a heart problem when he, the doctor, could find no evidence of it, Mr Biggin, now much reassured, scratched his head and said, yes it was funny: he didn't drink much, never smoked, ate sensibly, exercised, and he was not under stress. In fact his job was pretty damned boring after thirty years with the same firm.

Already the workshop members and I were wondering if the meaning of 'heart attack' for Mr Biggin might be 'punishment for high living'. We'd wait and see.

CONTEXT (PRESENT)

Dr X asked Mr Biggin to elaborate on work, not knowing for the moment what else he ought to ask. Then, as he seemed so relieved by talking, the doctor sat back while the patient gave lots more contextual information. Mrs Biggin was getting very involved in charity work now the children had left home and was thriving on the esteem of her colleagues and the admiration of the vicar. Mr Biggin was not religious and felt left out.

After an awkward and lengthy pause, which Dr X wisely refrained from interrupting, Mr Biggin 'spilled the beans'. His wife had lost all interest in sex while he seemed to want it more. 'But it's not just sex,' he said. *'I am not a monster.'* (The subtext here must be something approximating: *sex is very wicked.*) 'You see, I've never travelled like other people, painted the town red, bought posh clothes, a flash car. I'm sick of insurance, it's downright boring. I want to live before it's too late!'

The workshop group saw the beginning of conflict already: how to be a good husband and citizen yet live it up a bit if the wife wouldn't co-operate? Was he contemplating an affair and feeling guilty, we wondered? But why the 'heart pains'? We decided to hear more from Dr X to see if we were making things up or there was any real evidence.

Dr X told Mr Biggin that physically he was as fit as a fiddle but for some reason he was undergoing panic attacks. Would he come back for a longer appointment next week?

CONTEXT (PAST)

Mr Biggin was a very obliging and trusting patient so in the next session Dr X asked straight away about his family history. By keeping silent but attentive during embarrassed pauses, and asking the odd question, the meaning of Mr Biggin's panic attacks became clear.

Mr Biggin was an only child whose mother was a member of a strict religious sect. She was always anxious for his spiritual welfare, and very possessive. Dad was big in local Labour politics, posing as a man of the people, a man of integrity and justice (which was what had attracted Mr Biggin's mother), but it gradually dawned on the young Mr Biggin that his father was a womanizer and bon-viveur, to put it at its politest. His mother eventually admitted the truth behind his stopovers at hotels and late nights at the office, and became embittered and more religious.

For years the atmosphere at home was unbearable, mother tight-lipped and stoical, the boy studying hard and going daily to church to please and console his mother. Father was mostly absent, but when home he regaled the boy with tales of the high life, encouraged him to get out for a bit of fun. The young Mr Biggin was in tremendous conflict, wanting to be loyal to his mother, yet craving the excitement his father described so vividly.

After college, encouraged by his mother, he got a safe job and married young. The marriage had been happy, if not wildly exciting, until the children left home and his wife seemed to lose interest in their relationship.

Dr X asked what happened to the father in the end. 'He died of a sudden heart attack, found dead in a hotel room after the woman involved had scarpered.'

Mr Biggin described his mother as a 'magnificent widow'. She had triumphed. The wages of sin truly were death, and now her adulterous husband had got his come-uppance.

At fourteen, and deeply involved with his mother's religious sect, the young Mr Biggin wept alone and in private for his father, knowing no one else would understand his grief. When he finally accepted his father was gone for ever, he tried to put out of his mind all the illicit desires and curiosities that his father had planted in him. From then on, he resolved to look after mother.

THE CENTRAL CONFLICT

The loved and respected, but now sexually cold wife, and Mr Biggin's mother had become one in his mind. He loved but unconsciously hated both for depriving him of his manly rights and pleasures. Equally, albeit at different times in his life, he feared losing both if he fought for those pleasures. This is the central conflict. The link between past and present is clear.

Till now his marriage had been a successful compromise between the respectability his mother wanted for him and his own desires for a sexually warm relationship. But his mid-life preoccupations (he was two years younger than his father had been when he died) and the withdrawal of warmth from his wife had combined to turn a sleeping conflict into a full-blown one. His desire for excitement and fear of the consequences were both much heightened.

Mr Biggin's identification with his father, plus the continuing effect of early religious indoctrination, produced fear of retribution in the form of a heart attack, should he dare, in his own words, to become a 'monster'. The night before he appeared in surgery, he had wanted a showdown with his wife and was going to demand they take a proper holiday in the sun to put things right. She had gone to bed early, refusing to talk and he had then found himself fantasizing about ringing a prostitute.

THE DYNAMIC FORMULATION

There is enough evidence here to suggest the following. The rage Mr Biggin had for some time felt toward his wife could no longer be contained. Her indifference to his plea for help, preferring (like his mother) her 'good works', almost certainly de-repressed rage at mother too, resulting in his vengeful fantasy of the prostitute – a slap in the face for both of them. The function of the timely attack of pains and panic was to warn him about and protect him from *really* contacting a prostitute and ending up dead and disgraced like his father.

The workshop group finally offered this Dynamic Formulation to Dr X, who included it in his referral letter for short-term psychotherapy (marital counselling having been refused by his wife):

Mr Biggin is a decent, dependent, guilt-ridden man, tormented and tempted by dreams of mid-life regeneration which he is afraid to act on for fear of joining his father in a deserved early grave, and at the same time losing the security/esteem of his more independent wife, who represents the mother to whom he was so ambivalent.

A non dynamically-oriented GP might have written: 'Middle-aged hypochondriac. Prescribe tranquillizers'.

119

The next example is taken from a different GP practice where I was locum psychotherapist for a short time.

Toni, twenty-five, suffered from vaginismus. She was referred to me for Assessment by her female GP who concluded her note: 'Sorry Wyn – pain in the neck.' Handing me my appointments, the female receptionist said 'Poor you. She always shreds up our magazines with her bare hands you know, complains they're out of date. And she shouts if she's kept waiting more than five minutes. Round the bend if you ask me.'

I arrived a bit early as usual, set up the room, skimmed the referral note. Over the past year there had been genital warts, vaginal discharges, sore breasts, PMT and several minor motorbike injuries. Now it was vaginismus with no physical abnormality or infection in evidence. Toni had been jubilant at the diagnosis, demanding to see a woman 'shrink'.

TEXT

Toni looked like the Michelin man with her crash hat and goggles, and bulky head-to-toe motorbike gear; though I later realized she was in fact quite small. She proffered me a leather-gloved hand, calling out, 'Hi there!' as if arriving at a party. Then she made a joke about the flimsy furniture, saying she wouldn't sit down lest she break something. And so, in a booming voice and standing up, she delivered what sounded like a prepared speech, beaming heartily the whole time.

'So you're the shrink, huh? Well my problem is I beat up men, ha, ha! Had two at least in hospital. Really warped, I am. One had to go in intensive care for a bit. Trouble is, I've got myself a nice feller at last and don't want to hit him. But I do it in my sleep see, and he's black and blue. What do I do that for, eh? He says providing I can stop it, he wants to marry me. What should I do, doc, eh? What should I do?'

For a moment I wondered if she was mad or just having me on, but I thought on balance I'd use my own golden rule: when in doubt, wait.

She stood and stared at me, clearly expecting some pronouncement from me, but all I could manage was: 'What do these blokes do to make you hit them?'

She peered at me as if *I* were mad, then guffawed: 'They're *men*! Isn't that enough?'

SUBTEXT

My guess (I awaited confirmatory evidence and turned out to be wrong) was that under the awful cheeriness, the music hall male-impersonator behaviour, and the cynicism, was a real terror of the men she so mocked. Perhaps her subtextual demand of me was to confirm she was right to beat them up before they beat her – literally or metaphorically; I wasn't yet sure which.

CONTEXT
I enquired about the boyfriend. 'Aw, he's a softie. Likes to cuddle. Doesn't mind about my vagi-whatsit, but *I* do. I'd like, well, to be like other gals, you know?'

I sensed she was softening toward me, so I hoped I might get her to sit. But I still worried she might bolt. I commented that though I felt sure my chairs could hold her without breaking, did she really want to keep all that gear on? It must be uncomfortable, so wrapped up on a summer's day.

'Wha'd'ya mean, exactly?'

'It's hot,' I said, 'And I'd like you to feel cool, but I don't want you to sit down and take your things off if you need to stand up and wear them for, well, protection or something.'

Had I gone too far with this trial interpretation? But this was a busy GP surgery, not an analyst's consulting room. I had to work fast, but without alienating her.

She stared at me in the most unnerving way, and I knew she had read between my lines ('Trust me as you can trust my chair; if you take off your protective clothes I will protect you instead.'). To my great relief she stripped off the leather gear and helmet and sat down, her many carrier bags arrayed in a (magic?) circle at her feet, just in case. I waited.

She kept looking at me and I held her gaze. Slowly she crumpled and started to cry.

Her father had regularly abused her as a child but what she remembered most was her mother's failure to protect her: she would hear nothing bad about her husband, called Toni a tart, a little Lolita who asked for all she got. Her distress was pitiful as she recounted this, all her toughness gone.

THE REVISED SUBTEXT
I began to see I had got the subtext wrong. It wasn't that she wanted to hurt men before they hurt her. Indeed her men all seemed incapable of hurting a fly. Her more pervasive and all-encompassing construction of the world was: Be big. Be a bully. The world is made up of victims and aggressors so make sure you are on the right side. Hence the butch behaviour and the motorbike. Women were as big a let-down as men (whom she saw as rapists or 'wets'), though in asking to see me she must have harboured some slender hope that somewhere, some-time, perhaps some woman could do for her what her mother never

121

did. The receptionists had completely missed this bit of subtext, offended by her criticism of their magazines.

I guessed the many visits to the surgery, always 'playing up' when women were about, were desperate unconscious attempts to get her real problems noticed by mother figures, but as she was only aware of psychic pain without any clue as to its cause, her bizarre efforts went ignored. She was simply seen as an aggressive nuisance. The vaginismus, however, gave her a legitimate reason for asking to see a specialist.

CENTRAL CONFLICT

Toni needed and wanted attachment, love, protection, as we all do, but her experiences had taught her that attachment only came with the most terrible strings attached. She therefore decided (unconsciously) to avoid attachment in future; but as this proved equally difficult in that it produced intolerable loneliness, she opted for a compromise whereby she would attach providing she was in sole charge (so a machine or weedy man would do). The conflict between wanting and simultaneously not wanting (or 'The Wish versus the Fear', as some textbooks have it), was thus made bearable – until she fell in love.

Toni saw other happy couples and wanted a proper relationship with her boyfriend, but her body and her unconscious were not willing to take the risk even if her conscious mind was – hence the vaginismus and kicking him in her sleep.

DYNAMIC FORMULATION

I referred Toni for the longest therapy available at the local outpatient psychotherapy department. My Formulation, which was much longer than usual – two paragraphs (one for each parent? or was I just tired?) – went as follows:

> Under her loud, defensive behaviour Toni is a lonely, sexually-abused woman, doubly betrayed by her parents. Mother not only failed to protect her from her father, but trained her to hate her femininity, blaming it and not the perpetrator for the abuse. Consequently, out of self disgust at her female-ness and a need to avoid 'attracting' further abuse, Toni has made herself the very caricature of a man.
>
> Till now her short-lived relationships with men have served the unconscious purpose of getting her revenge: after a major physical assault on them, she's roared off on her motorbike (which sadly she regards as her only true friend), only to compulsively seek the next victim. Perhaps in identifying with the original aggressor in this

way, she can feel she is powerful, in charge? All her men have been 'weedy'; that is, experienced by her as effeminate and contemptible, as I suspect she unconsciously sees her childhood self. And like herself when young, they have all proved quite unable to stand up to abuse. However, she is now in love and wants help to discover her womanliness.

I ended with a recommendation that she have a senior female therapist.

A common technique for vaginismus is the gradually increased dilation of the vaginal entrance by a lubricated doctor's finger, while listening to relaxing music or engaging in soothing talk. Toni's vaginismus was one *result* of her problems, not their cause. Her muscular spasm was evidence of profound distrust and the body/mind's need to protect itself from further trauma. How could a lubricated finger possibly cure that?

## My third case comes from my Student Counselling days.

A twenty-one-year-old female Indian undergraduate of quite outstanding beauty was due to take finals in three months. She said she was having trouble working, haunted by thoughts that she might have been sexually abused as a child in India.

An uncle had kept lifting her on his knee when she was five and six and she had felt uncomfortable without knowing why. Then at fourteen or so, there had been a boy of her own age from a relative's family who wanted to kiss her all the time and when she tried to avoid his attentions he would tease her and keep digging her on her arms and shoulders, saying she was just a spoilt baby, she knew nothing about the real world.

I wondered aloud why all this was bothering her *now*.

TEXT
The text was: 'I am worried about sex,' and, 'I am worried about finals.'

SUBTEXT
I wondered (and awaited evidence) if the subtext might be: 'Being so young and beautiful is a problem for me' or, 'I am conflicted about sex and exams; thinking about one is drawing energy away from the need to think about the other' or even, 'My past bothers me. I don't know whether to put it away till exams are over, or face it now.'

She seemed stuck in the past, telling me about all the boys who had tried to win her favour since she was very young, and her many older male relatives (Mother had eight brothers!) who praised her beauty and brains and always wanted to touch her to show their appreciation. I noted this material did not affect me emotionally. It felt very factual and dead. It seemed to cause her no pain and there was no pride or conceit in her report either, just a vague puzzlement. Stuck, I decided to go for the context, past or present, whichever might unblock us.

CONTEXT (PAST)

Her family down three generations had always been affluent political Hindus, very Westernized, yet in some ways very traditional. Arranged marriages were still the norm, and disgracing one's family was about the biggest crime imaginable. She loved her parents and siblings as they loved her. In the main, her childhood, surrounded by adoring servants and countless relatives, had been very happy. I found no clues to the central conflict here so I encouraged her to talk about her present situation.

CONTEXT (PRESENT)

The salient points from her wandering account seemed to be: (a) she had always lived with her family before coming to a British university, so England and English people still felt new to her; (b) her parents had recently written to say they were arranging a marriage for when she finished her finals: the supervised courtship was to begin on her return home, which till now she had been looking forward to; and (c) in the evenings she was seeing one of her tutors for pre-finals 'coaching', but they were clearly enamoured of each other. She giggled, seemed excited whenever she mentioned him, yet was horrified when I asked if anything other than academic work had passed between them. 'I am not one of *those* sorts of girls,' she protested.

Now I had the Dynamic Formulation, which I rigorously tested by gentle questioning and subtle trial interpretation till I was satisfied I had got it right.

DYNAMIC FORMULATION:

A developmentally immature young Indian woman whose beauty from childhood has made her aware of and frightened by her sexual impact long before she was ready to cope with it, has now come to England to study. Unchaperoned, she is discovering – to her alarm and delight – her *own* sexual stirrings rather than other people's.

124

Sexual abuse has been much featured in the press of late and she is seizing upon this as a possible explanation for the guilty but pleasurable inner turmoil which, in her home setting, she would be able to talk over with a trusted relative.

In our remaining three sessions we looked at how frightened she was by the prospect of an arranged marriage, with its threat of sexual intercourse. We looked too at how she might handle the situation with her tutor, should he become overly amorous. I pointed out that though we could never know absolutely accurately what happened in her childhood, the one thing that was clear about it was her terror at not knowing how to say 'no'.

I encouraged her to regard herself as an adult who was in charge of and responsible for her own sexuality. What she did or did not do with it was not up to parents, tutor, uncles or newspaper pundits, but to *her*. The idea of being in control of any aspect of her own life had never occurred to her. She felt better immediately she realized she did not have to go along with *or* rebel against her beloved parents. All she had to do was ask to be allowed to wait until she felt more grown up, more ready for the serious business of marriage.

Here was a young woman who needed help certainly, but not formal psychotherapy. A GP to the Mind does Assessment with a view to preventing people unnecessarily embarking on a psychiatric career, as much as to getting the right kind of treatment for those who need it.

This student passed her finals and returned home, leaving a heart-broken tutor behind. She trifled with his feelings as she trifled with his body, for she was not yet ready for full intercourse. I suspect that had she not learned from me how to say no, the poor man might have stood accused of rape, had their relationship culminated in her ambivalent participation in sex. If tutors (and therapists?) insist on crossing boundaries like this, taking advantage – however well meant – of their *in loco parentis* position, they face some very dangerous consequences indeed.

When the proud new graduate came informally to say goodbye to me, she told me her parents were perfectly happy to delay an engagement they had seen as a reward for her degree. She was to have a new car instead! After a long holiday with her family she planned to move away from her home city and do postgraduate research elsewhere in India. She appeared self-possessed, confident about her future, and – thank goodness – not remotely interested in therapy or sexual abuse.

A useful exercise for the practising of making Dynamic Formulations is to utilize one's personal material. Picking a time in the therapist's own life when she felt distinctly wobbly – and any therapist who denies ever having felt that, ought not to be doing the job – assists her to make the Formulation quicker, as she can 'cheat', having access to subtextual and contextual information already in her memory store, whereas operating as a real Assessor she has to work 'blind', with no clue save what can be divined from the text.

In addition, practising on herself allows her to take chances, make daring leaps she would avoid in daily practice; for if the Formulation of her own historical problem turns out to be way off the mark, it isn't going to matter too much. Whatever the problem was at the time, she knows she has lived to tell the tale!

On the grounds that I have no right to ask colleagues to do anything I am not prepared to do myself, I shall take my sixteen-year-old self off to an imaginary therapist (me) and see if I can get a Formulation.

I am reporting the incidence of my second depressive episode, though neither I nor my family recognized it as such at the time. It was 1958 and we lived in a Northern working-class culture where psychological ideas had no place at all. If anyone did know about such things and valued their standing on the council estate, they would keep very quiet indeed.

TEXT

Sixteen-year-old Wyn arrived, over made-up and dressed in the latest fashion, including six-inch stiletto heels. She took a long time to trust, being moody and sullen at first. Then she became suddenly articulate, as if normally starved of conversation and glad for a chance to speak.

She said that, though she did not begin to understand why, she felt restless, discontent: her life was pointless despite good friends, a nice boyfriend, a coveted part-time job in a popular coffee bar and a nice home on one of the newer estates. She was expected to get at least eight O levels at the local Grammar, but school seemed to fill her with the same sense of pointlessness and discontent as the rest of her existence and she was doing no homework. Anyway, her parents weren't interested in 'posh' things like Latin and French. Lancastrians from the shipyards concentrated on survival, not trotting off to Paris for a weekend orgy, aping the rich; or burying noses in useless books full of dead languages. Airs and graces that was, just airs and graces!

Toward the end of the session the patient admitted to recurrent horrible dreams about nuclear war (the H-bomb had recently been invented). She could just about cope with her own death in them, but the death of the whole world and all its animal and plant life was just unbearable. She tried to stay awake to avoid the nightmares, but they always got her in the end.

SUBTEXT

On gentle probing the patient explained her 'moodiness', as she called her depression. There was something she was not getting that she thought everybody else got automatically. But she felt very guilty that she was so greedy for it, especially as she had no idea what it was she was missing. Maybe her mother was right: she was just highly-strung and imagining things.

She said so often to the Assessor, 'You must think I am mad', that it became clear part of the subtext was a fear that she was indeed mad, or at least marked out as 'different', so cutting her off from acceptance by 'normal' people. It turned out later in the session she had been mocked all her life for thinking so deeply, and this family 'joking' had been taken very seriously by her. She felt she had got everything in life wrong, that she was stupid in the extreme.

The thing she was not getting turned out to be permission to be herself and not some distorted version of a self that the family and especially her mother could approve of.

The next bit of subtext concerned her appearance. She explained that her clothes and make-up were vital to her. Without them she felt plain and tiny and almost invisible. Her mother and sister were both very beautiful and attractive to men, and she could never compete. On the other hand they seemed pleased with her if she made an effort. They never understood her moodiness, her absorbed reading for days on end, or her 'brains', but did reward her for looking glamorous.

CONTEXT (PRESENT)

Miserably bored by schoolwork, the patient was seriously considering leaving but the coffee bar (the busiest and smartest in town) was also becoming boring, so how could she live?

Her parents' marriage was dead, the house oppressive. Perhaps she would go to London? But she knew no one there. Only the cinema, novels and rock'n'rolling till she wore her body out and she could sleep ever distracted her from her guilty feelings of futility.

CONTEXT (PAST)

Her father had left home the night of her birth, and did not return until she was five. She worshipped her mother, but realized that as the youngest of the three, and born when her mother was unhappy, she was the least favoured. So she dedicated her life to becoming deserving of her mother's love. While her elder brother and sister were at school she listened to her mother's stories of *her* childhood, over and over again; knew the clothes she wore, the friends she had, the essays she wrote at school, every step of every dance she danced in the maternal grandmother's amateur dancing troupe.

She came to appreciate her mother's obsession with *her* mother, a manic depressive sounding theatrical artist who died in her fifties in a mental hospital. The patient in turn became obsessed with protecting *her* mother from sadness, hiding any sadness of her own for fear of upsetting her mother's mood. In short, the child created and maintained a universe of two, till father returned and at the same time she had to start to school. Eden was gone for ever.

Despite a passionate interest in dance, drama, music and painting, all were abandoned by the time she went to Grammar school, unconsciously given up to pacify the family, while more and more the patient tried to be like her sister and mother.

She had loved the Grammar school at first, but hated being seen as different, a snob, an upstart, by her 'What use is Shakespeare?' family. In the end she drifted away from academic interests toward boys and clothes and dancing, but all that palled too, till she could see no point to her life at all.

CENTRAL CONFLICT

This teenager wants to be loved by her family but this conflicts with her satisfying her intellectual and artistic interests. The solution is to give them up but this gives her bad dreams. The solution is not working.

DYNAMIC FORMULATION

This depressed adolescent girl with artistic interests is out of kilter with her working-class family who seem to have coped with her strangeness by laughing at her. There is great repressed rage at having to deny all her natural propensities and become a pale imitation of the feminine, non-intellectual, idealized mother to whose favour she is still trying to be restored, after her father's first appearance on the scene at five. This rage surfaces in nightly dreams of annihilation of the human race. The desolate world of her dreams is also the desolation of the inner world she has till now been prepared to put up with in return for a place in the family from whom she now needs help to separate.

A referral letter or report from an Assessor should always contain a Dynamic Formulation, even if it does not appear under such a formal heading. There is nothing to prevent the Assessor from airing hunches, sharing the evidence for her conclusions, issuing warnings about intransigent or difficult defence mechanisms, or giving relevant chronological history. But this should be done in other paragraphs. It is that brief but potent *Dynamic Formulation*, that distillation and interpretation of all that has passed between the therapeutic couple so far, that will provide the jewel in the crown of subsequent therapy.

Surely that merits a paragraph all its own, if not a formal heading as well?

## CHAPTER 7

# Making the Contract

If the Dynamic Formulation is the meat in the sandwich of the Assessment, then the bottom slice on which it rests, and by which it is supported is the Therapeutic Alliance, while the top slice, enclosing the meat and sealing in its goodness, is the Contract.

The Contract represents much more than an agreement as to where, when, and for how long the therapeutic couple will work. A Contract used only for administrative convenience or as an information leaflet treats the couple's relationship as if it were as empty as a marriage contracted to get someone a passport. It has been reduced to a mere formality.

The Therapeutic Contract, not unlike a proper marriage, stands for a *commitment* between two people, a commitment to stick together till the work is done, no matter the obstacles, to be true to the Alliance made in Assessment, to abide by the conditions, psychological and practical that both have agreed are the most conducive to the patient getting well and the therapist being able to perform the best treatment. The therapist needs to find a way of conveying to the patient that though the Contract is not a legal document and cannot be policed, nonetheless it represents the parties' word of honour, each to the other, and in that sense needs no policing.

When working privately, I always give the patient a written Contract, which he can take home to read at leisure. In the next session he can discuss any points raised by the document after which he may decide he is now happy to put our meetings on a formal footing, the Assessment having been completed.

I have a basic document, which is suitable for most once-a-week patients, but those on irregular work schedules, such as pilots or nurses or those obliged to travel as part of their work, those needing more than one session a week, and couples who have to sort out what is going to happen when one can't or won't come, will need the Contract trimmed a little.

Though most patients are content with a first reading and are anxious to get on with the therapy itself, I find the handover and discussion of the document, even when it only takes a few minutes, has rich significance. It clearly marks a new phase in therapy, separating the more active, exploratory Assessment from the painstaking, thorough, and sometimes slow or stuck periods

130

during post Assessment therapy. The acceptance of the Contract instils hope for it demonstrates that the first major hurdle has already been jumped.

The Contract also underlines the seriousness with which the therapist takes her patient: it ensures all is in the open, that the patient can renegotiate any condition with which he is not happy. The very existence of the written Contract suggests partnership, collaboration, not a hierarchical relationship between an all-knowing parent and an ignorant child – there will be enough of that in the transference. The Contract functions to maintain the Alliance, not to induce transference.

There are no secrets between the pair about how each is to behave. They can see plainly written down what is expected of them. (Alas though, many Contracts stipulate in some detail what the patient must do with regard, say, to missed sessions or holidays, or illness, but say nothing of what the therapist will or won't undertake to do should she find herself in the same position!) The Contract should be unambiguous but should not read like a book of one-sided school rules.

I do not find a verbal Contract nearly so satisfactory, especially in longer-term therapy where there is so much more time for 'misunderstandings' to occur, and the original agreement gets lost in the mists of memory. No matter how clear the arrangements are at the outset concerning leaving messages, lateness, absences, or holiday periods, a difference of opinion against a background of strong transference often springs up.

'But you said ... ,' complains the patient, off on holiday with only three days notice.

'No, what I *actually* said ... ,' replies the therapist.

'Well, you may have *meant* that, but what you actually *said* was ...'

A Contract, read and agreed to, cannot be argued with. It is at once clear whether or not the patient (or therapist for that matter) has broken the Contract and if so the reasons for this can then be analysed and understood, often yielding up much forgotten material from the patient's past.

The invitation to take part in such a solemn business as making the Contract in itself constitutes a test of motivation. Many patients need help to explore their deeper reasons for delaying or avoiding involvement. I have known patients go to inordinate lengths to 'lose' their Contract document before having had chance to read it. One patient managed to lose three in as many weeks!

Any hitherto undetected conflicts around issues of trust and commitment will surely rise to the surface on production of the Contract document. For certain patients the very idea of *contract* suggests unwanted responsibilities, a trap, even loss of individuality. Such fears need to come into the open early for they are going to considerably affect post-Assessment therapy, should the patient eventually decide he does want to go that far.

I once had a nineteen-year-old private patient referred for 'authority problems'. Apparently there were frequent arrests for disturbing the peace and occasional fist-fights with his father, though in therapy he refused to discuss either topic. Two psychiatrists had already given up on him because he was 'uncooperative'. Naturally, the Contract I made with him made clear that physical assault on me or my property would result in termination of therapy.

'Can I shout then?' he asked, full of cheek, but nervous.

'How loud?'

He grinned.

I explained that though I didn't mind shouting myself, I was unwilling to have my elderly neighbour frightened out of her wits.

He scowled down at the carpet.

'But you may have noticed, it is a detached house.'

He looked up, caught my eye. We were in business again, just.

In fact he never did shout (though I very nearly did, in sheer exasperation). He fought me, like an obsessional lawyer, over every sentence in the Contract document, refusing to agree to anything till he had argued out why it was written down, what really lay behind it, whether it was unfair, unequal or just plain bossy.

As he relaxed a little, he offered me a few ideas about what I might add, too, suggesting things other patients might get up to to make my life difficult that I would not be able to deal with by recourse to the Contract.

'Will you just look at this,' he announced disgustedly, slapping the now dog-eared Contract document with the back of his hand. 'There's nothing to stop us screwballs writing hate mail, or sending you stolen goods as presents.'

All this was taken up in terms of his relationship with me, his need to test me out, find – and push – my limits, his mixed feelings of anger (hate mail) and hope that I might really care (yet still not accept the stolen goods, thus humiliating him as he felt all adults did). He would grin or scratch his head when one of my comments made an impression, but he would never openly admit I had made a valid point.

He steadfastly refused to share what he regarded as weaknesses (that is, his private fears and hurts), and would only deal with me in terms of the Contract. By the time he had gone over it with several fine-tooth combs and could find no more fault, he announced he was leaving. The rewrite had taken him four months.

In spite of our long haggle, which was not without grimly humorous moments that we both non-verbally acknowledged, we had made good contact. He had learned much about the way he operated in relationships through conducting a stormy one with me. I was certain his leaving was because there was no more Contract to fight over (and through which he could covertly get help while continuing his self-esteem-maintaining rebellious role): the time had come to make the commitment of which he was terrified. When I suggested this to him he replied: 'Nothing in that Contract says I have to agree with what you say.'

His relations with parents and police had improved though were still hostile. We shook hands (at his instigation) and agreed that if he ever came back maybe this time we'd manage without a Contract and just trust each other.

In very short-term therapy, three or five sessions say, the Assessment *is* the therapy, but a Contract of sorts is still required. Indeed, if only one session is offered (perhaps the new patient is using up another's cancellation), the therapist still needs to make clear how much time she is making available for that session, so the patient can pace himself. She should state clearly what any next step might be with regard to referral, or if she will be sending the patient back to his GP. If there is to be a letter or report, how long will it take and does the patient get a copy? If not, how will he know the therapist has dealt with his case? Should he visit his GP in a week, two weeks, to enquire after progress? If he has taken advantage of a cancellation when is he likely to be seen again, and will it be the same therapist?

One might argue that it is particularly important to make this miniature Contract in short-term work, because it is under just such circumstances that the patient will feel rushed, unimportant, not taken seriously. In units where there is an established policy of short-term work, so renegotiation of the Contract is not feasible in any case, it can be very helpful for the patient's mental preparation as well as for reassurance that he does indeed matter, to have the arrangements under which he will have to work spelt out to him in a letter well before his appointment date. An enclosed map and details of car parking can make all the difference between a calm and calamitous (as well as late) interview.

When the Assessment of a potentially medium- to long-term patient is running into difficulties, there is no reason why interim miniature Contracts should not be made. The patient can be contracted to come along for a set of three or four more Assessment sessions, closely clumped or spaced out according to therapist availability and the patient's work commitments, so as to concentrate on particular issues or fill in specific gaps, before making a final Contract.

Such a 'mini' arrangement can give the patient the feeling that the therapist really is prepared to take her time and do things properly, but if Assessment just drifts on indefinitely, with no conditions or timetables attached, no offer of further treatment in sight, he may begin to suspect his Assessor is not too good at her job. If Assessment has to be lengthy the patient needs to know why.

Interim Contracts are very useful for newly qualified therapists, who can thus take time to review Assessment so far with their supervisors. An extra couple of sessions now could lead to a better Dynamic Formulation, a firmer Contract, and a lot less strain in post-Assessment therapy.

The sequence of treatment phases in broad spectrum psychotherapeutic work is not therefore simply beginning, middle and end. First the therapist where needful operates as GP to the Mind, which means intervening in a crisis, and/or managing, educating, containing the patient as appropriate, till he is ready for the next stage, that of Assessment. Assessment in turn requires the making of an Alliance, a Dynamic Formulation and then a Contract (with or without interim Contracts). Only then can post-Assessment therapy start, culminating in termination of treatment – for some patients the most significant part of the whole endeavour.

There is also the termination of the Assessment phase to consider, often extremely distressing for the patient if the Assessor herself is not to continue with the treatment, and/or there is to be a wait for the post-Assessment vacancy to become available. The patient is often so preoccupied, sad or angry at having to bid the Assessor farewell, that he cannot give his full attention to the Contract: he ends up agreeing to something he later finds he does not understand or is unhappy with.

Part of the Contract-making stage also requires the therapist to be an educator. Unless a patient is conversant with psychoanalytic practice he has to be helped to see the difference between the exploratory work of Assessment that pre-dates making the Contract, and the more traditional, less interventionist approach that usually follows it. This is especially important if the post-Assessment work is to be carried out by a different therapist. If not advised, the patient may well confuse the more traditional *technique* of the second therapist with his *personality*, and hence resist a technique that would be just the same had his (favoured?) first therapist carried on with his treatment.

The whole subject of changing therapists after Assessment is highly controversial and beyond the scope of this book, but it is vital to remember that some patients transfer less easily than others between one therapist and the next, so preparation for the changeover, and a properly attended to farewell, is essential. I believe it really does help if the first therapist can truly say of the second that he or she is known to and trusted by her, and that their way of working is similar.

If the Assessing therapist is fortunate enough to be allowed to complete the work she has started, how should she prepare her patient for the next stage? In some instances, where Assessment has been straightforward and the giving and joint processing of material comfortable and free flowing, with little need for questions or interventions designed to structure the material, the therapist may simply elect to continue as before. But what if the Assessment was turbulent, or hostile perhaps, or very wandering, the material having to be gathered and sorted and then re-sorted by the therapist in order to find the Formulation, while simultaneously trying to cope with a fast developing transference?

Assuming an Alliance was eventually made and a Formulation arrived at, the therapy post-Contract can be taken much more gently, and with much less interference from the therapist. However, the patient might construe this change of tack as lack of interest, or perhaps exhaustion, if he is not forewarned.

It is at this stage that many therapists invite the patient to begin lying on the couch, while others no longer believe in the value of this practice. I usually let the patient decide for himself whether he is more comfortable lying down or sitting up. The reasons for his choice are always interesting! Whatever he decides, if the tempo of the therapy is to be different from Assessment it is useful to explain to the patient that now Assessment is finished, he will not be asked so many questions, or interrupted nearly so often. The therapist will listen more and talk less because having had the overview, the time has now come for the couple to appreciate some of the detail.

Some patients will need more reassurance than others, that the therapist's lessening contributions in the post-Assessment phase indicate her preparedness to give the patient more room to manoeuvre, more say in the direction the therapy will take. This reassurance is deliberately given at Contract-making time (a short period during which the therapist operates almost exclusively in the here and now, like a manager or administrator) so that any other construction later placed on the change of tempo can be confidently analysed as a piece of transference distortion.

Every condition set out in the final Contract constitutes a boundary, a constraint within which both parties agree to work. If any boundary is ruptured neither can profess ignorance of it or protest the rupture has no psychological or transferential meaning. Without the firm boundaries provided by the Contract, and an understanding of what these boundaries represent for the patient, much deep material that could otherwise be contacted very fast is lost or its appearance in the treatment greatly delayed. In hard-pressed units this has financial as well as clinical implications.

What might a typical Contract consist of? Different clinics and hospitals will naturally generate different styles, but the areas covered should still be broadly similar. Most important of all is the underlying *tone* of the document. Without reading like a sermon, the Contract should convey to the patient the seriousness with which the unit or department take the job ahead, and the seriousness of purpose they expect from him in return.

Regular attendance is therefore required of both parties for the sake of continuity and containment. Again, if this is spelt out in writing, no patient or therapist can claim they genuinely believed one trip to the races and a single missed session would scarcely matter: this is indeed 'acting out' and constitutes material for analysis.

Under this section can be written details of where and with whom to leave messages, under what conditions sessions will be re-scheduled or replaced, how much notice is required for such changes, and what the policy is about cancellations and the taking of holidays. The therapist's obligations in these matters should be set down too.

Both patient and therapist must behave ethically toward one another for the project to best mature, but many patients are unaware of such matters and frequently get into difficulties that might have been avoided with a clearer Contract. If there is no prohibition to begin with, a patient contacting another therapist, for example, could insist her main therapist is jealous, or fears competition, or is just plain possessive. To the patient, getting a 'second opinion' may seem perfectly reasonable.

The patient may be involved in activities regarded by his therapist as incompatible with the treatment offered. Unless the Contract alerts him to the possibility that these activities could lead to problems from which the therapist wishes to protect him, he may fail to raise the matter until complications have set in.The Contract might therefore request patients starting psychotherapy to discuss with their therapist any other treatments, healing agencies or 'alternative' groups in which they are involved, or considering becoming involved.

Some patients attach themselves to all manner of belief

systems, cults, diets and classes. Therapists should not interfere, in my view, just because the activity makes no sense to them. They should discuss the matter in depth however, where they genuinely believe the activity to oppose the spirit and values of psychotherapy, or where there is intense emotional involvement with the leader or other member(s) of the organization.

I have been known to change sessions so patients can attend what to them are critical spiritual health festivals, and I once changed a Druid's early morning session following the summer solstice. People's views demand respect. But if they are choosing, or being seduced into relationships with organizations the therapist regards as undermining of or antithetical to psychotherapy, this needs sorting out honestly with the patient before post-Assessment work begins.

It should go without saying, yet I am amazed how often supervisees in the non-hospital field forget, that the therapist needs to know about any psychiatric medication and to have the patient discuss with her any plans for changing it, stopping it, or beginning new medication.

The therapist needs to preserve freedom of consultation if she is not to be manipulated by patients' unconsciouses into a state of clinical paralysis that does nothing to assist the therapeutic process. Whilst respecting day-to-day confidentiality it is important that the therapist can contact the patient's GP or referring psychiatrist in an emergency. It is no use approaching a patient for permission to contact his doctor when he is too paranoid, depressed, personality disordered, psychotic or out of the country to give it. Much wiser to build some phrase into the Contract such as: 'The therapist reserves the freedom to consult with the patient's GP or covering psychiatrist as appropriate.'

If the patient is not reassured by a discussion of the kind of unusual circumstances in which such a consultation would come about, then perhaps serious questions should be asked about treating such a patient at all.

Departments catering for special populations; couples, groups, families for example, will need to build in therapist and patient undertakings peculiar to their setting, in addition to the above.

When working with dynamically oriented groups it is essential patients are advised not to make relationships with one another outside the group. All therapists understand the reasons for this, in terms not only of preserving a 'clean' field of therapeutic operation, but also protecting vulnerable people from harming themselves in ways that brought them to therapy in the first place. The cure must not be allowed to be worse than the disease.

Working with family members, the unit's policy about who will talk to whom about what and with whose permission, must be crystal clear. Only then is the patient or family sufficiently informed to be able to decide if he/they will commit himself/themselves. Under-eighteens also need, want and are entitled to this information from their counselling and therapy services. This again underlines the need for a balanced Contract, therapists' undertakings to the patients as important as the patients' to the staff.

Patients who fall into the category of 'behaviour problems' or 'substance abusers' (though I dare say there'll be new terms in use by the time this book is published) should be offered a Contract that states clearly what the consequences of turning up to therapy drugged, drunk or physically aggressive will be. Then they too have a choice (at least consciously) about whether to sabotage their treatment. Neither can they justifiably claim they are being singled out for 'punishment' no one else has to endure.

It is not for me to prescribe the exact phrasing of Contracts. Each department/clinic/private practitioner will wish to ensure their own 'personality' shines through the document, otherwise it becomes just one more bit of bureaucracy. But on reading other people's Contracts I always feel the tenor is right when I see sentences like: 'With regard to holidays the therapist undertakes to ... ' or, 'With respect to medication the patient agrees to ... ' or sensible explanations like, 'Both parties will give maximum notice of summer holidays, so that patients have the opportunity to fit holidays round therapist availability if they wish, and the clinic can make optimal use of the therapist's time while the patient is away ... '

The careful way the Contract is composed, taking into account the particular population using the service, is just as important as the information it contains.

The Contract loses value and credibility if the therapist assumes no comment means no problem and fails to invite the patient to discuss it. Many patients are unused to being treated as equal human beings and assume the Contract (or whatever title appears on the page) is bound to be a set of instructions or rigid rules that should not be questioned. In making the Contract the therapist aims to disconfirm rather than reinforce the patient's earlier experiences of inequality and non-consultation.

However, a patient eager to start post-Assessment therapy who has no qualms about the Contract should not be made to wade through its administrative minutiae just for form's sake. Let him get on with the work he has come to do!

PART THREE

# Following Assessment

## CHAPTER 8

# Making Interventions in the Longer Term

I start this chapter with a confession. Once I have made a good Alliance with a patient and we commence the post-Assessment phase, I rarely make complete and elegant interpretations, the like of which are reported in learned papers and books. I am guilty of 'ers' and 'ums' and frequently omit verbs or full stops from my utterances because I am too involved in the business of thinking as I speak to worry about the grammatical niceties. This is largely because I now know the patient and am prepared to sacrifice precision if sharing my thoughts as they occur involves him further in his own treatment, including the making of his own interpretations. This is especially the case in short-term work.

All the same, my interventions in sessions must be rendered readable for the purposes of this book. But I do not want the reader to imagine that because I attempt proper syntax on paper, I always speak to the patient in the same way. Psychotherapy is an exploratory, experimental, amorphous business and often the patient gains insight despite the therapist's inexactitude. He follows her thinking-aloud productions and elaborates, corrects, modifies or pounces, depending on how close her wanderings might be to the truth for which he is searching.

I do not condone intellectual or verbal sloppiness or lack of technical rigour; but neither do I feel comfortable with therapeutic practice that only allows the therapist to deliver herself of a statement when she is absolutely certain she is correct and there can be no argument, play or further exploration of what she has just said. By that time the patient's enthusiasm and patience may be all but exhausted, and what could have been an idea for both patient and therapist to develop and toy with while simultaneously strengthening the Therapeutic Alliance, turned into a finished, sterile product packaged by the therapist for admiration and unqualified acceptance by the patient.

I am a great believer in the 'Deconsecrated Interpretation' (this term will not be found in any textbook: it's one of my little jokes). To offer *any* interpretation to a patient is to suggest a hidden *meaning* in what he is saying, feeling or doing. This suggestion of latent layers in my view should be felt by the patient as part and parcel of normal conversation with his therapist, not experienced as Moses in awe-struck receipt of the Tablets. An interpretation delivered as an oracular statement from a therapist who rarely speaks or reacts at all may have tremendous force (because of its scarcity value if nothing else), but says more about the practice of domination and indoctrination than the facilitation of insight and understanding.

It is true that sometimes the therapist can see with crystal clarity what the patient has a vested interest in missing and the therapist must enable the patient to consider that same vision, without waffle or ambiguity. But the willingness to hear a confident interpretation should come about via the collaborative spirit inherent in the Alliance, rather than out of transferentially induced obeisance.

Often the most helpful interpretations are those arrived at as a result of both parties endlessly building, discarding, modifying and arguing over hypotheses till a meaning (interpretation) is arrived at that the patient knows in his *bones* is right. I make no apology for placing great faith in bones.

The patient should be able to trust the therapist's honesty absolutely. If she is tentative it is because she feels uncertain and is consulting him, or asking his forbearance while she thinks aloud: if she is direct and specific it is because she is confident she has hit upon something important which, if the patient is to properly consider, must be delivered accurately and without circumlocution or decoration.

Many years ago, wanting to be seen by patients as tactful and non-doctrinaire, I got into the habit of prefacing all my interventions with: 'Could it be that ... ?' or, 'It seems as if ... ' or, 'I find myself wondering whether ... ?' This is perfectly acceptable technique for the therapist who genuinely wishes to communicate lack of certainty while issuing an invitation to the patient to help her take the issue further; but regular lack of conviction in her interventions can damage the patient's confidence in her. I was cured of the habit when a very irritable patient said to me: 'When are you going to bloody well stop wondering and start *knowing*? I'm paying for this, you know.'

This highlights the theme I want to develop in this chapter: the manner, timing and purpose of an intervention is as vital to therapeutic success as its content. Not all interventions are concerned with latent meaning (interpretations) but that does not mean they are any the less important, as I trust the clinical illustrations in this and particularly the following chapter will show.

The early post-Assessment phase can be a very exciting time in psychotherapy. Following a full Assessment, patient and therapist are sufficiently familiar to use a bit of joint shorthand, share jokes, take risks, ask questions and confront each other, knowing the Alliance that is between them will ensure their mutual safety. Both find it easy to say things and share ideas they would not have dreamt of bringing into the open during their first meeting, because they can now predict the other's response. In other words, now the Contract has been agreed the honeymoon can begin.

Some honeymoons go wrong of course, but often this is a time of real mutual exploration and discovery within the safe boundaries of the Contract. There is often a proliferation of insight at this time, symptoms vanishing with miraculous speed, the therapist feeling buoyant, effective, the patient feeling empowered, his self-esteem soaring.

As with marriage, though, the honeymoon cannot last for ever and reality testing sets in. Can the Alliance survive the slow, even boring times when there is very little progress in evidence? On occasion each will disappoint the other, in reality as well as in the transference; they will grate on each other's nerves, maybe even doubt the commitment they have made (this is one of the unconscious reasons why many therapists restrict themselves to short-term work: either they cannot face necessary mutual disillusion, or they cannot trust the strength of the Alliances they make). Successfully negotiating such doldrums in therapy, as in marriage, can lead to a deepening of the bond between the couple and an even firmer commitment to the job in hand.

The whether, when, how and why of making interventions, as well as the way patients' interventions are dealt with (see Chapter 9), determine to a huge extent whether the therapeutic 'marriage' will wither or thrive.

Patients differ vastly in personality and so the therapist must have a repertoire of intervention 'styles' available, which, while still maintaining authenticity, she can tailor to suit individual needs. With one patient she is verbally precise, measuring her words. With another she falls into associative wordplay, thinks and speaks 'as it comes'. With yet another she deliberately introduces contrast via her interventions: calm reflectivity to his emotional explosions, injections of warmth to his tomb-like inner world. With one her interventions draw the boundaries tight to protect him from his own excesses; with another she shows that flexibility, even rule-breaking, is possible without the world ending. One patient needs everything spelled out, while another responds to a raised brow, a sucked in cheek, a twinkle in the eye.

In post-Assessment therapy, especially in its mature stages, the treatment as a whole has shape, distinguishing features, a *history*. Interventions can be constructed and delivered in the light of all that has gone before. A patient's episode of depression, or rapid growth, or fatigue, or a sudden longing to terminate therapy will mean one thing in one therapy and something quite different in another.

For in addition to being unique, a fresh start, every separate session represents the continuing flow of the one long session that constitutes the whole therapy. When a supervisee feels very stuck about material brought by the patient in the session she is reporting, I often ask her to go back to the end of the preceding session, and the mystery is solved. For the patient, the intervening week has not occurred: he is carrying on from where he left off last time.

No textbook or new supervisor can state categorically that a patient threatening to leave is really doing or meaning X and the correct intervention is Y. Only the therapist who knows the therapy's history and who therefore possesses the joint psychological context in which these remarks are made can finally judge their full import and hence design the most appropriate intervention. With Mrs Jones she may wish to call her bluff; with Mr Smith she may feel more like calling an ambulance!

I remember a young, socially-isolated male postgraduate student who talked most of the time about killing himself, the how and when and where and what pills were best. He sounded very serious about it and for many weeks I heard him out each time he pored over his plans. Eventually I told him his preoccupation with how to die sounded to me like a miserable but effective way of avoiding the much more difficult problem of how to live. He had somehow got hold of the idea that to die, though scary, was noble and romantic, whereas admitting 'I don't know how to live' would mean facing he was weedy, a coward, a no-hoper.

He was furious, refused to speak, then missed a session. I wrote and told him to come back. He did. He sulked. He fumed. He argued. Then he cried – and cried and cried. Then he started to get better, as we looked at his fear of women, his inability to be assertive, his refusal to accept his academic limitations.

Had I made the same intervention to another patient thinking of suicide the results could have been disastrous. But I had completed an Assessment and made a firm Dynamic Formulation about this man. I felt I knew him, and that with my support he could just about take the intervention I believed to be necessary, after diluted versions had failed to touch him.

As a teacher I am sometimes asked why 'deep' interventions are more effective than superficial ones, or put another way, why comments on there-and-then events in the patient's life rather than here-and-now ones are more therapeutic. I reply that this is by no means always the case. The rule of thumb for the therapist is: 'Intervene where it feels hot'. This usually means where it hurts, be that past or present.

Let us say the therapist is concerned about the frequency and intensity with which her patient gets himself involved in triangles where he is always the excluded, unhappy one. She may be well aware that the blueprint was laid down in childhood, may even have graphic accounts in her mind of the poor patient locked outside the parental door while they were having intercourse; but to the patient that is just so much dead history. Harking back to it when he falls for a married woman who encourages him to follow her about while she hangs on to her husband's arm does not help him.

Let us suppose this triangular situation is occurring at work. Fed up with humiliation the patient decides to get a new job to avoid the enforced witnessing of the couple. The post is tailor-made for him, he can do it standing on his head. But he fails to win it. The man who does is underqualified, personally and technically, nothing better than a smooth-talking, empty-headed charmer. Why, didn't the patient see him sucking up to the secretary soon as he was told he had the job? Didn't she give him tea and a big gooey smile, silly woman? How come she couldn't see through him?

The patient is angry and hurting, *now*. He cares only about his current life, not the distant past. The therapist needs to link what is 'hot' with what else is simultaneously 'hot'.

The therapist sees that in trying to put one painful situation behind him the patient has created another by processing the new one in terms of the old. By making an intervention that links the job application and its aftermath to the situation with the married woman, who, like the secretary, chooses the lesser, unworthy man, the patient begins to recognize his pattern of seeking threesomes and reacting violently to them. After all, he did not need to spy on the rival applicant to confirm his suspicions, any more than he had to torture himself by ingratiating himself with the husband so as to satisfy himself the man was inadequate as a consort. Both situations (and others previously reported) are the same: this is more than coincidence.

Though the intervention leaves out his past and his parents (and we must assume the therapist's Formulation is based on more than a single painfully excluding episode in the boy's life), it does make him look at himself and his relationships over time, their repetitive pattern, which points eventually to the past. If this is missed and the therapist goes straight to the parental exclusion he may say: 'So what? Kids do get in the way of sex. The door does have to be locked. It happens all the time. What's all the fuss about?' Until he is put in touch with the compulsive and repetitive nature of the pain he creates and maintains for himself *now*, he will not be able to take on board interventions about *then* except in the most cerebral, therapeutically meaningless way.

However, therapists should guard against the popular but erroneous notion that only interventions of a *feelings* sort are worth while. The rule of thumb this time is to go for what is missing. If the patient emotes endlessly, spillage may need to be mopped, the rate of flow lessened. The patient may need interventions that will help him *think* about what he is *feeling* and what purpose or gain there may be in so swamping himself. Is constant emotional reaction to the past helping him avoid conflicts in the present, or vice versa?

At the other extreme, a patient with a rational, exasperatingly logical mind might benefit from interventions that lead him to dare test himself for emotion. The attempt to *feel* in the here-and-now of the session may be much more valuable than the *thinking* about how his there-and-then experiences made him the person he is.

### What is the Intervention For?

An intervention by the therapist is anything she says, does or provides that comes between the patient and his material. Generally speaking, an intervention is designed to: (a) temporarily stop the production of material; (b) further the production of material (as with questions, partial interpretations, confrontations and hunches; also the making of links and comparisons, the amplifying, organizing, categorizing, simplifying or selective focusing of the material); or (c) adjust the material's course (as with the intervention called interpretation).

The material is stopped so it can be clarified, inspected, interpreted or linked with other material. It may be halted because if allowed to continue it will cause the patient to lose control, become psychotic or perhaps violent, or will lead to a panic attack: he will no longer feel contained by the setting and the therapist. Sometimes, however, it is halted because the therapist, not the patient, is afraid of further revelations she feels ill-equipped to handle. This is a matter for supervision.

The material may be halted because it is defensive – the patient is leading the therapist 'up the garden path', seducing her into one area so as to avoid another; or he may be stuck in a demoralizing circular debate with himself, that only the therapist can break, and perhaps by reframing the issue enable him to take a fresh direction.

It may be stopped by the therapist because she is getting lost and needs to ask a question. Or she may intervene to prevent the patient from skating over one vital issue and hurtling on to the next.

For example, a garrulous, health-conscious patient once talked to me about frying some new-fangled fat-free sausages for his breakfast, followed by a discourse on the merits of semi-skimmed milk, followed by a comparison of the various 'fresh' orange juices on the market. I interrupted the flow to enquire if he was aware of the tears pricking his eyes when he mentioned the sausages. He was embarrassed, tried to change the subject, but eventually recalled memories of his now dead but much loved mum cooking sausages for him as a kid (he was the youngest and her favourite) and making eyes, a nose and a mouth on each banger, with ketchup. He thought this memory was sentimental nonsense. He had not yet seen that though he was fifty-two he had not finished grieving.

When it is the patient who stops the flow and the therapist does not feel she has enough data to make an interpretation, she may wait calmly and patiently (often the best strategy) for further associations that come to the patient's mind in his own and not her time, or she may sense the patient needs and wants help to continue. After she has intuited the reason for his tapering off, her intervention – even if only a grunt or change of facial expression (assuming the patient is not on the couch) – is constructed so as to assure him of continued interest and attention, that she will not be shocked or disapproving, or that she will not take things personally.

But this is by no means always the cause of the material's fading away. The next association, should the patient allow it to come, might be too frightening, or too despairing, or too angry. It might even concern the therapist: you don't bite the hand that feeds you. The therapist takes a delicate decision about whether to hint at what maybe waiting, giving her patient the choice to continue or not, or whether to respect the defence in view of the patient's current vulnerability and leave him to change the subject.

He may not be blocked at all, merely puzzled and in need of a collaborator. The therapist reminds him of earlier material similar to this, makes one link so that he can make others, which in turn will remind her of yet others, back in their shared history. This I call 'chaining' – therapist and patient co-operating to call up previous bits of material, maybe passed over as incidental or unfathomable at the time; then each associating to what the other has recalled, thus recalling more, associating to one another's associations before together arriving at some interpretation of it all.

The therapist may sense that her patient has stopped because he is confused, unsure whether it is he who is speaking or the parent inside him holding the remote control panel. Her intervention is designed to enable him speak in both voices, his own and the parent's, and conduct a dialogue or downright argument between the two, while she acts as referee to make the row safe.

The therapist sometimes enables the patient to further his internal explorations by picking up the gauntlet thrown down by an angry and/or exhausted cessation of material. Perhaps he cannot sustain his indignation, self-justification or blaming any more, needs the therapist to rescue him from the rationalizations he is fearfully preparing to give up. Before letting them go however, he may need one last fight to re-enact that other avoided fight (be this within himself or with a significant other). Once fought to the end – the enemy this time being also an Ally – the unconscious duel that has dogged him for years can be jointly analysed and understood.

## Who is Making the Interventions?

In my view it is not possible to design, construct and deliver interventions totally neutrally, however desirable this may seem. Attaining such neutrality would involve such flattening of feeling and withdrawal of involvement the therapist would be about as useful as a robot. Yet to prevent abuses it is vital that during sessions with patients she is at all times honest with herself about just who, inside her, is making the intervention, irrespective of how the patient's transference-perceptions will read that person.

From my own experience I would say every intervention is made by a God, Friend, Surgeon, Teacher, Parent or Sage, all operating under the rubric of 'psychotherapist'.

## The God

Few of us admit, for fear of being seen as arrogant, grandiose or dogmatic, that in some instances we are *absolutely sure* about our interventions at a given moment. Plainly, any therapist who claims to possess the one and only Truth all of the time is deluded, but at the other extreme a therapist without any conviction at all as to the veracity of what she professionally practises is equally dangerous. She would feel free to practise anything!

Many interventions are of necessity hesitant, exploratory, and need further joint work. But sometimes an insight pierces the hitherto fogged brain of the therapist with visionary intensity; that, 'of course, of *course!*' feeling. The accuracy and precise nature of such certainty cannot be demonstrated scientifically – but neither can love, beauty, music or art, yet people understand them to exist, feel life would be infinitely poorer without them.

When this therapist intervenes I call her *the God* (capital 'G') because she is acting on absolute conviction and this cannot help but affect the patient. The intervention may frighten him because he senses its rightness but is unsure if he can bear to acknowledge it yet. He must be given time. Alternatively, he may be greatly inspired, his faith in therapy restored after long weeks of apparently unproductive slogging. The recognition that it is his personal material and his own thoughts and feelings about that material that have contributed to this new light, is esteem-building and Alliance-firming.

However, if the patient already sees the therapist as a god (small 'g') in the transference, and if the therapist already has a similar, so far unresolved transference to some central psychoanalytic figure on whom her training was founded, the situation is potentially harmful. Therapist and patient may become locked in a god–disciple relationship that pleases them both but does little to shift the neurosis of either. The doubtless well-meaning therapist is confusing the therapeutic God with the transference god. Both parties are destined to perpetuate the authoritydependency tie in all future relations, never finding their own voice.

Worse, if the patient does not oblige such a therapist with associative offerings acceptable to and decipherable by her particular analytic religion, the patient may be seen as 'unsuitable for treatment', or a dutiful attempt at treatment is made but the therapist unconsciously rejects or demotes the patient who cannot participate in her ideological view and thereby confirm its rightness and her sense of security, even superiority, in having chosen it.

False gods abound in therapy as in every other area of human experience. The God inside the therapist referred to here demands no followers, just waits to be discovered: is not an icon to be placated, prayed or sacrificed to, but a vision of the unconscious Truth in a piece of material that comes fresh each time, direct to the therapist, awaiting the packaging of language and theory

149

merely to give it form and communicability. Many different languages and theories can express the same Truth.

In therapeutic practice the God inside the therapist speaks only rarely, indeed often seems to have deserted her. When a patient or therapist hears every intervention as divine they are deep into a transference that has nothing to do with the God here described.

## The Friend

*The Friend* inside the therapist can be both a help and a hindrance. When operant she behaves very like the person-centred counsellor. She tracks the patient's feelings, checks with him occasionally that she is following him correctly, makes empathic comments like: 'That must have felt very lonely'; or, 'What a lot you had to carry, before you were really old enough.' The Friend is also there to mentally hand-hold when penetrating and/or confrontational observations have to be made; her support makes the incisiveness of dynamic interpretation bearable.

The Friend inside the therapist champions the healthy aspects of the patient, reminds her when she is low, or facing tough insights, that there are other sides to her that don't need treatment, that are fine just as they are. When the patient loses hope, the Friend points out how far the patient has already come, despite the distance ahead. She acknowledges the patient's courage in facing unpalatable truths, lets her take rests, have a moan or a gossip while she recovers her strength for the next piece of hard work.

The Friend can be an unwitting saboteur, however, for friends are biased people: they always take our side, give weight to our way of seeing the world. They like us the way we are, warts and all, and certainly do not risk the friendship by challenging us, making us change. A too-solicitous Friend in therapy, by making the patient too complacent and comfortable, undermines the necessity and motivation for change. The Friend wants to cushion pain, whereas the Surgeon sees it as an inevitable precursor to the healing process.

## The Surgeon

*The Surgeon* inside the therapist, inspired by the God (who only rarely speaks directly to the patient, the therapist more often taking time to decide how best to translate and present the 'revelation') cuts into the deep layers of her patient's mind the way a hospital surgeon cuts deep into his patient's body. He aims to isolate, inspect, cut away, rebuild or replace diseased tissue. In so doing, the body undergoes trauma and will need recovery time, rehabilitation and a friend at the bedside. The same is true in psychotherapy except Friend and Surgeon are one and the same person. And it should be remembered that psychotherapists do not use anaesthetics!

I had a very intelligent and dynamically-minded patient who quickly recognized the importance of some deep issues which my Surgeon longed to get at. I probed carefully and respectfully, but though he agreed with my interpretative 'cuts' he became more, not less miserable. I sensed resentment under the misery, which he finally agreed to explore.

He expressed it all in one angry outburst, after which the therapy moved forward. He was seeing me as a sadistic surgeon, dissecting him with relish, waking him up from his anaesthetic to make him poke at his own wounds and share my pleasure in his pain.

Though exaggerated, this fantasy had elements of truth in it. Because he was so intelligent and often joined with me in the sorting out of his material, I had assumed this situation was no different. But it was. He needed the Friend in me to show him that I knew what he was going through in facing these awful internal experiences, that I recognized his bravery, would give him some encouragement. He made it clear that though he had wanted to go into just as much depth as I did, I should first have attended to the frightened child inside him who was terrified of my 'operation', needed a reassuring cuddle before 'going under' without having to be a sissy and ask for it.

We looked at his real experience of being hospitalized at three and a half, his mother going out to work and not able to visit as often as they would both have liked. But before making this connection I acknowledged that I had underestimated his fear and paced the therapy too fast, just as his parents always treated him as a big, independent brave boy when underneath he felt wobbly as a jelly. Once I admitted my neglect and spent some time appreciating his jelly-like feelings, the patient himself took up the metaphorical scalpel and recommenced the surgery I had abandoned.

## The Teacher

*The Teacher* is a controversial figure in psychotherapy. Received wisdom dictates that tired therapists teach and alert ones interpret. It is true that a clear interpretation given to a therapeutically

151

experienced patient at the right time, and deploying his own vocabulary, should need no elaboration, and certainly no 'persuasion' to accept it.

However, this is a counsel of perfection, and patients (especially those trying to adapt to ten- or twelve-session work, or those who never normally address matters from a psychological viewpoint) still ask for explanations. It is not so important to decode any specific interpretation for the patient, as to educate him generally about how to think dynamically.

Even very sophisticated, long-term patients fail to grasp interpretations sometimes. Assuming they were correct and properly framed, there will be sound psychological reasons for the patient's incomprehension so there is little value in forcing the issue. If the matter is as important as the therapist believes, then new material that is in effect a re-emergence of the old in different form will surface at some later date, leading to a similar interpretation that this time can be assimilated.

If the therapist has only a few sessions to offer, though, and the patient is one who needs educative help to get used to the idea of an unconscious at work in him, then interventions may need to be simpler, less subtle than usual, and the Teacher willing to explain them. The spirit of these explanations is that of helping a student master Japanese characters and the way they are laid out on the page before expecting him to write sentences. Or like showing a toddler how to use a knife and fork with a view to him eventually feeding himself. It is not about indoctrination or coercion. Such teaching represents an invitation to learn, not a requirement to agree.

Again, the patient may have a transference to the therapist that is already pupil-to-teacher (small 't') and it is important the therapist who loves teaching does not over gratify this ('act in'), such that transference becomes inseparable from reality and the patient is prevented from ever having to struggle alone with difficult concepts and take pride in his mastery of them.

Some therapists are natural teachers and this leads them to engage in much valuable training work. When they are doing treatment, however, they sometimes find it hard to shift the emphasis away from comforting and protective explanation to the more challenging interpretive domain. It is entirely understandable that a teacher-by-temperament will respond warmly to a willing pupil, but in therapy this has to be seen in terms of transference and countertransference and resisted. For it is quite possible the patient has come to therapy precisely because he needs to learn how to stop being everybody's pupil and start being his own master.

The Teacher in the therapist then, is but one function among others, discharged sparingly, judiciously, very consciously, to assist the patient to find out how he can make best use of the treatment situation. Teacher interventions should never be used to satisfy the therapist's own need for a pupil.

## The Parent

*The Parent* inside the therapist is the healing function most tugged at by the patient's needs and again should be dispensed with great awareness and care.

In some way or other all patients feel bruised, deprived, misunderstood or damaged by their upbringing. This is not a simple matter of parents being to blame (though it cannot be denied that cruel, neglectful and abusive parents do exist). It has more to do with how the child *construed* what happened to him in the light of other events and relationships at the time, when and how such constructions were subsequently firmed up and elaborated, the necessity for their application repeated by or unconsciously solicited in new relationships.

All but the most despairing patients are on the unconscious look-out for all they feel they have missed. Much of the so called honeymoon effect of early therapy is due to the patient's realization that someone has at last appeared who really does listen, attend, attempt to understand. For the therapeutic hour he alone in the whole world counts, is the absolute centre of the therapist's concern. Bliss!

The inexperienced therapist is often convinced she made an instant Therapeutic Alliance when what has really happened is the imagined reconstitution of the paradise lost (or never gained) in infancy, when mother and child were one. The therapist no less than the patient yearns for fusion but is wise enough to see the fantasy for what it is, and philosophically awaits the necessary disillusion that hopefully precedes a proper Alliance.

It is true that for both parties the mature Alliance will contain some element of the 'corrective experience'. Why do therapists become therapists after all, giving to other what they so crave themselves and getting vicarious satisfaction?

But other features ultimately matter more. Paradise cannot be sustained, for disappointment on both sides will soon set in (the perfect patient and perfect therapist, like the perfect parent, having yet to be invented).

The Alliance, dependency-based at first, grows into an adult-to-adult bond based on the results of actually relating rather than projecting idealized qualities; based on the testing of one another, the grown up acceptance of each other's imperfections as well as abilities.

The Parent in the therapist cannot and should not hope to replace or compensate for all the patient's bad growing up experiences, but does need to inspire and maintain hope in him by showing that parental qualities (containing, managing, letting herself be used, teaching, listening properly, respecting his separateness yet need to attach – to name but a few) do exist in the world and are available to him.

The aim in therapy is to enable him gradually to internalize these, carry the feelings of worthwhileness such parenting inculcates in children along with him; so that, though he needs a top-up occasionally like the rest of us, he no longer wears the chip of not being adequately loved on his shoulder, nor compulsively or dependently seeks from the therapist and others what his parents failed to provide, so finding himself unable to enjoy or even recognize the non-parental aspects of relationships that can be so fulfilling.

Parents, like therapists, must with all their shortcomings do the best they can and then let the child go. Every good therapist I know had a difficult time of childhood and consequently has a need to put right in others what was not right and not given to her. Most conscientious parents feel this way about their children. Unlike many well meaning parents, the competent, properly analysed therapist is very aware of this need, its potential use and abuse in the treatment she offers.

She must not adopt the patient; it is a lie that he can ever be her child. She must not obsessively nurse her own hurt through his, nor constantly use him to prove she is a better parent than her own mother or father was. But how hard to resist when the patient is crying out for precisely what she longs to give and possesses in such abundance! This underlines the absolute necessity for the therapist's own therapy and supervision.

The therapist is not a substitute for an inadequate parent. She must help the patient come to terms with whatever parenting he had or missed having, not dupe him into false hope by seeming to promise a second chance that does not exist. Therapy cannot make fairy tales come true, change parents or provide new ones. Rather should it give patients the courage to face their disillusion, bitterness and loss, instead of denying or avoiding these, leading to symptoms and wrecked relationships.

Neither treater nor treated can put back the clock: the patient must be helped to let unrealistic dreams die. After the mourning for those dreams comes the assistance to go on living, scars or no: living, relating, working, growing in wisdom – and because he is now free from the encumbrances of emotional problems, perhaps lucky enough to sometimes love and be loved.

## The Sage

The Sage is rather different from the God, Friend, Surgeon, Teacher or Parent in that all good therapists contain these in one combination or another, know how to utilize them when required and restrain their influence when not. But not all therapists are Sages (though some patients, because of their transference, see a sage where a sage is not).

A true Sage is rarely conscious of this quality – though arguably she should be. It is a difficult quality to pin down but is something to do with her accumulated wisdom, the depth and breadth of her personal as well as clinical experience and what she has made of it, that somehow *shows*, without any effort on her part. Her patients and colleagues tend to see her as a shaman-like figure, an example of where, in outlook, they themselves might one day want to be (though I know a few Sages I would not want to be like because I am aware of suffering and endurance in their earlier life that I could not bear, whatever the rewards in terms of personal growth).

The therapist who is also a Sage, or near-Sage, does not allow private philosophical concerns to interfere with or take the place of the treatment for which the patient has come; but in the mature stages of therapy, as termination approaches and for technically proper reasons the therapist is diluting the transference, exchanges of views not directly related to the patient's problems become possible. Long after therapy is over, extracts from these conversations are often quoted by patients who realize they have been privileged to receive much more than symptom relief and an understanding of their personal history; their life has been enriched and changed by a relationship with a very special and rare person.

The Sage affects people – patients, colleagues, friends – more by what she is than by anything she says or does. Her special qualities are often not recognized before long and intimate acquaintance. She is not given to dramatics.

Patients and trainees should watch out for aspirant Sages. A true Sage lacks any ambition to take over people's lives or unduly influence them over and above what happens in treatment. Alas, there are some therapists with unresolved personality problems who long to be 'charismatic' and work very hard at it, both on the lecture circuit and in the consulting room. They are especially dangerous when given charge of suggestible patients whose problems include a longing to be swept up into the arms of certainty by a powerful figure who will take all responsibility for them.

## GOD, PARENT, TEACHER, FRIEND, SURGEON – AN EXAMPLE

Zoe had been coming to see me twice a week, then once a week, for four and a half years. Only one hurdle remained in therapy and we had been trying to jump it for nearly a year.

Zoe, twenty-seven, was an only, unplanned child from an airforce family. As a young child she had travelled all over the East with her parents whom she rarely saw as they were always socializing. There had been a series of governesses and nannies, followed by boarding school in England (which she experienced as a foreign country) where she was mercilessly bullied.

Bouts of self-starving, months of lassitude and refusal to speak, attacks of psychosomatic inability to breathe properly, not to mention attempts to run away were all treated as naughtiness by the governesses and either not reported to her parents or her parents ignored the information. The boarding school was having financial problems so hushed up a year's worth of anorexia.

Not surprisingly she grew up into a woman beset by feelings of uselessness, convinced no one would ever want her. She made terrible relationships with men, in which she allowed herself to be treated like a doormat before being abruptly left. She spent the first three years in therapy waiting for me, too, to throw her out.

In spite of the long and serious history, Zoe progressed well. By our fifth year, she had ranted and raved at her parents, poured out her grief for the loss of her childhood, dispatched sundry exploitative males after our careful inspection, worked through a good deal of idealized transference to me, recognizing the profound distrust that lay beneath it, and exorcized the various nannies and the boarding school by talking through the recurrent dreams related to them till the 'hauntings', as she called the dreams, finally ceased.

However, Zoe still constantly scanned her environment for the prospect of a friendship with an older woman who she was all too aware represented the mother she never had. The more she disentangled herself from undesirable men, the more she felt the need of a woman friend.

Zoe was rich, overly-generous, beautifully turned out and well connected, so found it easy to attract companions. She knew whenever a woman took advantage that it could not go on. She would allow herself three or four months' worth of inferior companionship in exchange for extravagant meals, presents and introductions to the most exclusive hotels, then bravely end the relationship, after which she would come to therapy and weep copiously for weeks on end, angry and miserable that all the insight I had provided her with could not stop this compulsive behaviour.

We worked for months on her conflicted feelings towards me: gratitude that she had learned to respect herself and no longer wanted to die, as she had at the beginning; but fury that I could not work this last miracle, solve the problem of these older women by standing in for the missing mother myself. She claimed to understand the transference situation completely, accepting I was not and could not be her mother, but she could not stand the pain that went with such an acceptance. He head accepted while her heart rejected. This was where we had been stuck for so long.

One day, particularly low, she fantasized how it would be if I just held her and rocked her, while she cried over the latest fiasco with a woman she was about to send away. 'Don't worry,' she said sadly, 'I won't get you struck off. I know it's impossible. It's only a fantasy.'

I pointed out how, as always, her own needs came second to mine. She was looking after me when I was supposed to be looking after her.

'I know,' she said. 'We've been over it all so many times before. This time it isn't transference though. This is the big, sensible me talking. I need you as my therapist. I can't risk losing that. I must not put you in an invidious position. I've read the books. I understand perfectly well why you can't touch me. *You would if you could, but you can't.*'

At last my long-sleeping God woke up. I saw what I had avoided seeing for months. It was imperative I stop being so 'helpful', sack my sabotaging Friend and allow the patient to feel bitter disappointment in me. Clearly she had been living in a fantasy world where, were it not for 'the authorities', the consulting room would be a cocoon of mother–baby bliss. As it was, she believed we were having such a relationship secretly, non-verbally. The other older women were stand-ins for me. Our relationship had to be illicit, but with them she could for a while 'go public'. So much for my belief we had worked through the idealized transference!

'You believe the *rules* prevent me from holding and rocking you?'

'But of course.'

'I'm not intimidated by rules, Zoe. I could break them. I have before, when it was needful.'

She was aghast. 'You *what?*'

'This is not about the rules, Zoe.'

'You mean that you *choose* not to hold me, not even *once*, knowing I would never split on you?'

My Surgeon said: 'Yes. Because to get well you have to face she will never come. These women you befriend are not her and I am not her. *She will never come.*'

A heavy silence hung over the couch. The Surgeon had hit home, the patient was in shock. How to Parent her without pretending to be mum, giving her false hope?

The Parent in me teamed up with my Teacher, and we addressed her softly: 'I can't give you your heart's desire, Zoe. To hold you now would be to play let's pretend. It might make us both feel nice for a bit, but would only put off the evil day when you have to face the truth.'

Zoe sobbed, then became very angry. What was wrong with a bit of let's pretend, providing we both knew? It was now, when she really needed me that I was letting her down. I was no different from her awful mother. I too had betrayed her.

On and on it went, the *therapeutic* Parent in me giving her space to ventilate her rage and despair, while resisting the strong *personal* maternalistic pull she exerted on me.

The Teacher in me came into play again as the atmosphere calmed and melancholy took over: the mourning for the mother she never had, and now never would have, had begun. She bade me explain again and again why I could not hold her in my arms. She understood fleetingly, then lost it, became angry again, refused to accept it, then begged me to explain again.

Eventually she started to absorb the idea that no mother would ever appear, but that in giving up the search for her, she could start giving to and taking from other women what *was* on offer; real rather than fair-weather friendship, loyalty and comradeship, the dignity of sharing not just receiving support, equal not dependent status. She saw that our relationship was a model for such exchange, but because of the professional nature of our association, it would always remain an example, a prototype, not the finished article. Still, it would always be important because it was the *first*.

Had I given in to her – and to some extent my – need to hold her in my arms, I would have robbed her of what she came to therapy to learn.

She fought bitterly at first, rejecting the emotional independence I seemed to want for her on the grounds it was too painful to bear, too lonely; she would rather take what crumbs older women could offer – including me, of course.

When she was strong enough my Surgeon had to get her to see

that I was going to remain a therapist no matter what. She had stopped the other relationships, for a time hoping such fidelity would persuade me to metamorphose into a new mother, now the rules issue was out of the way; but in her heart she knew I had to be given up too.

My Parent–Teacher took great pains to show her that unlike the other unhappy attachments to women that she had broken, this was going to be a parting between equals, who had a high regard for each other, who together had achieved great things, were grateful and well disposed to each other, not angry and resentful. It was to be a necessary, if sad, ending so there could be a new beginning in her life, instead of fruitless compulsive repetitions.


## The Setting as Constant Intervention

By the post-Assessment stage in psychotherapy, the patient is used to the therapist, her consulting room and its environs; but even so this physical setting continues to come between him and his material, triggering associations, memories, feelings, especially when he detects change, even minute change, in what the therapist is providing for him. The therapist should maintain a predictable, non-distracting environment in which the patient can do his work, but even the blandest and most consistent of surroundings can affect him, often without warning. Such reactions can often be turned to therapeutic advantage.

I pride myself on always having fresh flowers from the garden, however humble, in my private consulting room, but this is a little difficult in the depths of winter. Over the Christmas period I generally manage by using indoor bulbs. One December evening, as I prepared the room for my weekly group, I realized I had no flowering plant for the centre coffee table and the shops were shut. Patients seated in a circle must be allowed to see each other across this table, so the tall green plants adorning window ledges would not do.

In a flash of inspiration I brought in from the living room a basket of large, unbroken, beautifully formed speckled stones, collected from the wildest shore of the Cumbrian island where I grew up. I thought they looked lovely.

Normally the flowers were ignored, or the gardeners in the group would pass the odd comment before moving on to the serious business of Group Analysis. On this occasion, however, we very nearly had a revolution.

'Stones. *Stones!*' cried one patient. 'Is that all we deserve, all we mean to you?' Another disgusted group member said that no flowers at all would be preferable to being palmed off with stones. It was just plain insulting. Another wailed about a child's story concerning a mother who fed her children stone soup and they got no nourishment.

I did not apologize as I had done nothing improper. But I had certainly succeeded in drawing a very powerful transference reaction. I resolved not to waste it.

Everyone had discussed maternal deprivation in one form or another at some time in the group, but on this occasion there was a positive chorus of complaint. Group members became even more angry with me and the mother I stood for, when it became clear I was not even going to say sorry. Each patient felt supported and understood by the others, through their shared 'neglect', so much fresh work was accomplished on the theme of bad mothers – work that any apology of mine would have blocked.

Another example. One recent Autumn I had to have the old apple tree outside the consulting room window radically pruned as it was cutting out light from most of the garden. Grass and flowers were failing to thrive. A recovering patient rejoiced at the amount of light that now flooded the couch on which she lay. A depressed patient obsessed with his own mortality went on and on about it being the end of an era, how he had loved those gnarled branches which he would never look upon again. A man full of repressed anger saw the pruned tree as spiky, threatening, lightning-struck, something out of a halloween poster.

No matter how careful the therapist is to make the surroundings neutral, they cannot but come between the patient and his preoccupations, even when month after month they remain unchanged in every detail. I have had several patients over the years who insist on using every facility every session; toilet and toilet cleaner, soap, towel, glass of water, phone book, tissues, rug on the couch, all light switches, spare pillow covers, books from my waiting room shelves, scrap paper from the desk – and one who in addition used the front lawn on which to meditate for twenty minutes prior to each session. This is valuable material for analysis when the right time comes, and should not be missed.

I have had patients who breeze in without noticing their environment at all, and patients who take off shoes, hang up their coats, mount the couch as if it were all some sacred ritual, the room some kind of temple.

The couch itself produces a wealth of fantasies. For one person it is the lavatory where he dumps his shit and feels lighter after; for another it is a holy altar. Yet another rolls onto it and announces he is ready for his blood-letting, while another sinks down with a sigh awaiting his 'mental massage'. For several it becomes a baby's cot. For some it has distinctly sexual connotations.

I remember one man who was progressing satisfactorily and for whom the immediate environment seemed unimportant. One day, in the middle of a series of stories about his sad childhood, he suddenly shot from the couch to the window, which it faces, frantically gesticulating at me. 'Quick, quick, come quick!'

I did as I was told, seeing it seemed so urgent and there would be plenty of time for analysis afterwards. I got to the window to find him pointing, goggle-eyed. There on the fence, not six feet away, a heron stood poised, ready for flight. In slow motion it gathered together all its strength, lifted head and neck to the sky, before launching itself and its huge elegant wings into the air. We watched it traverse the sky and disappear. When it had gone, the patient and I turned to look at one another, sharing a few moments of speechless wonderment.

Then we crept back to our places and recommenced the treatment. It was too precious and intimate a moment to spoil by discussing it. But I reckon that that rupture in the predictable environment for which I had striven so hard did more good for the Therapeutic Alliance than months of hard labour.

Unusual clothes worn by the therapist, the hair cuts she has, the fatigue or private joy that sometimes shows in her face, the weight she puts on or takes off, the colds and flu and days off sick, are all disruptions of the setting and should be taken very seriously. I have known patients convinced their therapist was dying of throat cancer when the real trouble was a short-lived cough.

I had a patient who could do no work at all on any day I was attending a lecture or meeting and so wore 'respectable' clothes rather than my usual comfortable, casual gear. I became then a powerful castrating woman who must be avoided at all costs. It is important not to be embarrassed about discussing such things, as the patient himself will rarely bring them up for fear of causing offence.

CHAPTER 9

# Making Interventions:
# Clinical Illustrations

In the previous chapter, interventions were grouped loosely under three headings. 'Stop–start' ones are designed to inhibit the emergence of more thoughts, feelings and ideas from the patient because the therapist is uneasy or muddled about the course these are taking; or they are couched so as to get the flow of associations re-started after it has stopped of its own accord.

The second group of interventions aim to help the patient develop, extend, elaborate on or organize existing material so as to generate yet more data.

Thirdly, the allocating of unconscious meaning to a body of material (an *interpretive* intervention) attempts to provide for the patient a platform of insight from which he can launch himself into a more accurate trajectory for the locating of specific associations which will lead to even more concentrated interpretations.

But this pathway to self-understanding is rarely so straightforward as it sounds. For, in order to follow the overall direction of free association, intervention, more association, interpretation, then more focused associations, followed by more penetrating and inclusive interpretation, some types of intervention not comfortably fitting the above categories need to be made.

For instance, interventions that maintain the security (or flexibility) of the boundaries within which the couple work may be more important at certain times than the race for insight.

Sometimes well meant but misguided interventions take the couple in any direction *but* insight. This often happens when the therapist believes her intervention is strengthening or repairing the Alliance when in fact it serves only to foster an unacknowledged transference. Other therapists so earnestly pursue and make interventions about the transference they fail to see the fear or irritation building up in the patient that outweighs any desire for self-knowledge and destroys whatever Alliance has been achieved.

The function of some interventions is to redress a balance within the therapist; when her Teacher or Friend must hand over the mouthpiece to the Surgeon or the God, for example.

Other inputs by the therapist serve to help the patient bear a bad time, be this an internal matter – for example, a depressive episode where no work can be accomplished for a time – or an external one, such as a stunned response to bereavement, the shock of un-expected physical disease or perhaps a bad car accident.

Maybe it's just a question of holding out together till exams are over, till the patient has settled in his new job, or finally moved into that new house. We therapists, so habituated to pathological signs and symptoms, tend to miss the degree of trauma induced in our patients by 'ordinary' life crises such as illness, being burgled, failing the driving test *again*, being made redundant, or a teenage child leaving home or getting pregnant. It is right and proper that these incidents, and the shock that follows in their wake, temporarily take precedence over the Dynamic Formulation as the centre-piece of therapy.

The task for the therapist is finding interventions that turn a necessary waiting interlude into a constructive rather than marking time experience, while resisting the twin temptations of turning the patient into an over-dependent invalid, or encouraging him to tackle therapeutic work he cannot cope with at the moment, because the therapist erroneously believes she is not doing real therapy unless she is 'digging deep'. The therapist's professional pride should never count more than the patient's crisis needs.

There are many little but important interventions whose job it is to clear the cluttered pathway to interpretation. Such humble but essential interventions represent a regular tidying-up exercise that speeds up the therapy (hence, in the public sector, saving money). Extraneous material is discarded; the rest is sorted, occasionally even ranked in relevance to the Dynamic Formulation (this is especially important in short-term work, if the therapist is not to be tripped up by too much material). Everything is dis-entangled from everything else and dusted off.

The inspection that follows determines what is restored to its original site on the path and what is placed with other items relevant to it, by hedge, stream or tree, available for retrieval if needed but no longer blocking the route to new finds. To steal from Milton: 'Those interventions "also serve" who only sweep the path'!

Playful and experimental interventions can make patterns or bits of patterns with the material left after the tidying up, seeing where one pattern mirrors, suggests or amplifies another, putting the patterns in some kind of pattern of patterns, locating areas where bits of the pattern or patterns are still missing, so giving the therapeutic couple ideas about where to look next.

Often, when a treatment seems clogged and worsening, I perform this tidying-up operation in my own mind outside the session. It frequently leads to better interventions and this in turn succeeds in getting the patient's material to flow more freely.

With the right patient a joint sweeping of the shared pathway to insight can do wonders for the Alliance while creating space for further therapeutic developments. It is amazing, too, what valuable material often lies hidden among ancient debris, or is just obscured by more recent, colourfully distracting data that has to go into the bin with the rest.

Lastly, there exists a set of interventions that do indeed fit the category of 'furthering the material', that is, making it possible for the patient to build on existing productions; but I have included clinical examples of them in this chapter about miscellaneous interventions, rather than in the previous one, because their success relies on specific techniques and/or vantage points, that are not required in the run-of-the-mill 'furthering' intervention.

*Reserved Interventions*

Although the therapist may understand, or partially understand, a piece of material in terms of its unconscious determinants, she will sometimes refrain from checking out her understanding with the patient on the grounds that it is premature, or that made at any time it might disturb an equilibrium in his mind that could result in further damage rather than development. Or it would simply send him away in fright.

Knowing what is going on does not oblige the therapist to comment upon it. Indeed, such comments can be positively harmful. Keeping her cards close to her chest may be very frustrating for the therapist who has not realized that there are other uses for cards than throwing them down on the table. A psychodynamic understanding of the patient's material can inform the therapist how to manage and contain a disturbed person without necessarily discussing her reasons with him. I did this with Guy, the borderline American student, raped by his uncle, in Chapter 3.

Providing the patient wants therapy and appears to be benefiting, the therapist's first duty is not to *do* therapy but keep him *in* therapy, even if she has to reserve many interventions for a later date or for ever.

Neither should the opposite situation be forgotten. Patients sometimes finally leave because the therapist lacks the necessary boldness to offer challenging interventions that could unstick a chronic problem, or liven up a dull and pedantic treatment. Holding off and pitching in are two ends of a continuum; most therapists feel comfortable sitting in the middle, but the journey out to either end is sometimes clinically essential.

Between these two extremes lies the technique of what I call 'crabwise' interventions. These, too, are important throughout the therapy and not just at Assessment. The therapist is clear about the intervention she wishes to make, but is doubtful as to its reception by the patient. She makes a series of comments or gestures – small, subtle – that sidle up, one at a time, to the main intervention. Like a crab she stops whenever she senses danger, but does not necessarily retreat; she waits hopefully instead for the moment when it might become possible to make another sideways step toward her goal.

## 'Acting In' Interventions

These interventions commonly occur when the therapist is presented with a choice of working with the Alliance or the Transference. In good faith, but unconsciously gripped by her own transference to the patient, she chooses the wrong one!

Delia, still in her twenties, recounted a life of extraordinary academic success, followed by a prestigious job in the City, which she privately scorned as she longed to be a painter or poet but was aware she lacked the life experience yet to say anything significant about the human condition.

Highly literate, she knew all about the theory of psychotherapy, and proceeded to describe her formative influences as well as her family members going back three generations. Both her parents, especially her mother, had always enjoyed high-powered jobs in international aid schemes and were passionately committed to the Third World. Though they had helped Delia and her brothers with needs and problems whenever they could, the children had often to wait weeks before their parents returned home, by which time the problem had passed or they had sorted it themselves.

I encouraged Delia to actually contact some of the loneliness and anger she had felt as a child, rather than simply talk about it in abstract terms. She allowed herself to cry occasionally. The therapy forged ahead quickly.

Next, she wanted to talk about boyfriends, how they all admired her, found her strong and capable and brainy, as well as attractive. This annoyed rather than pleased her. Eventually, contempt for her men led to a messy ending of the affair that left her feeling lonely and in the wrong. Girlfriends, too, tended to look up to her, asked her advice. Some developed erotic attachments to her that at first flattered then irritated her.

I felt I should ensure the Alliance was one in which she could see I respected her abilities, but was not overawed by them; that in fact we had much to offer each other. Already it felt as if Delia was comfortable in her intellectual domain while seeing me as ruling the emotional one: we were thus equal and separate so could do business together and not end up like her other one-up, one-down relationships. I was sure she saw us as equal – it was certainly how she behaved – and I wanted to keep it that way. I was wrong. I should have monitored the transference more closely.

I had sensed at Assessment that her greatest fear, yet hope, might be that one day she would meet someone who would turn the tables on her. She would then be the dependent one, the admiring one, and at last the looked-after one; but alas, she would also be the one in receipt of contempt and rejection. This, not the maintenance of the Alliance, was what I should have pursued.

One day Delia gave me some fascinating material about her most recent boyfriend. His personality, despite being very different, almost opposite on the surface, to her father's, was in fact very like his. She was re-enacting much of her childhood through this young man, trying to show her father how to this time get it right. She wanted the boyfriend to be emotionally available to her as her father never was, yet to have an equal relationship with her, whereas all he seemed to want was his own enslavement.

Delia had adored this man at first, but now he had declared his undying need of and love for her, she felt the old contempt returning. I saw this as her loathing his dependency on her the way she loathed her father for depending emotionally on her mother, preferring his wife over his daughter, following her round the globe so as to avoid separation, while the emotionally neglected child pined at home.

Poor Delia was in a cleft stick. She so wanted attention she chose dependent men (and women), but then hated them for being as weak and clingy as her father. She wanted to be more passive and yielding in her relationships but her partners went on insisting (as had her parents) that she be strong and self-sufficient so they needn't feel responsible for her.

When all the material about the boyfriend was on the table – it took about half an hour – and we had both taken a little time for silent thought, I made my mistake. Believing I was respecting her intellect, protecting her from getting too dependent on me too quickly, reaffirming my understanding that equality in relationships was vital to her – believing, in other words, that I was maintaining the Alliance – I asked her what she made of it all.

To my astonishment she stared long and hard at me, her eyes filling with tears. Then her face became grim, angry. I thought she was going to swear at me, but she bit her lip, hesitated, then marched out of the room. I heard the front door bang and her engine start up before I had chance to collect my thoughts.

I am relieved to report that she returned the following week and we began to mend matters. Foolishly, I had ignored a powerful transference in deference to the Alliance. Delia had walked out hating me for doing what all bosses, teachers, girlfriends, boyfriends and her parents had always done – namely, expect her to do her own work; look after her own needs.

Delia had known perfectly well what interpretations I would have made of her material about the boyfriend. The interpretations themselves were not the point. She needed to hear me say them. She wanted me to be a good caring mother who would not demand she sort out her own problems, even though she had the ability so to do. I had let her down. I was just like all the others. She wished to God she weren't so bright, then maybe someone would look after *her* for a change!

In missing the hungry child beneath the bright, co-operative adult I had confirmed all her worst fears. She had prescribed how I should behave (treat her as Superwoman), as she did with everyone else, and I had foolishly obliged (acted in). She was especially embittered at my making her do her own interpretation (that is, mother herself) because she knew from our earlier work that I was well aware of her neediness. I must therefore have done it on purpose.

The uncomfortable question that remains in this case is: Did I really invite Delia to share her ideas about the material with me because I was preserving the Alliance, respecting her oft-quoted longings for equality? Or had I, like so many others, fallen under the spell of her intellectual glamour? Was this error due to my own transference to my patient?

Occasionally, skilled therapists deliberately act in so as to reconstruct for the patient what typically happens between him and significant others, bringing about an inevitable denouement. When the interaction is complete she offers an 'action replay', demonstrating for him how he contributed to an outcome he generally blames others for. The Teacher in the therapist is consciously using acting in as a *technique*. This could not be more different to the unconscious *error* I made with Delia.

Sometimes therapists use their Parent function to make listening, respecting, supporting qualities lacking in childhood available to their patient. Their aim is to provide a 'corrective experience', show him not every relationship has to replicate an early damaging one. However, susceptible patients will easily confuse the qualities offered with the therapist making them and the idealized mother he longs for. Gratifying (acting in to) such a transference, basking in the patient's love and gratitude may be pleasant for a time, but the therapy is headed for trouble.

*'Acting Out' Interventions*

Ideally, the therapist becomes conscious of two way transference so acting in is avoided. Supervision can be a great help here, providing the supervisee trusts her supervisor enough to confide her personal feelings about the patient, and her feelings about the patient's way of experiencing *her*.

Whether she is conscious or not of her own transference – and I think most therapists have a sliding scale of awareness, depending on what is happening inside and outside the consulting room at any one time – therapists, like patients, do also act out. They do things – take decisions, say things – outside the therapy frame that properly belong within it, though in all sincerity the therapist believes she is acting for the best.

I had two patients following each other every Tuesday morning, one named Jonathon and the other Jon. Jonathon was a musician who frequently went on tour and was scrupulous about letting me have dates in advance, which I would then write down in my diary.

Jon, on the other hand, never missed a session. At forty he had still not left home and most of his therapy had involved his preparing to go. He had a job now and a few friends and was going to evening classes. Until recently I had always been very fond of him (in fact I had had to watch that I didn't take over his mother's position).

One day, to my surprise, I found 'cancel' written by both their names, so went off to the supermarket to get some much-needed supplies. Jon duly turned up and was devastated to find me not there. He looked all round the garden, then in the garage, realizing my car had gone. He left a note through the letterbox and went away.

On my return I felt dreadful, wracked my brains for some explanation. My practice was at that time full to bursting and I was tired. Had I confused the names? But why would I write 'cancel' twice, once by each name? And Jon had never been away before, so why hadn't I questioned it? Naturally I apologized and encouraged Jon to express his anger with me.

It was only afterwards that I made myself face how fed up I had been with him lately. This was the fifth or sixth time he had packed his bags to go, and always he funked it at the last minute. I had really thought he would make it this time, but he came to the session before the missed one full of excuses. Had I been more honest with myself about how cross I was with him, I would never have done such an unforgivable thing as cancel his appointment.

He accused me of acting out and would not believe that the similarity of names and their proximity in the diary could account for it. I asked him what kind of denied feelings he thought might lead me to such aberrant behaviour and he then confessed how fed up with himself he was, for not making the move. He could well understand me feeling the same, but all the same I was in the wrong and he was very hurt.

Fortunately the Alliance was strong. We made up and he did in the end get better.

## Reconstructing Interventions

Far into treatment many patients still cannot recall, or recall only dimly, memories they know would be helpful to the therapy's progress. Patient and therapist may use the patient's transference as it occurs in the consulting room, plus the available historical facts and not a few hunches, to reconstruct what might have happened in the patient's earlier life. This is not the same as guessing what happened, or distorting and embellishing facts to fit a pet theory. It is more like making a police photofit picture, accepting it can be very useful but is nonetheless only a crude simulacrum.

Just as this artist's impression sometimes leads to a successful arrest, so a reconstruction of the patient's past does occasionally result in the reclamation of real memories. It is essential, however, that the therapist does not inadvertently provide the patient with a false version of his early life that might comfort by appearing to explain everything, but leaves his current symptoms and conflicts untouched because the 'screen' memories are absorbed cerebrally, not re-experienced as with true memory recall, so they can be properly worked through.

Only rarely do I use reconstructing interventions to entrap rogue memories. If they are determined to stay hidden there must be good reason, so I usually leave well alone.

Generally speaking, I have different purposes in mind for such interventions. I might run a mental film of a self-blaming depressive's childhood for him in the consulting room, asking him as a capable, controlled, intelligent adult to witness the vulnerable, confused, unhappy or lonely situations in which he once found himself, and the childlike solutions he was forced to find, in the absence of adequate environmental supports. As I take him through the film he corrects any scenes I may have got wrong, or under/over-emphasized: be becomes a co-director in fact.

If I have timed it correctly the patient will have that, 'No wonder I am the way I am', revelation. He sees it rather than being told about it. He learns to have compassion for the child he was, lessens his self-criticism as a result, feels more worth while. He is parenting the wretched child he saw on film and who still resides within, rather than persecuting him for being so weak and useless.

Reconstructing interventions can also relate to the very recent past. The patient has no trouble remembering people or incidents, who said what and to whom; but cannot re-create the actors' feelings, reactions, wishes or fears. Where the Alliance is sufficiently strong to withstand mistakes, the therapist may ask the patient for licence to reconstruct the internal experience of some person important to him with whom he is having difficulty. The technique is not so dissimilar to psychodrama.

A supervisee brought the case of a young woman with maturational problems, who hated her ex-soldier father but could not resign herself to this. It seemed wrong to detest one's own family, especially as he had been taken prisoner 'in some grubby Asian war' and left to moulder in a camp for some months, if not years: it was all very vague. Neither parent talked about this, though hints and gossip in the neighbourhood suggested torture at worst, filthy and starving conditions at best. The supervisee had to quarry for this information: it had never occurred to the patient to enquire directly.

Lack of curiosity (denial) on the patient's part was the source of the supervisee's problem. She didn't want to interrogate the patient about her father's history, even supposing she knew anything more, yet as the patient was so preoccupied with her guilty hatred of him, she felt she ought to do something to help her understand the distress he daily caused.

Though in her mid-twenties, the patient had had no sexual experiences, having led a sheltered life in a private boarding school. She was now attending a genteel ladies' college just down the road from home. She found her father surly and uncouth, disgusting in

170

fact. He urinated and defecated with the toilet door open, never flushing after use. He smelled of sweat and grime, burped and scratched all the time, left the towels filthy.

Once safe in her bedroom, she was reduced to tears by all this, but it had never occurred to the patient to leave home.

Apart from these gross habits her father could be sociable and relaxed when he chose. He was never physically abusive to her or her mother. In her opinion he was not suffering from any mental disorder and was not depressed. Enquiries from the supervisee to the patient about the parental marriage yielded very little; the girl (for so she seemed despite her years) had noticed nothing untoward between them (more denial?).

The supervisee and I worked out a way to reconstruct what might be happening from the father's end, in order to enable the girl to express some of her true feelings about him rather than remaining stuck in her miserable guilt and long unproductive silences. We had only a few facts about him but the reconstruction would put them together into a story of his subjective experience that might provoke a reaction in his daughter, even encourage her to find out whether the story was true.

Next time father left the toilet door open and the patient confessed (rather than expressed – an important difference!) her hatred of him, the therapist did not adopt her usual, understanding look. It had always led to a complete cessation of material before.

Instead she said: 'When he does these disgusting things in front of you, I try to imagine what he could be feeling and thinking. I am saying this not to condone or condemn his behaviour, but to try and make sense of it, from what little I know of him.'

She waited for a cue, positive or negative.

The patient replied warily: 'Go on, then.'

'Well, maybe he thinks: "Here am I in the autumn of my years. Washed up. Unemployable. No use to anybody. But there you are, my precious little daughter; young, unmarked by experience, all your future ahead of you. You have never lived in a human sewer, never eaten pig swill, never been stripped and humiliated before your mates. What do you know of life? I can't bear your innocence, your hope, your simple faith in a benevolent God. I am angry at the world, at God, at you. I want to show you how the world really is, how obscene it is, what it can do to a man. What it did to me when I was your age."'

'You mean the war made him bitter? He needs to get his own back? He's *jealous* of me?'

'Perhaps. It could be something like that. What do you think?'

The patient cried then, obviously moved by her father's possible

171

plight, but furious that she and not someone else (mother?) should be the butt of his envy and hatred. She kept saying: 'But it isn't my *fault!*'

Reconstructing a confrontation reported for the dozenth time, but on this occasion from the father's point of view, helped the patient access a sense of injustice, hurt and fury so far muffled under monotonous guilty grumbling, while simultaneously enabling the therapist to see how the mother, too, might be involved in the patient's unhappiness.

Anger at the therapist for showing father in a more sympathetic light – in the patient's eyes, taking his side – also needed working on. In supervision we speculated about whether this might be because the girl experienced her mother, too, as colluding with her father, agreeing to ignore or forgive his obnoxious habits. We suspected she must have horrifying fantasies about the sexual union that resulted in her own birth, and much fear for her own sexual future.

But perhaps the mother was totally estranged from her husband, pretended his behaviour was not happening, so he did it more? Did the patient feel angry and disappointed with her mother for failing to protect her from his angry 'messages'? And were the messages for the world in general or the two women in particular? Why was the patient afraid to complain to either parent about her father's behaviour? Did she fear she might be just exaggerating what others regarded as normal? If that was normality, how could she ever live with a man?

Suddenly a deadened therapy had come alive with possibilities. Now that the patient was more in touch with her feelings and curious about them it seemed possible for the supervisee to contemplate asking her about these previously taboo subjects.

Perhaps she might even assist the patient to reconstruct the childhood so far undiscussed, re-imagine it piece by piece, filling in the memory gaps with what could have happened, what she might, should, could have felt and done or said, rather than just issuing a few facts about her history. Such a reconstruction would occur within the safe confines of the consulting room, with two capable grown ups looking on, able this time to comfort and explain to the child why she was being exposed to such masculine brutality long before she was able to comprehend it.

The therapist might also gain a glimpse into the child's mind at that time, see what kind of meanings she attributed to what was going on around her, without having to ply her with questions.

**Carried out unambiguously but sensitively, a reconstructing intervention can help unstick a therapy that more conventional**

interventions have failed to budge. This includes interpretive interventions, which may be technically correct, but do not reach the patient because of the impersonality or prematurity of their delivery. It was the supervisee putting herself in father's shoes that brought the issue so alive for the patient, making interpretations about fear of growing up (that is, dealing with aggression and sexuality) possible later on.

Clearly, both therapist and patient must be aware that the reconstruction does not necessarily replicate the truth, but the active reconstructing of possibilities might help the patient search out the truth that is missing, as this patient did by starting to talk to her mother about her father's experiences in Asia before she was born.

Reconstructions stimulate the flow of further associations from the patient and provide a new agenda for him to work on. But they should never be attempts to rewrite history.

### Translating Interventions

It is not enough for an intervention to be 'right'. The information it contains must be translated into the kind of words, attitude and presentation from which the patient can learn and progress. If he feels attacked, disliked or undermined, the chances are he will recoil from rather than make use of what has been said.

A supervisee brought a South American student who had come to her university counselling service after a spell of psychoanalysis in his own country, which he had not found helpful. The supervisee could only offer a once-a-week contract, and as the student's stay at the university was limited, she was rather doubtful about her ability to help if the analyst, with much more time, training and experience to hand, had not been of use.

After two sessions her impression was: A man of twenty-five going on sixteen, constantly assailed by sexual desires, restless and angry, yet believing himself too inadequate to find a girlfriend. At the same time he was needy, helpless, regressed, had lost the ability to iron or boil an egg. The supervisee felt he was appealing to her, tranferentially speaking, on two counts. He wanted her to be mum so as to fulfil his childlike needs to be looked after. That way he could avoid the whole humiliating business of girls, and growing up in general. But his older, teenage self wanted a mum to give him the education, advice and sympathy over his adolescent sex/love failures that his actual mother, chronically ill, had never given him.

Not wanting to act in and intensify a transference there was going to be insufficient time to work through, the supervisee concentrated on the Alliance, inviting the student's healthy self (the one that wanted to make a go of rather than abandon maturation) to 'share her chair' and look with her at the poor man – child really – who couldn't boil an egg, think with her about why he might be in such a state. It wasn't so much that he was bad or weak but that because he lacked confidence and was bruised by failure, he had withdrawn, as we all do under stress, to the safety of childhood dependency, a time when he could legitimately expect maternal rescue.

The supervisee showed the student to himself as a lonely, insecure and inexperienced chap striving mightily to do normal healthy male things, but in a foreign land, with no backing from his real parents or any imbibed parental influences that, had they been adequate, would have given him a sense of worth, power to act, and the resilience to bounce back from failure.

When the patient recognized this picture of himself as lacking the tools for the job, rather than just being intrinsically useless, he began to get indignant on his own behalf, became his own champion. He started to use the therapist not as a substitute mother to boil his egg but as an ally, someone who could show him more pictures of himself, perhaps help him paint in some new features, paint out or adapt others.

He became eager to contribute to these pictures, and so found himself talking about his mother and father, his painful memories of their marriage, his father's constant absence, his mother's illness, the way he had been left to his own devices as if he was not important. At one point the supervisee said something like: 'Yours wasn't the sort of family a kid could learn to be a man in, was it?' and the student was enabled to weep.

This proved to be a turning point in the therapy. Formerly refusing to discuss the analysis, he now told my supervisee that he had felt his analyst (like his father?) had not been interested in his wish to have a girlfriend, career, be a man. He had constantly taken up his material in terms of the part of him that couldn't boil an egg. 'You feel you are a baby. You want me to be your mother. You tell me how helpless you are so I will be your mother and give you advice.' The student felt criticized, even less of a man. He believed the analyst did not respect the part of him that despite his regression did want to be a successful adult in the world.

Because the supervisee *had* respected that part of him, his self-esteem improved such that he was able to tell her about, and with her help use, those insights he had formerly been unable to accept from his analyst.

Many of the analyst's interpretations seemed to have been correct in their content, but ill-conceived in the manner and timing of their delivery. The supervisee had been unable to find any evidence of a Therapeutic Alliance between patient and analyst that might have made unpalatable truths bearable and usable.

In building her own Therapeutic Alliance with the student, she had diluted (rather than interpreted) his transference demands, restored hope and pride in him, before translating, taking the shame out of, the insights from his analyst that he had not till now been able to assimilate.

An intervention is delivered in the context of a real as well as transferred relationship, the therapist having a choice as to which relationship the intervention should address. As the therapy develops it becomes possible to make an intervention that covers both simultaneously while translating the content of the intervention into a language and attitude acceptable to the patient.

For example, my supervisee might say to this student: 'Given the way things were at home, I can understand you experiencing me sometimes as the mum you never had, who'll boil your egg and iron your shirts. But you and I both know we must find a way to help you face and cope with your feelings about her, not find a substitute for her. Our work together has shown us, too, that a girlfriend is a girlfriend, with needs and problems of her own. She can't stand in for mum either. You and I, and you and the potential girlfriend, have to find a different form of relating that will have different rewards.'

From the student's account it seemed the analyst only ever addressed the transference and did not pause to translate his interventions before delivering them. Neither did he appear to value the notion of Therapeutic Alliance. No matter how technically correct an intervention, it has no value if the patient is too demoralized and unallied to hear it.

## World-Assumptive Interventions

Some patients 'transfer' not just to the therapist, the consulting room, to particular situations or figures (authority figures, for example), but to the whole world. Their most intense relationship is with the world as a whole.

As a result of childhood experiences they have developed theories about how it all works and have accordingly designed behaviours and emotional responses that will ensure survival in such a world. They have arrived, too, at fixed unconscious beliefs concerning the inevitable consequences should they fail to properly 'play the system' they have created.

From time to time we all say things like: 'You have to look after yourself in this world, no one else will' or, 'It's dog eat dog; you've got to fight.' These are theories about the world that govern people's behaviour and decisions but they are consciously held, adaptational attitudes that tend to be reserved for stress situations or emergencies. In better times, or within the bosom of family and friends, a more loving philosophy takes over. But the patients referred to here spend their entire lives acting on assumptions of which they are not aware and which never shift, irrespective of circumstance. They are neither easy to treat nor easy to like.

Their unconscious, hence initially inaccessible, world view colours all their dealings with everybody including their therapist, who is working from the basis of a different world view: this makes emotional resonance between the pair almost impossible. Weary supervisees bring unsatisfactory sessions with such patients to supervision, complaining that all attempts at building a Therapeutic Alliance have failed, that despite their best efforts they cannot like the patient, and they are certain the patient detests them; indeed, the therapist cannot understand why the patient still comes.

This question can only be answered if the therapist perseveres in finding out what is his transference to the whole world, rather than just to her. Underneath his courtesy and behavioural correctness, how might a patient really view a therapist's attempts to understand him if he assumes the world is a place where, 'If you are not for me, you must be against me'? Or: 'The world is a place governed by hidden rules. If you break them you are out on your ear.'? How does he experience the therapist's attempts at making an Alliance if his assumption is: 'Everyone acts as if loving your neighbour is what counts, but when the chips are down it is the one with power that wins: control or be controlled.'?

And what about the patient whose world is based on science, logic, rationality? How can he trust someone who so invests in feeling, symbolism, 'inner worlds'? For him, that direction leads to madness, and in his version of his history there will be good evidence for such a construction. No wonder he is suspicious; she is not acting the right way; that is, in accordance with his view of the world.

Too often the therapist worries about her own relating abilities, reacts defensively against her patient's coolness or hostility, or becomes discouraged and depressed at his lack of regard for her, instead of seeing this very fact as material to be understood. She is not there to gratify her own need to be appreciated, but to investigate her patient's unusual attitude (for most patients share the therapist's basic assumptions about the world, so display a collaborative demeanour from the beginning). What kind of non-collaborative world did he see as a child and what meanings did he ascribe to what he saw? What laws determine the way his unique 'system' operates? He treats the world and the people in it as if such-and-such were the case. What, precisely, is this 'such-and-such'?

In other words, great difficulty in forming the Alliance may itself constitute the chief symptom, rather than being evidence that this patient is not suitable for dynamic work. When he sees his own distortion of the world, how it is affecting all his relationships, so is enabled to make that Alliance, he is ready to leave therapy.

Class, race and gender are also relevant here. A man may believe, without knowing he believes it, that: 'Us blokes are supposed to be the stronger sex but the truth is it is women who break you.' I have had several female feminist patients whose unconscious assumption about the world was: 'I'd die sooner than admit it, but men really are superior.' How is a female therapist to overcome this prejudice? She must begin by seeing it as a symptom, rather than just an unpleasant personality attribute.

Unwarranted reactions to other people and to their therapist make sense, once these patients' underlying assumptions about the way the world works are brought into the open. If what they believed about their 'system' were even half-way true, their 'negative' behaviour would be absolutely appropriate.

Millie's mother brought her up on welfare benefits and money from scrubbing floors. She scrimped and saved to give Millie a good education so she would never have to be poor. She died of cancer in her early forties, which Millie was certain had been brought on by stress. Dad had deserted them when Millie's mum was six months pregnant.

At twenty-nine, Millie lived alone in a tasteful flat, and was steadily climbing the ladder of a publishing career. She was well dressed and smartly groomed, was seen in all the right cultural venues, but had never kept a boyfriend for long and had few friends. She said tersely that she had no idea why she felt so depressed. If she knew she wouldn't have come to me would she?

In our sessions she was polite, obliging but cautious with her material, prompt with her fees and emotionally cool. I sensed how lonely her life was but found it hard to warm to her personally, not least because in some subtle way she always looked down on the people she talked about. She seemed to have a chip on her shoulder: it turned out that others had said this – 'behind my back' – in a work context. She regarded them as inferior human beings who just couldn't stand her capacity to go for what she wanted.

It was this remark that made me invite her to elaborate upon her career philosophy, which she did with considerable pride, if not hauteur. I linked her views to her profound sense of injustice with regard to her mother and hinted that perhaps she coloured the rest of the world, too, with her resentment. She sniffed dismissively but said nothing.

Millie had found no personal happiness or even job satisfaction on fulfilling her mother's career ambitions for her. She did feel a grim satisfaction, however, that the sorts of people who had once looked down on her mother now looked up to her daughter, envied her. Her mother had been vindicated.

Such was her construction of human relations, she believed her unpopularity with colleagues and dismissal by boyfriends was just the inevitable price she had to pay for worldly success and refused to be fazed by it. It never occurred to her that some people managed to be admired and liked as well as being successful, or that her unpopularity was due not to others' envy of her, but her childhood envy of others persisting into the present.

Fiercely loyal to her mother, anxious to assuage her depression, terrified of exciting her envy in any way, Millie had stayed home from the school she loved, refused to make friends or go to parties. She never asked anyone home. As a teenager she had not had boyfriends, eschewed new clothes, not travelled when she longed to, always reassuring her mother of her gratitude and devotion. Her dream had been to do pottery or sculpt in Italy but she'd agreed to a business course in Croydon.

She must have had to repress every ounce of natural longing for the pretty, the glamorous, the expensive, the exciting. Behind the devoted mask, how she must have envied other children, hated her mother for putting her in this position. Yet how guilty such hate would have made her, had it been allowed to surface. At all costs, the envy and the hate had to be crushed, were still being crushed, years later. For hadn't her mother died anyway, proving her efforts inadequate? She must try harder.

In therapy, Millie's mother had to be removed from her shrine and properly mourned, which included the difficult task of accessing those repressed resentful feelings at being deprived of a normal upbringing. Then the child was able to emerge who had so longed to have what other children took for granted, who had dealt with her envy by becoming contemptuous of their shallow lifestyle, who had grown up into a woman who sneered at anyone capable of drawing the love and friendship she would die rather than admit she wanted for herself.

Without any attachments except her mother, young Millie had set about constructing a world in which the Haves reigned supreme and the Have-nots, like her mum, were humiliated. All she had to do was become a Have, which would appease her mother and at the same time provide a legitimate reason for her inability to make relationships. In Millie's world, so long as you were a Have, love did not matter.

From the start, before I knew any of this, Millie related to me in an aloof, almost haughty way. Sometimes I sensed her sneering at me but fortunately suppressed my angry reaction in order to take time to think out what might really be happening between us. For it was bound to mirror other relationships. If she could get it right with me, then perhaps that could be extended to workmates?

In her role as patient she was definitely the envier and myself the envied. Were she to accept any intervention I made it would only make her position worse; she would envy me more – hence her self-protective sneering attitude. But if she succeeded in making me envy her; if she turned me into a useless Have-not, how was I ever going to help her with her depression? It would be yet another Pyrrhic victory.

As understanding began to dawn, I put this dilemma to her but again she could not consider it, because if she accepted anything good from me she would feel humiliated, one down, a Have-not. So I commenced a series of 'what if' interventions. What if the world were not divided into these two populations of envier and envied; how would a conversation between us work out then? What if I, a Have in her eyes, felt no desire whatever to be envied? What if she as a Have-not were not contemptible but merely somebody who needed something that I could provide? What if we both shared the same world assumption: 'The world is one family, we've got to prop one another up'? How would that make either of us feel when we shared ideas and feelings?

Millie could not conceive of such a world. She asked me sarcastically if I was some sort of religious nut. But she took up the 'what if' challenge (she relished any challenge, the more impossible the better), going through conversations with me that could happen were we batty enough to believe such sentimental nonsense about the world being a family. We had made a start.

## Other Types of Intervention

Patients themselves, and sometimes their relatives, intervene in the work. It is not uncommon, for example, for a therapist to find herself acting as mediator or interpreter for an abandoned spouse who is not in treatment. Where the patient has failed to successfully communicate to the partner or the partner failed to comprehend or believe the reasons for the marital split, the therapist may have to put the marital Dynamic Formulation in simple terms which the partner might understand, while helping him/her absorb the shock.

Introducing him/her to a therapist of his own is a separate issue from the one of explaining to the partner why what has happened *has* happened. Too often a therapist is reluctant to give an honest professional opinion to a relative or partner, for fear of causing distress, when in fact the soliciting of such an opinion can represent a first real attempt by the relative to come to grips with what has occurred.

Effective treatment always disturbs the patient's closest relationships to some extent. And so the patient, too, might need a review of treatment from time to time. 'How am I doing?', or, 'Is it usual to get worse before I get better?', can be processed by the therapist in the same way as any other material, but this can be and often is a legitimate request for a progress report, and needs to be treated as such, the patient's questions answered as honestly as the therapist is able.

Patients intervene in their own sessions, deliberately or not, by making bodily contact, an alarming development for many therapists who fear accusations of abuse, or are themselves conflicted about their bodies being touched, or who feel that in this particular case manipulation of their feelings is being attempted.

Touching can be 'innocent', as when patients from other cultures take handshaking at the end of a session as normal procedure, or when, after a long and very moving treatment concludes successfully, they hug their therapist with no motive other than to demonstrate affection and gratitude.

These are exceptions rather than the norm, however. Generally speaking it is advisable to avoid touch, while remaining sensitive to and willing to talk about the patient's desire for it. Avoiding the whole area altogether by sending the patient disapproving cues each time the therapist senses an impulse or longing to touch, cuts off a vital area of investigation and the therapy will be greatly depleted as a result. Whatever else psychotherapy patients suffer from, there has almost always been an insufficiency of loving touch in their child-hood, and without acting in, this issue must be fully addressed.

The same general principles apply to the giving of presents. Each patient should be discussed in supervision, though; for rigid rules about such matters, while serving to provide a code of conduct for the therapist, can also deprive her of creative oppor-tunities in the session.

One bleak February a patient brought me a bunch of snowdrops that I put in a pot on the table between us. They looked so brave yet vulnerable and we both stared awhile at them, the atmosphere between us sad but companionable. I decided not to comment on her 'breaking of the rules', certain it would spoil some developing theme that had not yet been put into words.

This patient's husband had died fifteen years ago. That much I knew. What I did not know was that his grave was far away so she had dedicated a tiny plot in her garden to his memory. Each year these snowdrops had been the first flowers to bloom, the first sign of spring, the first lifting of her spirits after yet another grieving winter.

Eventually, life had picked up and she had married again, letting the memorial site become overgrown.

She hated winter, was always more depressed, lethargic then, but had this year found herself vigorously lifting and dividing the now overcrowded snowdrops that still bloomed in spite of all the weeds and rubble. She smiled sadly, recounting this, saying no one could ever take her first husband's place; letting his memorial ground become neglected hadn't cured her of her love for him.

After a little silence, she sighed. Life has to go on, she said. She could not live with a dead man for ever. The morning of our session she had divided and replanted the tiny bulbs so as to spread some of the hope they represented all over the garden. She very much wanted me to have a share in these little flowers of hope. She was telling me the therapy and our relationship was helping her mourn properly at last.

Thank goodness I'd kept my counsel about the 'rules.'

Although it can be embarrassing, I am always encouraged when a patient feels confident enough of my response to ask 'nosy' ques-tions. It shows the Alliance is in good condition! He may inter-vene in the material that is developing between us by asking me if I, too, ever get depressed. Do I really know how bad it can get? What it really feels like?

I am aware that if I say yes, he might lose confidence in me: 'Well, what's the point in the blind leading the blind? I need a therapist who knows how to enjoy life so some of it might rub off on me.' If, on the other hand, I were to stoutly deny any depressive episodes, he might then feel I could not possibly understand him, am bound to look down on him, so am equally useless.

Whether or not I actually answer his question (that is a matter for fine judgement, though as I get older I find myself increasingly able to tell the truth) I might ask him to consider, in the interests of his therapy, how he would feel if I answered one way, and then how he would feel if I answered the other. His answers will be most revealing.

Many people coming for marital/couple therapy eventually find themselves able to ask me, as I don't wear a ring, whether I am single, widowed or divorced. Again, soliciting their reactions should I answer one way or the other, rather than reacting defensively on the one hand or confiding my life story on the other, always yields rich material.

Suppose I say yes, I am divorced. Some feel that if I, a supposed expert, have failed to make marriage work, there is no hope, whereas others are comforted that even experts can get it wrong and maybe they should be less hard on themselves.

In the subsequent discussion, some even come to see that marriage for certain couples might not be a question of success and failure at all, but that given the two people's psychological make-up and history they were as fated to be drawn to each other as they were destined to part. Separating can sometimes mean the healthy refusal to go on with a repetition compulsion that threatens to make one or both parties chronically miserable at best, psychiatrically ill at worst.

Some come to realize that many so-called marital 'successes' are due not to closeness and mutual love but the total surrender of one party. He or she may be required to constantly inhibit, or completely deny their healthy needs for communication, support, reassurance. He or she may have to give up much-needed sex altogether, or endure participation in sexual acts that revolt them, so as to maintain marital peace. They may be a slave to the other's job, the other's mother/father. Where one party's autonomy is constantly denied and that person finally rebels, this too may be a declaration of health, the very opposite of failure.

These philosophical meanderings, consequent upon questions about my private life, often guide the couple gently and safely into the murky waters they have to come to explore. They begin with a general, safe discussion about marriage (which nonetheless contains hints of stresses in their own) and progress gradually to the specific marriage we are met to study. This process should be

allowed to develop at its own momentum. Unnecessary interventions will only slow it up.

Many couples want to know my personal beliefs about marriage
and divorce, and often about sexual practices, too, if this is an
issue for them. I think it only fair these questions are answered
truthfully. For many patients have told me of experiences with
couple-therapists determined to keep the pair together at all costs,
and others who seem opposed to marriage in principle and hell-
bent on breaking them up. It would seem from some of these
patients' accounts that some therapists cannot talk about sex at all
and others cannot talk about anything else.

Working with couples, I usually say I am divorced if I am
asked, my tone making it clear, I hope, that I am neither ashamed
nor proud of this: it is simply a fact of my life. Always my open-
ness about this has let the pair to discuss coupledom and its
problems with their own relationship in mind. They know they are
talking in front of someone who knows the hell as well as heaven
that marriage can be. Seldom, if ever, do my own marital affairs
concern them further; they have too much business of their own.

The same is true once I have been asked about depression, or
loneliness, or if I have children, or ever had an alcoholic/schizo-
phrenic in the family. No patient has ever 'grilled' me, once the real
query behind their initial question has been properly dealt with.

*'Fingers Crossed' Interventions*

Interventions discussed in this chapter cannot be all-inclusive, for
a whole book would be required to enumerate every one. Eliciting
and describing more of them would make an interesting project
for a weekend training workshop.

I would like to mention one last intervention though – the
'fingers crossed' intervention. The therapist either has a creative
hunch, an informed guess in mind; or, completely at sea, she
senses a response is being demanded of her but she doesn't know
what to say. Fingers crossed, she wades in. If she is right, well
and good. If she is wrong or just filibustering, it won't matter too
much, providing the Alliance is strong. The patient will forgive
her, even tease her about it at some future point. But if the
patient is suspicious still, or the Alliance weak, better by far to
stick to my Lancashire maxim: when in doubt, say nowt.

Saying nothing can be facilitating or unintentionally persecuting. Both consequences can be worked with. It is important not to
infantilize the patient by protecting him from negative feelings

from which he could learn. The discomfort of the silence might drive him to produce more material that this time the therapist really can make sense of; or his anger and disappointment with the therapist for not meeting his need on demand becomes the new focus for work. Either way the therapy has moved forward.

Not making interventions is just as important as making them!

## CHAPTER 10

# Dealing With Transference in the Longer Term

Like love, transference is something that is fallen into rather than chosen. It cannot be willed into being, though like the less dramatic forms of love it sometimes grows with time and familiarity. It comes in all shapes, sizes and degrees of intensity, waxing and waning throughout the therapy. The therapist is as much prone to it as the patient, though the therapist's own therapy and clinical experience should enable her to monitor and manage her own transference to the patient without it intruding upon his treatment.

The therapeutic situation is one in which the therapist holds the boundaries and is therefore in charge of things. She also has special knowledge which the patient needs. In addition she keeps private her own inner world, concentrating on the patient's. The execution of this role, combining as it does both the care and control elements of parenthood – the wanted love and feared power – will 'draw' any transference that exists without artificial aids.

Many years ago, some of my trainers criticized me for being too open with patients, showing too much of my personality, thus denying them their right to a 'blank screen' on which to project their old feelings for parents. I still doubt this advice today. If transference is there it will find its way out, no matter how much it is contradicted by reality. Like falling in love, falling in transference is so powerful, irrational, all-consuming that it cannot be stopped. It will demand expression in the conducive environment of the consulting room just as lovers, however illicit and guilty their love, are unable to resist consummation given the intimacy of the bedchamber.

When the transference to herself is weak, the therapist is advised to work where and with whom it is strong – the patient's spouse or colleague, son/daughter or parent-in-law, for example. Just as one does not fall in love with everyone one meets, neither does one fall into transference with them, even when nudged by conducive circumstances.

In this chapter I shall look at some of the transferences that occur mostly, though not exclusively, in established therapy, and how these might be dealt with.

## The Reciprocated Transference

### The least discussed transference of them all!

Iris had been supervised by me for three years. I was impressed with her work and professional integrity. Imagine my surprise when she came for supervision as usual, and after much nervous preamble burst into tears and told me she was deeply ashamed and shocked, but there was no denying it: she was in love with a male patient.

Currently six months into therapy, the man had been brought for supervision during the Assessment stage, but not since. He was a very cultured man, well travelled and with private means. He had published some poetry a few years ago and was now working on a serious play which he could neither finish nor abandon.

He had endlessly discussed the creative process with my supervisee, herself a great reader and theatre-goer. I had drawn to her attention how these intimate and mutually flattering talks might be the patient's avoidance tactics. Exchanges of ideas with an attractive woman are much more thrilling than examining non-functioning relationships. Had he discussed the state of his marriage, or his relationship to his son? Or maybe he was simply demonstrating the way in which he always related to women. Instead of reacting to it (falling for it) perhaps she should be standing back to analyse it?

Iris took the point, reporting thereafter that all was proceeding satisfactorily if slowly. The patient did indeed have marital problems but found it hard to admit to any discontent, still insisting the creative block was the main problem. She'd bring him for supervision again as the need arose.

Iris confessed there had been a strong mutual attraction from the first moment they met, but she had of course quickly disguised it. Six months on, she now realized how all the discussions about art had been a respectable way for both to get close without breaking any therapeutic rules. She knew she had to stop her collusive part in it but did not know how.

When the patient finally admitted problems in the marriage his attachment to Iris greatly increased. Instead of connecting these two occurrences in appropriate interventions, she had fallen deeper into her own warm feelings for him, longing yet fearing to hear more of his infatuation with her.

Iris was greatly distressed, knowing she had lost control of the therapy and her own feelings. Things had got so bad she even felt jealous of the 'frigid bitch' of a wife, found herself falling over backwards to point out good things about her to hide these feelings from the patient, who then criticized his wife even more. Iris hated herself for enjoying this criticism.

She couldn't bear to ask him to consult another therapist, for fear of never seeing him again. Anyway she'd have to tell him and the new therapist why; that was unthinkable. She cherished totally unrealistic fantasies of completing the therapy herself, then admitting her feelings afterwards so they could start up a new life together. She wanted me to help her control herself during this interim period.

Iris was certain he was in love with her too, for he was now reporting daydreams of living with her, commenting on her clothes, saying he knew patients felt this way about their therapists sometimes and that she could never, never reciprocate, but he just couldn't help the way he felt.

As supervisor, I needed a good sorting out of all the material to hand concerning his key relationships, to see what this attachment might mean, what it was he was re-enacting, or what other problem a love affair with a non-available figure might solve. At the same time Iris and I needed urgently to construct a range of interventions that would enable her regain control of the situation while assisting him to look *inside* at his motives and conflicts, rather than dealing with them by soliciting gratification of his needs through his all too willing therapist. As things stood, both therapist and patient were acting in.

Both these tasks were accomplished and monitored over many weeks, but for the purposes of this clinical extract it was our third task, that of searching the therapist's past, that was so critical in enabling Iris eventually to fall out of love.

I do not normally ask about a supervisee's private life, but this very serious situation warranted it in my view and Iris was keen to co-operate. She had been analysed some years back, and as a single self-supporting mother with two children, going into therapy again was just not feasible.

I wanted to know what Iris's patient was tapping into, what it could be that rendered her so susceptible to his appeal. I knew Iris had divorced a physics teacher five years ago, basically because he was emotionally so withdrawn she could no longer bear the loneliness. I knew her father had vanished before she was born but that she had an excellent relationship with her mother. That was all. I could make no links here.

'Tell me about all your important men,' I said. 'What has this patient got that they had too?'

We started from age fifteen. Every man was different: artists, scientists, rich and poor, one tough businessman, and the withdrawn physicist. Some were outgoing, some withdrawn, some full of self-doubt, some great show-offs. Unlike the patient, none of them was married when Iris met them. I was puzzled.

Working from hunch, I asked Iris to tell me about each man's mother. They were all possessive, full of love and attention but very controlling. In each case the man was the favoured or only son. This also applied to the patient's original family, and to his marriage, where his wife subtly but powerfully controlled his every move. Now we were getting somewhere.

Next, I asked Iris what the unwritable play was about. She said well, it was sort of philosophical. Its central question was: Can humans only fulfil their true potential if they are free of all ties? Do they have to choose between being a lonely but wise hermit, or a socially happy but spiritually depleted family/group member? Was there any hope for a third state that connected independence with interrelatedness without compromising either? ...

Her voice petered out here. She was realizing that she had been too infatuated, too keen for literary discussion, to notice that the play told her everything she needed to know about why her patient had really come for therapy. The play contained – albeit in lofty language – his own Dynamic Formulation.

Iris had succeeded in enabling the patient to admit to himself the marital disquiet he had been denying for ages (by intellectualizing it in a play), but in the process had uncovered his profound fear of aloneness. As a child he'd had a love–hate relationship with his mother, ran away several times, but always came back in the end, scared by his premature independence. He wanted to run away now, from what I must admit sounded a very controlling wife indeed, but he could only contemplate this by seeing his therapist (for his wife made sure there were no other women in his life) as an alternative. Real freedom was just too terrifying. With tabooed Iris he could be free and attached at the same time!

For her part, Iris was in the grip of a common syndrome, an unfathered daughter growing up to look for impressionable men she could fashion into husband/father material. Being in charge of the design process made her feel safe: her own very creation would never want to leave her as did the original. Iris wanted to lovingly 'groom' a talented man to her emotional specifications, while the patient wanted an attentive mother with all the best of the original but none of the worst: they were a perfect match.

Iris groaned when I offered this idea. Now she recalled what it was that all her men had held in common. 'Potential,' she said. 'They were all gifted, but *unfinished* in some way. I was the woman to complete the job. Fell for it every time.'

'Then what happened?' I enquired.

'They all let me down didn't they? When I wanted to step out of that position of benevolently running their lives for them; when I wanted to stop being mum and get a bit of fathering for a change, just be listened to myself, they either switched off, walked away, or professed not to know what I was talking about.'

'So what evidence do you have,' I asked, 'that this patient would be any different, should you risk your career and his mental health by having an affair with him? How do we know that part of his wife's need to control isn't because she, too, feels his withdrawal and incomprehension each time she needs from him what you want from your partners and never manage to get? What makes you so sure he is capable of thinking about *your* needs? In the consulting room you are not allowed personal needs; your job is always to put the patient first, and he thrives on that. But in a real relationship with him you *would* have needs – and moods, and tempers, and sulks, and complaints. What will he do then?'

This may sound unfair on the patient but it was his health and his treatment I was fighting to preserve. I was also trying to get Iris to see she had chosen another in a long line of similarly structured dependent personalities. She would improve his confidence, shower him with the love his wife denied him, turn him into a great poet – then he would let her down and eventually she would leave him. Neither could benefit from such an affair.

Eighteen months into therapy, Iris had recovered control, interpreted the patient's need for a special relationship with her in a way that did not criticize or punish him, and had helped him see how he relocated his central conflict about attachment/separation in his play. She also helped him see their abstract discussions as pseudo-intercourse and acknowledged that until she had understood their meaning, she had mistakenly encouraged him.

Soon the patient began to show interest in other women, though this remained at the level of fantasy. Iris brought her jealousy to supervision. He was increasingly determined to leave the now love-less marriage, but always had an excuse. This Iris worked on in terms of his earlier terror whenever he tried to leave his mum. Outwardly Iris behaved with all professional propriety but I sensed that, inwardly, anger and disappointment in him was growing. I had to be quite firm to make her honestly examine her feelings.

Then came a long stuck period. The more the patient moaned about how awful life was, yet refused to budge from his secure and cosy family, the more furious Iris became in the supervision sessions. 'He's just like all the rest, needs constant propping up. He was keen enough to leave her when he thought I was waiting in the

189

wings. He could kid himself and poor sucker me *then* that he yearned for independence. I see now I was nothing more than a trade-in, a more accommodating mother-figure to the one he's got. He won't leave her but blames her for his emotional starvation, his inability to create anything. He clings like a leech, all the time saying it's her fault! God, what a wimp!'

Iris's transference became as negative as it was formerly positive. This once adored patient was now in receipt of hurt and rage left over from all her previous partners. She must not allow such feelings to colour her interventions or behaviour in the session.

After some months, these feelings having been discharged in the safety of supervision, the work settled down and the patient improved steadily. He could look back to the time he was madly in love with Iris, discuss it with some humour, see it for what it was and feel gratitude that she had not exploited his emotions at that time (if only he knew!).

When the patient started an affair Iris was jealous but relieved. She saw he was doing with the new woman what he had been doing with her, using her to make separating from his wife easier. This time she was able to work on it with him, without her own desires getting in the way.

The affair was brief, the patient having become aware of and impatient with his idealization. He prepared to leave his wife in earnest rather than just dreaming about it. He said there would be no more women until he had faced life on his own for a bit. Iris had a new problem now. Her patient was begining to turn into the kind of man she really could respect. She feared she really had, at last, groomed a man to her specifications and that she was in danger of falling in love with him all over again!

In this case two erotic transferences dovetailed, rendering an otherwise able therapist completely useless to her patient for a time. Other reciprocated, or locked transferences that occur include the mother–therapist finding a daughter–patient, a sadistic patient finding a victim–therapist, a therapist–priest being found and maintained in his position by a never-graduating novice.

Opportunities for unintentional abuse of patients are rife when two transferences complement one another. The situation is especially difficult and dangerous because the therapist is too emotionally engaged to be objective. Mercifully, Iris knew herself well enough to see she was out of control.

*The Attitudinal Transference*

Some patients transfer neither to a particular person nor the world as a whole (see previous chapter) but somewhere in between. They have developed special categories of people and institutions about whom they hold irrational but unbudgeable (because unconscious) attitudes.

The commonest one I encounter is in the GP's surgery. Doctors cure you, protect you from death, have special knowledge and power. Therapists work alongside doctors so they, too, should give advice, tell you what to do, make things better. Many patients are frightened and/or angry to discover that I want to hear from them and not the other way round. In many cases a bit of education sorts out the problem: this is ignorance not transference. But some are absolutely certain I should be dispensing magic advice and become most upset that I am 'holding out' on them. They would not dream of attributing the same power to their bank manager or solicitor.

When working with a marital problem, the patient's unconscious assumptions about what and who the institution of marriage is *for* have often to be challenged, otherwise therapist and patient are constantly at cross purposes.

Peter came to see me in the GP's surgery holding the note his wife of twenty-three years had left on the mantelpiece. 'I am leaving you for ever. Don't look for me. I am very sorry.' For a month he had carried it everywhere, because unless he re-read the letter he still could not believe it was true. He was naturally shocked, but most striking to me was this sense of absolute disbelief, of impossibility, as if the sun had forgotten to rise one morning.

'I don't want to brag,' he said, 'but lots of women would give their right arm to have a husband like me. I don't smoke or drink. I make all my own furniture – beautiful workmanship if I say it myself. I help with shopping and do all the gardening, and I've brought home a decent wage the last twenty-odd years. And if she feels we're getting a bit past the bedroom stuff, I never press her.'

Peter's parents had run a fish and chip shop in London and seemed to have had a reasonably happy, traditional marriage. His childhood seemed very average, his schooling and friends unremarkable. He married Shirley after a six-month courtship, when she was pregnant. He was convinced she was the girl for him and had never questioned that throughout their marriage.

He had 'let' Shirley have a part-time job when their son grew up. He 'let' her go out with girlfriends to the pub. He 'let' her take

191

holidays occasionally, with relatives or friends. Peter himself loved his home. He constantly made furniture, then accessories – carved boot-scrapers, an elaborate cat basket, coathangers. He extended the loft. He converted the cellar to a shower room. He never took holidays – no point, had everything on tap at home, and anyway house security was a major problem these days (Peter's job was installing burglar alarms).

I began to see that Shirley had run away from a luxurious fortress, the very embodiment of Peter's concept of marital bliss. For him marriage meant a completely sealed off, self-supporting environment – psychologically and domestically – in which both parties were but an extension of the other. Nothing else was necessary. He could not begin to understand Shirley's need of friends and holidays. He 'let' her have them, saw no threat to him in them, because he simply found them irrelevant.

His enduring disbelief that Shirley had left him resulted from his conviction that she had no cause. He *knew* what a good marriage was. He had kept every single rule. He had been perfectly content with what they had, so why hadn't she? He was genuinely bewildered about this.

I tried to make his unconscious assumptions about marriage conscious so he could start looking at and comparing them with other views, but he grew impatient. Clearly my job was to assist him to get her back, not try to change *him*!

Soon, he started a relationship with a woman at the local post office, entertaining her in his home. Nothing had changed. The post mistress moved into the literal and psychological space Shirley had once occupied. Peter's attitudinal transference remained untouched by brief therapy.

Another man, holding identical views, *but at a conscious level*, might have been persuaded to see things from his wife's lonely, bored and imprisoned point of view. Peter could not see why she might be lonely and bored in the first place because his *unconsciously-held* attitude to marriage told him she had been given everything any marital partner could possibly need.

Other common unconscious assumptions about partnerdom are: 'Partners carry on where caring parents left off'; or, 'Partners should make up for all the bad things that once happened to me'; or, 'He/she will be everything my mum/dad was not'; or, 'Marriage will be the one place I can truly be myself. He/she must be just the same as me.' Many marital therapies suddenly steam ahead, the blaming dramatically reduced, once one or both partners see what they have been really demanding of the other, because of these assumptions.

Therapists, too, are gripped by prejudice, often about themselves. Such assumptions usually show up in supervision. A therapist might be constantly reassuring her patients, not because they cannot stand their suffering but because the therapist is working on some assumption to which she is oblivious, like: 'If I fail to reassure adequately, a calamity will occur and it will be my fault. I *must* prevent it.' The original real or fantasized calamity which she is still avoiding has been lost in the mists of time, but the *attitude* to patients derived from it stands out when she presents her cases to the supervisor.

Therapists who, on top of earlier conflicts about their brainpower, only train in mid-life, and/or who never had a university education are often prone to over-intellectualizing and over-theorizing in treatment and in supervision. Though unaware of it, it is clear to the supervisor that they feel obliged always to display their 'credentials' – of which they remain highly uncertain. Patients more intelligent than they frighten them, in case they are 'caught out'; intellectual scoffers and point-scorers can terrorize them into impotence.

Whether any threads connecting up such an attitude to early familial experience remain intact or have long since disintegrated, what remains critical is that such therapists work at managing and protecting themselves and their patients from such powerful prejudice. To do that they must first become aware that it exists.

All therapists have a need to heal that is not entirely altruistic. When this need is thwarted, it is all too easy for them to retaliate, reacting to the patient as if he wilfully refuses to get well. Or they lapse into depression or guilt at not having produced a miracle. Such a frame of mind is not going to be useful to other, more helpable patients.

## The Mediated Transference

A supervisee brought Brigid, thirty, a very damaged girl from a now broken family that had always malfunctioned. She covered her vulnerability with a tough, sometimes sarcastic exterior.

After only a couple of sessions it was clear Brigid had become attached to the supervisee but could not say so directly. The summer break approached and Brigid produced a small teddy bear, complete with kilt and bagpipes, plonking him on a bookshelf, 'where he can look down and watch you work'.

Brigid's therapist commented that this was to be their first separation. Perhaps Brigid wanted to leave a little bit of herself here for safe keeping, in the form of McTavish (for such was Brigid's name for him). She did not hand back the present for fear of this being seen as rejection.

As therapy progressed McTavish was used more and more to carry hidden messages from the patient to the therapist. Interpretations were made about this but the patient would not or could not use them to help her speak more directly. Each time she changed the subject. While the teddy bear felt sad or lonely or neglected, she could cope, but saying she felt that way was just too risky.

Sometimes Brigid looked up at McTavish and asked the therapist what kind of a weekend he had had, knowing full well McTavish had been on his own (as she had). She could only complain through the bear. In her more agitated states she would ask after the bear's health, needing reassurance that her therapist knew she, Brigid, was feeling terrible, and would help her cope. At Christmas Brigid declared that McTavish needed new music for his bagpipes and a red cushion to sit on.

It was useless explaining projection to this patient, taking away the one avenue through which her therapist could contact her true feelings. On the other hand, to reinforce the defence mechanism would do nothing to assist her to relate more authentically with others, who only saw a hostile exterior. The therapist sometimes replied or even interpreted through the bear, thus playing along with the 'joke' as a way of preventing the patient veering away from a too directly addressed topic. At other times she intervened directly, trying to 'wean' Brigid from the bear.

Early on in the supervision, I was unsure if the patient might be rather near the psychotic end of the spectrum, but I was reassured when, after the Christmas break, no red cushion was provided for McTavish and the patient accepted this sadly but philosophically. She knew the difference between fantasy and fact.

In supervision we looked at how the supervisee might deal with Brigid's disappointment. While declining to provide the red cushion – implying promises the therapist could not keep – she could nonetheless make clear, by referring to and playing with the idea of 'new music' (new sorts of interaction between the therapeutic couple?), that she had heard and remembered the request for a Christmas present of special attention. This in turn might lead to a recall of earlier Christmases, and an expression of some of the sadness and neglect felt at that time, which was currently hidden by Brigid's bitter attacks on the commercial exploitation of Christmas.

**A mediated transference can be colluded with, the patient's dissociated state thereby encouraged; it can be rigorously interpreted thus driving it underground; or it can be playfully addressed by**

the therapist in a way that shows the patient she understands the communications being sent, and their disguise, but is not going to demand the patient 'come clean' until she is ready. All the same, a line has to be drawn, as with the red cushion, showing the patient the limits to which the therapist is willing to go in this very serious game.

In this case the patient needed to know her therapist understood that only the most special and important folk sit on red cushions. But if the therapist had actually bought one, she would have been acting in, possibly ending up spending a fortune on McTavish's wardrobe, while the increasingly dependent patient became less and less able to relate outside the session.

Some patients, on the edge of psychosis, would be devastated by non-receipt of the red cushion, because for them the concreteness of the gift is equated with its meaning: the cushion *is* the special love, rather than merely representing it. For them a mere interpretation about the cushion will not do.

During Assessment, gentle trial interpretations help to determine if a patient is pre-psychotic or, like Brigid, resorting to a mechanism of defence that enables them speak their mind but through a third party, who, if the therapist fails the test, can be dismissed as just a silly teddy bear, just a bit of fun.


*The Allowed Transference*

Some vulnerable patients for a time need their transferences preserved intact in order to survive. It isn't easy for a therapist to knowingly accept projections and contain them: everything in her training tells her to interpret and disown them. However, there are exceptions to every rule.

Marilyn's mother had died of slow cancer six months ago. An only child with no one to share her grief, she felt she could not recover from it, though outwardly she had soldiered on. She was twenty-seven and single. She had broken down at work a week before she came to see me privately, and was now off sick indefinitely, able to care for herself practically but unable to take the smallest decision or responsibility. She had her own flat but visited her father daily, vainly trying to get him to understand what was happening to her.

Marilyn's father had always been generous with money, a private education, clothes and presents but could stand no display of emotion, especially neediness. He believed that after six months Marilyn should have pulled herself together. He said she ought to be married with children like other women of her age. That would keep her mind off morbid thoughts. When she visited his home, he gave her food and they watched the news on TV, but if she started to talk about her feelings he became irritable, lectured her; even asked her to leave on several occasions.

In the early months of therapy Marilyn would not use the chair opposite me, but sat cross-legged on the floor, using the couch as a shelf for the drawings, poems, embroidery, photo albums and various soft toys she brought with her.

Soon she started wearing an Alice band in her hair and pleated skirts that reminded me of school uniforms. She came to the session carrying brightly coloured folders with childlike doodles all over them, the stains from coloured felt tips all over her hands. Clearly she was much regressed.

She liked to chatter about her day – shopping, cleaning the bathroom, the cream buns she ate – while showing me her 'treasures', such as her sewing. A point always arrived in the session when her face clouded over. She wanted then to talk, and often weep, about 'horrid Daddy' and/or 'my lovely dead Mummy'.

Occasionally I would venture the odd lightweight observation: 'I can see you sitting on the floor like this with your Mummy, all your treasures about you'; or, 'Oh dear, Daddy is all you have left and yet you can't make him understand.' These remarks were to assure her of my non-intrusive attention rather than to facilitate any insight. I let Marilyn use me as the lost mother until she could bear to start facing life without her. At the same time I tried to stand in for the sympathetic father she so badly needed.

Over time she wrote less and less sentimental poetry, brought fewer soft toys, instead bringing pages and pages of personal reflections: childhood memories of mother, school, nice and nasty outings and holidays; long standing hurts with regard to her loving but very distant father; what to do about a career, about marriage and babies, and her increasing awareness that she seemed so much younger than other women her age. I allowed her to move from floor to chair and back again as she saw fit, and to read aloud until she was less bashful about her thoughts.

Eventually, to my enormous relief, she took off the Alice band and started to wear lipstick. Now I could cautiously commence some interpretive work.

After a year or so she stopped reading aloud her essays on the preceeding week's feelings and talked 'off the cuff' instead. She sat on the chair and left her toys at home. Normal therapy had begun.

Marilyn's family conflicts went back further than her mother's death. A recent trauma superimposed on covered-over old problems often results in temporary dramatic regression where it is quite useless to try and force the patient to grow up. Nature's own healing time has to be respected.

Sometimes the allowed transference is between a couple.

Raymond was engaged in a mutually torturing, blow-hot, blow-cold relationship with a married woman. For five years she had promised to leave her husband and live with Raymond, only to withdraw at the last moment. Whenever Raymond determined to forget her and build a new life she followed him everywhere, threatening to take an overdose if he didn't return.

Raymond used therapy well, although the regular crises in his relationship – which always had a life and death feel about them – did interfere greatly with the attempt at calm analysis of his attachment to his mother. The parallels were clear and Raymond understood them well, as he understood how his problems about his masculinity had derived from a difficult relationship with his father.

The married woman's machinations drove him to despair at times, as his retaliations, including moving house and job (she still found him), clearly terrified her. Both partners had at times considered suicide on the grounds they could neither live with each other nor without each other.

Raymond was fifty and had been unhappily married before, to a cold woman who had controlled him. At least he felt this current relationship was one in which he was loved (and hated!) with equal passion.

In the end Raymond understood his problems but still could not solve them. He was confident about his masculinity, less shocked and depressed each time his partner 'threw a wobbly', as he put it, and, knowing the relationship would remain unpredictable indefinitely, had invested more energy in his job and started a photography course.

'I need a few permanent things in my life so I don't collapse each time this happens,' he said. He had decided he could never give her up but he wasn't going to let her destroy him either. He knew she stood for his mother, but he insisted he also loved her independently of 'all that'. He was prepared to accept the transferential aspects of the relationship rather than lose it altogether. 'I have to be realistic. At my age, I'll never find anything half so good again – even if it is ghastly half the time.'

Privately I felt disappointed I had not helped Raymond more, but who am I to judge what is right for him? He knows what he is taking on in allowing this destructive transference to continue.

More importantly, perhaps, he has learned through therapy how to generate strategies that will compensate for and comfort him in the bad times to come. He has the same problems he brought to therapy at the beginning, but a much healthier attitude toward them.

## The Split Transference

In order to get something untaintedly good from a person, that person must be idealized, all their faults denied, all their bad habits and cruel impulses relocated so they can be kept 'pure' in the mind of the subject. But as for every day there is a night, for every thing its shadow, so for every idealized person carried in the subject's mind there is a corresponding loathed person, full of poison and negativity. What happens when this split cannot be maintained, when the patient is forced to see that his mother, girlfriend, wife, daughter – or therapist, is in fact madonna and whore, saint and sinner, healer and charlatan, a mixed bundle of good and bad?

Aaron's single mother had treated him abominably, forgetting to feed him or wash his clothes, locking him in his room when he was naughty and forgetting to let him out again before she went out for the day. Yet she lavished attention on her several dogs which she proudly took to shows, and whose silver cups she eternally polished.

Understandably Aaron grew up craving the attention of women, yet hating and distrusting them at the same time – not that he was aware, until therapy, that he contained such a divide within him.

His sexual dreams featured either anal rape, which he found up-setting, or love scenes of immense tenderness such that he was moved to tears on recalling them. He had been promiscuous throughout his life, with women he now saw little worth in, but who at the time had been pursued because they were 'easy' – easy to get into bed and cuddle up with, pretending it was Mummy, easy to despise afterwards as money-grabbing sluts who deserved the sadistic fantasies he then started having about them.

His treatment progressed. He began valuing himself more, starting a relationship with a cultured paediatrician. He was overjoyed to dis-cover the rewards of intelligent conversation with a woman, loved how she offered to pay her way rather than sponging off him, how she took him to her flower bedecked flat, wining and dining him there. She became the Perfect Woman, Aaron refusing to explore further his non-enjoyment of sex with her. He said he didn't mind 'doing his duty'; it was the least he could give her, considering the new ways of relating with a woman that she was opening up for him.

He came to his session one day greatly distressed. For the first time in his life he had been completely impotent. Worse than impotent, for he had not even been able to go through her front door, let alone reach the bedroom.

I asked him to tell me about the evening. It had been the paediatrician's turn to treat him. They had seen a really good new film, dinner afterwards, and then a couple of drinks at a club. Drowsy and very pleased with each other, they had driven to her flat.

Though the relationship was some weeks old, it was only now Aaron told me about his girlfriend's dog, a huge drooling creature that followed her about like a slave and growled at him. He always tried to ignore it. Arriving home on this occasion Aaron stepped out of the car onto the drive, right into 'a great steaming turd, the size of a dinner plate'.

The girlfriend apologized, explaining the arrangements with her neighbour to let one another's dogs 'out for a necessary' when either of them was away till late. She promised to clean Aaron up as soon as they got in. 'She was trying not to laugh. She was *proud* of the brute. She thought it was *funny!*'

I had a distinct impression of the couch shaking under his rage and loathing. The dog excrement had pitched him full force into contact with the dog-adoring mother he hated. *The split between the idealized and the loathed had been brought together.* In allowing her dog to befoul him the paediatrician suddenly lost her ideal mother status: he could not bear her to touch him; he wiped his shoe on the grass and left.

The subsequent sessions made clear just how much her dog carried the darker side of his maternal transference. He derived great pleasure from telling me exactly what he would do to that dog if he ever got his hands on it. However, he resumed the relationship, longing again for her motherliness, but he could only give her the sex she expected if it took place in his house. Thus his venomous hatred of his mother could reside in the dog, leaving him free to see the paediatrician as at all times above reproach, the very model of what every woman should be.

In therapy the aim is to heal the split gradually over time, interpreting the black-and-whiteness of the transference wherever and with whoever it occurs, in the past and present. Aaron had been totally unprepared for the rejoining of his split and so was shocked rather than helped by the experience, although we got much therapeutic mileage and not a few chuckles out of it later on.

*The Confronted Transference*

As therapy draws toward its end, many patients, now aware of how their problems came about, wish to 'set the record straight' by speaking frankly at last with the person who originally so influenced them.

It is important such patients are helped to see that while this may be enormously releasing in terms of finally unloading a huge store of anguish, of 'having their say' at last, there is very little likelihood of the other party changing into the kind of mother/father/sibling for whom the patient longed. Leopards very rarely change their spots.

In the happiest of situations a truce may be reached with an old enemy, a little new light shed on old conflicts, but true reconciliations are rare, for the other party has not had the benefit of therapy and so is unable, unwilling or uninterested in seeing the past in a new light. Many cannot bear to be reminded of what for them, too, was a very painful period. Confronting a parent with childhood memories, many patients are confidently informed that they are imagining things.

Frequently the refusal of the other party to acknowledge the past despite a major confrontation helps the patient to accept at last that the relationship of his dreams will never be on offer. After the mourning for that lost dream is over, he can break an emotional tie that has bound him for decades.

Beatrice, fifty-six, a senior social worker, had been on and off antidepressants for some years. She said she was very puzzled by her illness and had always assumed it was genetic. Her father had been a rather gloomy type. Apart from that, she had enjoyed an ideal childhood, growing up in a large country house. Her mother, whom she admired inordinately, had been a magistrate and tireless charity worker. Even now, at eighty, she hosted garden parties and sat on committees.

Over many months of therapy Beatrice was forced to see how she constantly edited the past, picking out only the glowing memories and shelving the unhappy ones. She was often left with her uninterested father and the maid, while her mother travelled and lectured up and down the country. Mother also conducted several long-standing affairs about which everyone knew but never spoke. Underneath her admiration Beatrice felt unloved, unimportant and very angry.

In the meantime I, too, had been idealized and it felt very uncomfortable. As her disappointment and anger at her mother rose to the surface I became, by way of compensation, all that a perfect mother should be. I allowed this transference for a little while because I saw Beatrice needed an alternative security base temporarily, from which she could begin to critically assess the maternal image she had so carefully constructed and maintained at the cost of years of depressive illness.

When the time was right I began to help her look at how she was using the same technique deployed with her mother on myself. She always laughed this off as modesty on my part.

Just before her session I regularly saw a married couple, who one day had a furious row, leaving cushions and arm-rest covers flung to the floor. The phone rang as they left and by the time I had attended to the call it was time for Beatrice's session.

I collected her from the waiting room, forgetting about the cushions. She was absolutely furious that I had not bothered to tidy up for her, that she didn't matter enough (I later learned her father and even the maid didn't bother to tidy up when her mother was away; the house was always a mess).

After that no one was any good. She hated her mother, her father and the maid, God, her teachers at school who only took any notice of her because of her mother's intellectual reputation, and of course myself, playing havoc with people's lives. Why hadn't I left her in her fool's paradise?

Beatrice was now in the blame phase of treatment, where her rage had full rein. Under the anger dwelt despair that anyone, anywhere, ever could love her. Until that despair was in the open, the confrontation she threatened with the now aged mother did not feel appropriate.

When the long catharsis was over, Beatrice began looking at her mother's childhood and came to see why any intimacy had posed such threats to her, why she had put her trust in her brain and power to control others. But Beatrice's sadness about her own childhood remained; nothing could alter that. Her mother had done harm without intending harm. She had to be made to face up to what she had done, at the very least take responsibility for it, say she was sorry.

By now, through much work on her transference to me, she saw me as a competent but fallible psychotherapist rather than a wonderful mother. She hoped to come to terms with her real mother, too; find a way of accepting her with all her faults. But to be forgiven Beatrice said her mother *must* acknowledge her daughter's childhood loneliness. Yet mother was eighty and had a heart problem. What would such a confrontation do to her?

Each time Beatrice visited they would go through routinized conversations and eat together, pretending everything was fine, while

Beatrice raged inside. Along with the rage went a longing for a proper hug, rather than the peck on the forehead that she hated. Before she had commenced therapy she had talked herself out of such needs, assured herself that it was a generational thing: old people from 'good' families just didn't go in for emotional demonstrations. It wasn't fair to ask them. Yet after every visit she was depressed for weeks. Till therapy started she had never made the obvious connection, putting it down to work or the weather.

While she brooded on how and when to challenge her mother, and I encouraged her to explore honestly her unrealistic hopes for a sudden change of heart, her mother died quietly in her sleep.

A face to face showdown was now out of the question, though later on we continued the confrontation in the sessions, addressing not the real eighty-year-old mother who may or may not have responded, but the *childhood mother* carried in her heart and mind, very much alive and still influencing her, undermining her confidence, making her feel less acceptable than other women, pushing her to out-career her mother in some sad competition that drove her to overwork and exhaustion.

The source of transference is confronted from three directions. First in the current transference to the therapist, although this is problematic because the patient needs a 'good' therapist whose hand can be metaphorically held while the 'bad' transference source is being confronted. Second, it may be confronted in the flesh with an old person still injurious to the patient but who may well have vested interests in forgetting, distorting, or avoiding any reference to the past. However, that person's very recalcitrance can help the patient finally come to terms with his history. Finally, it is the *internalized*, young, vigorously active parent who must be confronted again and again in the consulting room, the one who is running the patient's life still, however old and frail in actuality.

Ultimately only the patient can decide whether a face to face confrontation is what he wants. It is the therapist's job to help him look at the possibility from every angle rather than act on impulse and risk a painful rejection for which he is not prepared.

In every case of sexual abuse where the abuser is still alive I have found actual, but prepared, confrontation to be enormously beneficial, whereas with elderly parents, when their 'crimes' are not so clear cut, patients vary on whether or not family upheaval caused by a showdown would be worth the effort, especially where the patient knows there is no hope for rapprochement.

Occasionally, the therapist wishes to help her patient face, inside the consulting room, a transference to someone outside it, and is frustrated that conventional interpretation has failed to get through.

Among other problems, Julian, a successful businessman, was having trouble with his son, Malcolm. He was the oldest child and had been very disturbed at the arrival of twins when he was three. The twins grew up to join Dad in the business and Julian was very proud of them; whereas Malcolm kept trying, and failing, to set up ventures of his own. He produced original, creative, if somewhat wild ideas, but they failed because he insisted on being in sole charge and couldn't deal with a team.

Every time a project went wrong Julian bailed Malcolm out by getting him a good job 'on the old boys' network'. Malcolm could do the work easily and well but always fell foul of the boss and had to leave.

Julian was exasperated and very angry with Malcolm. Every time he was jobless he borrowed one of his father's cars, left it filthy, scratched and without oil. He borrowed cash and 'forgot' to pay it back. Then he'd turn up with a scheme wilder than any previous one and expect his father to congratulate him on the plan. Julian admitted the scheme was audacious yet full of possibility (were it not for Malcolm's authority problems), but he was just so hopping mad about the third minor accident to his car, and the hundred-pound loan outstanding, that he could not work up any enthusiasm. He knew if he dared to remind Malcolm that this scheme, too, would be a five-minute wonder, the lad would fly into a temper and storm out.

I interpreted to Julian that while any father in this position might feel cross, the reason he was so *unmanageably* angry was that he was transferring his younger self to Malcolm.

As a boy Julian had been abandoned by his father. His mother had never encouraged him at school, always complained he was in the way, and finally threw him out on his sixteenth birthday to fend for himself. No capital, no job, no qualifications.

Julian responded to my interpretation. 'Too damn right. I've lavished money, time, special tutors, jobs in my very own company on those boys so they would never have to suffer as I did. Yes, I *do* put myself in his shoes. I would have given my right arm for a dad who cared about me, let alone one who also provided what I have given to that ungrateful little sod.'

'You are hurt he doesn't appreciate your efforts?'

'I don't want him to grovel or anything. I just want him to be like the other two, take and enjoy what I give, be glad he's got a good dad.'

'You try to make your own childhood right by giving them what you missed out on. But in return they must reassure you that you have corrected the past by displaying the joy and gratitude you would have shown. And Malcolm won't say his lines.'

'Look, Wyn, I know what you are saying and it's true. But the twins don't have a problem with it, do they? They adore me. It's only Malcolm who plays up. Judged by anybody's standards he's, well, arrogant and ungrateful. I'm not making this up.'

'You seem so intent on seeing your son as your younger self, showered with all the material and emotional goodies any child could want, that you can't stop and think how he himself processes the situation between the two of you.'

'I expect he thinks I'm a sucker, a soft touch. I've got to sort things out with him. Why can't he look up to me like the other two?'

I then made a reconstructing intervention, to try and show Julian the implications of his pervasive transference to Malcolm, his inability to see him in his own right.

'If I were Malcolm, I think I may well look up to you – in awe and admiration for your achievements. I might hate and envy my brothers, of whom you so clearly approve. I may want to prove myself better than them in your eyes, not by taking your offer of a job, but by making my own job, my own business, doing as well, even better than you. Then you would *have* to recognize me. I might hate it every time I am forced to work for somebody else, another Dad to patronize me and show how small I am. I may hate having to borrow *your* money and *your* car when the twins have both, and your respect as well ... '

'But I'm just a jumped-up, second-hand car dealer. The trips to the Far East, the yacht – that's just all show. I'm nobody.'

'To Malcolm you might be a hero. Look at all the projects he brings for your approval – the boldness, the daring, the latest research. Look at his need for independence, his demand to be recognized as his own man. He sounds just like you when you were making your way in the world.'

'A chip off the old block, eh? Wants to do it his way. The impossible way.'

'Yes.'

'I did well in the end, but I was scared stiff at the start. I didn't have an affluent father to bail me out. I'd have given my right arm ... '

'Perhaps Malcolm would give his right arm for a father, too.'

'What the hell do you mean by that?'

He soon worked out what I meant, and began to see things from where Malcolm might be standing.

Simply stating that a transference exists, even stating it repeatedly, does not necessarily diminish its potency. Sometimes the therapist has to dislodge a stubborn transference perception by speaking on behalf of the transferred-onto person in the patient's life and directly contradicting the patient. The therapist may have only caught the drift of that person's feelings, can offer no detail; but if her challenge enables the patient to go and find the exact truth about how the other person thinks and feels, much good has been done.

## *The Cross Transference*

It is a mistake to assume a female therapist will always stand for the female parent in the transference, and a male the father. Neither should it be forgotten that siblings, grandparents, nannies, neighbours and teachers played a more formative role in some patients' lives than did parents. In addition, the therapist may well stand for more than one figure and one gender at different times in treatment.

Sammy, from southern Italy, met a British academic holidaying there, married him and came to live with him in London. Soon after, she found he was having an affair with more than one of his students. Defiant and angry, she moved out, but came to see me in a state of tremendous shock. The early sessions were taken up with her expressions of grief and horror that such a thing could happen.

Later the husband begged forgiveness and asked to return. Every session was filled with her agonizings over this. I felt as if I were standing in for her absent mother, whom she greatly missed, just letting her talk and come to her own decision.

Eventually her husband was allowed to return and bit by bit Sammy began to recover. The benevolent maternal transference persisted.

I learned she had an adored but bullying father who did something mysterious and powerful in the business world (she made him sound like the Godfather), and a brood of brothers all keen to follow in his footsteps. She had struggled with all the men in her family to be seen as an equal despite her gender, and had read law at university until she met her husband.

Now her husband was back and she felt stronger, she was keen to learn about English people and their ways, find herself a career so that she could support herself if the marriage failed. She accepted my suggestion that she join my therapy group, where at first she seemed to settle well and make good contact with the others.

Then came a dramatic change. She began to arrive late or not at all. When asked why, she would offer outrageous excuses, such as having gone shopping or gone back to bed. She kept throwing down gauntlets, like listing all the things she refused to discuss with us, including her marriage. She never criticized me directly but there were many barbed remarks hinting at my inadequacy as a therapist. She arrived giggly with drink on one occasion, spoiling every attempt at work. Patient at first, the group became furious, then fed up with her.

I said I thought the group might be replicating her family, the members who could do nothing right standing for her bullying brothers, but this was dismissed. I assumed at the time that perhaps she was also rebelling against the protective house-bound mother I had for so long represented. Perhaps she was telling me she wanted to stand on her own feet now. She avoided talking about her family except in the most superficial terms, preferring to provoke and destabilize the group, so I was unable to elicit any transference material other than her behaviour.

Sammy became so histrionic the group finally told her she seemed hell-bent on getting them to drive her out and unless she calmed down a bit she would certainly succeed. She seemed triumphant yet upset by this ultimatum but refused to discuss it sensibly and soon stopped coming.

Some six years later I received a letter from Sammy saying she was now divorced, had made her own career, had completed another stint of therapy and felt her life was progressing well. She had gone over her experiences with me in her second therapy, and now realized that while in the group, I had stood for the father she admired but envied, while loathing him for his bossiness. Most of the acting out had been directed at me and she now wished to thank me for helping her separate from her father!

I kicked myself for not having seen that I had in her mind crossed from being supportive mother to powerful, controlling father when she crossed from individual to group therapy.

## Transference to Things

An inanimate object can come to possess a powerful significance for a patient, and because of its symbolic meaning is transferred onto as if it were a live being. Therapists on the whole find it easy to deal with the concept of a symbol, but balk at the idea of a human relationship with it. Yet they have only to watch a child playing with his toys, frequently talking aloud to them, now scolding, now soothing, now caressing, now throwing down, to see how much of his inner and outer world he attributes (transfers) to them.

Certain youngsters on pinball machines clearly attribute personal qualities to the machine, as do some computer operators. In both cases I have seen murder in the eyes of the operative, and in both cases I have seen them treat the machine as if it were the sweetest of lovers.

Pets come into the same category. I always prick up my ears when patients joke about their cat having acquired its first grey hair, or explaining to me the complex reasons why their dog is not eating well at the moment. When a pet dies I treat the situation with as much gravity as if it were a person.

Ingrid, Larry and Steve were members of my private psychotherapy group, who over many months had developed a special mode of communication the rest of the group could sense, and often envy, but no one could put their finger on quite how or why it worked.

Ingrid had recently left a bullying husband after thirty years and was trying to establish a life of her own. A gracious, cultivated and very feminine woman, she had captivated Larry and Steve who seemed to be dancing attendance on her without actually *doing* anything, much to the discomfort of other women in the group.

Larry was a middle-aged managing director used to organizing vast numbers of people and money without turning a hair. The trouble was he *managed* everything and everybody he came across, rather than pausing to try and *understand* them.

Steve was twenty-four and had lost his mother after a long wasting illness, emotionally cutting himself off from her years before she died to avoid the pain of watching her deteriorate. He had never had a girlfriend. I sensed in his emergent transference that for him Ingrid combined all the qualities of a mother and girlfriend.

One day, group members were chatting in the waiting room prior to the start of the session, and Steve mentioned that he was selling his car. Ingrid was delighted, for she had to part that same week with her big family car and find a smaller model for her own use, now she was on her own. She had often admired Steve's well maintained vehicle which would suit her down to the ground. Steve, who had been in the group a long time, was pleased and flattered but sensed a possible boundary confusion and asked Ingrid to bring up the matter in the session.

Ingrid was surprised and disappointed that apart from Larry, who offered to stage manage the sale, ensuring fair play all round, no one else in the group, including me, seemed to approve of it. A furious row ensued, as to whether buying Steve's car was just a convenient sale not relevant to the group or whether it constituted a special relationship between purchaser and provider that contravened the group's ground rules.

I wanted the group as a whole to take its own decision if possible, so members would not feel infantilized or bullied by me, and could take credit for having in the end done the best thing rather than the easiest. Accordingly, I invited them to imagine the sale had already proceeded and we were some weeks on. How did they now feel?

The group members and I were in possession of a lot of information about the three 'act-outers' that readers are not. Suffice to say that a group analysis of the proposed car sale led to a clear appreciation that the car, for the three involved, was not a car but a baby. No wonder feelings were so heated.

For Ingrid, who had raised her children in a foreign land with no help whatever from her busy husband, and whose adored children had now grown up and left her, this 'little red darling' must have felt like another baby, this time with two very solicitous males looking on approvingly. Acquiring another baby saved her from having to move away from the safe and known domestic role to a more independent one. In other words, she was saved from having to stand on her own two feet and get her own car, do her own bargaining. All her life men had been knights or bullies: Sir Larry and Sir Steve could not be experienced as real men until she dispensed with their services and organized her own transport.

For Steve, who longed for a feared attachment, here was a ready-made family: Ingrid the wife/mother; Larry the hearty, supportive dad in contradistinction to his own very cold father; and the car/baby, who also represented himself as a youngster. He was getting a second chance, via his car, of all the attention he had missed.

For Larry the situation replicated his own marriage: he had 'rescued' a single mother twenty-odd years ago and adopted her child. He was still playing the knight in shining armour, solving everybody's problems to deflect his own and others' attention from his own needs.

The rest of the group drew to the threesome's notice how tricky relations could become if the car broke down, or developed a fault. Who would believe whose story? Who would ring who? – phoning one another was also against the ground rules. And what about a trial drive before money changed hands? That would certainly mean relating outside the group. And what was going to happen each week as Ingrid parked her baby alongside Larry's and Steve's? Would there be little huddles, enquiries as to the health of the 'little red darling', pattings and pettings? Weren't the three of them (much to the others' envy) already playing happy families without adopting a baby as well?

The car never changed hands, but a great deal of therapeutic work around the theme of babies was achieved.

## The Dissolved Transference

Most therapists (though not all) try to divest themselves of transference trappings as therapy comes to an end. By now most of the transference should have been worked through, but the patient may be so used to seeing his therapist, at least in part, as some other key figure in his life, that his mode of relating to her has become an entrenched habit which a bit of disconfirmation from her will help him break.

The therapist's aim is to let the patient take his leave of a real person, the one with whom he made an Alliance all that time ago. The pleasure and sorrow in mutual acknowledgement that a solid, real bond has grown out of all the anguish and suffering entailed in therapy and that that good relationship has now to end, provides a powerfully emotive experience for both therapist and patient.

Every time I have to say goodbye after a satisfactory therapy, it always seems to me unfair, cruel, yet very necessary that, having made the bond, it must now be broken, at least outwardly, so that the patient can internalize the good experience, carrying positive expectations based on it to future relationships. As most parents will testify, one has to let go, but it is never easy.

Dissolving the transference is not dependent on doing anything special, or suddenly changing one's stance from sphynx-like inscrutability to chatting about the weather; it is more a process of allowing temperament, attitude, opinion – *personality* – to show, whereas before it would have been reined in as superfluous or distracting to the treatment.

Toward the very end it also involves allowing distress at parting, pride in, respect for and admiration of the patient to show, while still retaining sufficient control to hold the therapeutic boundary intact. After all, there's another patient in ten minutes!

Vestiges of transference dissolve quickly when patient and therapist do their stocktaking at the end of treatment. They pore over their joint endeavour, highlighting this and that: 'Do you remember when ... ?' and, 'Crikey, that was a tough period wasn't it?' They go over areas now completely cleared of difficulty, and areas where the patient will have to continue the work alone, now he has the tools.

Having together undone the past they look at what preparations for the future might be made, where the flashpoints of difficulty are going to be. The therapist here gives her professional opinion, rather than processing the patient's productions as she would have done in earlier stages of treatment. By now both parties are experts on the inner workings of this patient: they are consulting as equals about how to send him into the world with the best chance of success.

Another way to dissolve remaining threads of transference is to allow the patient, *as an adult*, to thank the therapist for her loyalty, dependability and respectful attention at all times. Patients often tell me at the end that it was these qualities that made all the difference. (Alas, rarely do they remember that brilliant interpretation or complex bit of psychological detective work that I thought had altered the whole course of treatment!)

I do not find it easy to receive praise or gratitude but I have come to see that I must not avoid it. It is one of the last important services that I must do for my patient if he is to finally leave the role of dependant behind him and make a clean break from me. When, because of my own neurosis, I have failed to make space for such thanks, I have pushed patients into giving me embarrassing farewell gifts in place of the gratitude they need and should be allowed to express, lest a sense of obligation, of unfinished business with their therapist, continue to haunt them.

# Afterword

I opened this book with a rescue fantasy. A resurrected Freud was invited to inspect and advise on our mental health services. I trust by now the reader would agree that this is about as useful as bringing back to life one of the famed Victorian naturalists – a leisured, affluent gentleman poking about contentedly in the cliffs for fossils, publishing only decades afterwards – and asking him to crack the problems of the modern scientist shackled to his lab and his technology, under ever-increasing pressure to bust frontiers before his grant runs out.

Without Darwin, Freud and company, the 'helping professions' and our Science today would not be anything like they are – the debt is immeasurable. But instead of harking back to the golden days of psychoanalysis, we therapists must try to preserve all the best aspects of the analytic tradition while adapting it to present-day conditions, with especial regard to the fact that mental health services must now address the needs of a mixed general population producing clinical pictures (not to mention financial pressures) unheard of a hundred years ago.

In recognition of this requirement, I have given the process and technique of Assessment a thorough overhaul. A therapy in miniature, Assessment may be, but I must caution against its abuse as a justification for giving patients short shrift: one of its chief purposes is to optimize resources so that each patient gets the short-, medium- or long-term help he needs, not the minimum number of sessions the clinic can get away with.

Also needed is a bringing together of different therapeutic disciplines. True, some concepts may be irreconcilable, but many others are not. Different schools of therapy often come to similar clinical and theoretical conclusions via a different route and using different language (when the chips are down there are only two kinds of therapist; good ones and bad ones). The rivalry and suspicion inherent in the ghetto mentality of those therapeutic extremists who believe they possess the one Truth have no place in a modern mental health service, which has enough problems already.

Each discipline has much to teach and learn from the others. A pooling of knowledge and experience is required, such that we can train, and then maintain via supervision, a new kind of therapist,

211

broad in technical, clinical and theoretical range, appreciative of and able to mine the psychic depths of their patients while flexible enough to work within different and difficult time frames, changing their technique accordingly.

Much is demanded of the Broad Spectrum Psychotherapist. To fulfil obligations Freud and his contemporaries never dreamed of, she needs first-rate training (which should *always* include her own therapy) and first-rate supervision. Current training quite properly stresses classical psychoanalytic texts but tends to fall short on pressing day-to-day clinical issues – the crucial differences between and uses and abuses of, short- and long-term work; the whether and whens of using group, couple or family techniques; the dynamics of the staff team/institution; the rationale for and minutiae of Assessment; the detailed management of the treatment setting along with the professional handling of referrals sent and referrals received; help to recognize and operate in situations where, in the patient's interest, a prevailing policy or practice should be challenged.

Some therapists work privately at home or more or less alone out in the so-called 'community'. They can become very isolated and demoralized – many even downright eccentric – without realizing it. A professional network is essential. Training should involve preparation for such alienating working conditions.

Clinical practice within a real treatment setting is a world away from the training course and the few specially-selected patients seen under sheltered conditions. It offers opportunity for the new graduate to spread her wings but also brings pressures to adapt and conform that can be as disillusioning as they are anxiety provoking. A good supervisor is essential. It is to the supervisory couple and their mutual roles and responsibilities that I shall turn in my forthcoming book *The Supervisory Couple in Broad Spectrum Psychotherapy*, Free Association Books.

# Further Reading

*Place of Publication is London unless otherwise stated*

Abram, J. (1992) *Individual Psychotherapy Trainings: A Guide.* Free Association Books.
Budman, S.H. et al. (1992) *The First Session in Brief Therapy.* New York: Guilford.
Casement, P. (1985) *On Learning from the Patient.* Tavistock.
—— (1990) *Further Learning from the Patient.* Routledge.
Coltart, N. (1992) *Slouching Towards Bethlehem ... and Further Psychoanalytic Explorations.* Free Association Books.
—— (1993) *How to Survive as a Psychotherapist.* Sheldon.
Corney, R. and Jenkins, R. (1993) *Counselling in General Practice.* Routledge.
Davanloo, H. (1978) *Basic Principles and Technique in Short Term Psychotherapy.* New York: Spectrum.
Davis, H. and Fallowfield, L., eds (1991) *Counselling and Communication in Health Care.* Chichester: John Wiley.
De Board, R. (1978) *The Psychoanalysis of Organizations.* Social Science Paperbacks, Tavistock.
France, A. (1988) *Consuming Psychotherapy.* Free Association Books.
Gray, A. (1994) *An Introduction to the Therapeutic Frame.* Routledge.
Gustafson, J.P. (1992) *Complex Secrets of Brief Psychotherapy.* New York: W.W. Norton.
Hobson, R.F. (1985) *Forms of Feeling: The Heart of Psychotherapy.* Tavistock, 1990.
Holmes, J. (1993) *John Bowlby and Attachment Theory.* Routledge.
Jacobs, M. (1988) *Psychodynamic Counselling in Action.* Sage, 1989.
Kernberg, O. (1980) *Internal World and External Reality: Object Relations Theory Applied.* New York: Aronson, 1994.
—— et al. (1989) *Psychodynamic Psychotherapy of Borderline Patients.* HarperCollins.
Klauber, J. (1981) *Difficulties in the Analytic Encounter.* New York: Jason Aronson Inc.; Free Association Books, 1995.

Kohut, H. (1977) *The Restoration of the Self.* New York: International Universities Press, 1993.

Lomas, P. (1963) *True and False Experience.* Allen Lane; New Jersey: Transaction Publications, 1995.

—— (1992) *The Limits of Interpretation: What's Wrong with Psychoanalysis?* Harmondsworth: Penguin.

—— (1994) *Cultivating Intuition: An Introduction to Psychotherapy.* Harmondsworth: Penguin.

McDaniel, S.; Hepworth, J. and Doherty, W. (1992) *Medical Family Therapy.* New York: Basic.

——; Campbell, S. and Seaburn, T. (1995) *Family Oriented Primary Care.* New York: Springer-Verlag.

Main, T. (1989) *The Ailment and Other Psychoanalytic Essays.* Free Association Books.

Malan, D.H. (1963) *A Study of Brief Psychotherapy.* Tavistock; New York: Plenum Press, 1975.

—— (1976) *The Frontier of Brief Psychotherapy.* New York: Plenum Press.

—— (1979) *Individual Psychotherapy and the Science of Psychodynamics.* Butterworth-Heinemann, 1993.

Mann, J. (1973) *Time Limited Psychotherapy.* Cambridge, MA: Harvard University Press.

Markus, A.C.; Murray Parks, C.; Thomson, P. and Johnston, M. (1989) *Psychological Problems in General Practice.* Oxford: Oxford University Press.

Noonan, E. (1983) *Counselling Young People.* Methuen, 1990.

Obholzer, A. and Roberts, V.Z., eds (1994) *The Unconscious at Work: Individual and Organizational Stress in the Human Services.* Routledge.

Peck, F.S. (1978) *The Road Less Travelled.* Rider, 1995.

Phillips, A. (1993) *On Kissing, Tickling and Being Bored.* Faber.

Rowe, D. (1988) *Choosing not Losing: The Experience of Depression.* Fontana.

—— (1992) *Wanting Everything.* Fontana.

—— (1994) *Time on our Side: Growing in Wisdom not Growing Old.* HarperCollins.

Salinsky, J. (1993) *The Last Appointment: Psychotherapy in General Practice.* Lewes: The Book Guild.

Salzberger-Wittenberg, I. (1970) *Psychoanalytic Insight and Relationships: A Kleinian Approach.* Routledge, 1990.

Sandler, J.; Dare, C. and Holder, A. (1973) *The Patient and the Analyst: The Basis of the Psychoanalytic Process.* Allen & Unwin.

Skynner, A.C.R. (1978) *One Flesh: Separate Persons.* Constable, 1990.

Storr, A. (1992) *The Art of Psychotherapy.* Butterworth–Heine-mann.

Symington, N. (1992) *The Analytic Experience: Lectures from The Tavistock.* Free Association Books.

Winnicott, D.W. (1971) *Playing and Reality.* Tavistock.

Yalom, I.D. (1975) *The Theory and Practice of Group Psycho-therapy.* New York: Basic, 3rd edition 1985.

—— (1991) *Love's Executioner and Other Tales of Psychotherapy.* Harmondsworth: Penguin.

# Index

'acting in'
  interventions, 165–8, 187
  projections, 23
alternative treatments, 136–7
analysis, treatment by, 95
anxieties, patients', 112–13
apprenticeship, 60
Assessment
  danger of repeated, 66, 96–7
  importance of, 33–4, 211
  and long-term therapy, 69
  notes about, 95
  protracted, 134
  by senior assessor, 66
  and short-term therapy, 68–9
  structure of, 97
  and Therapeutic Alliance,
    65–6
  trial identification in, 16
  using psychiatric background,
    97–102
asylums, need for, 98

boundaries, 70, 92, 125
  in Contract, 136
Broad Spectrum Psychotherapy,
  36–8, 212
  contrasted with
    psychoanalysis, 6, 37, 82
  importance of Therapeutic
    Alliance to, 86

common language, finding, 80–4,
  115
community care, limitations of,
  98

confidentiality, within team, 6–8
conflict
  defined, 93
  in Formulation, 116, 119
containment, 54–7, 104
Contract, 130–8
  importance of written, 130–1
  interim, 133–4
  and preparation for post-
    Assessment therapy, 135–6
  and short-term therapy, 132
  style and content of, 136–8
couch
  significance of, 160–1
  use of, 135
crisis intervention, 43–5, 163
cueing, 12–14, 32

dissociation, 102
drugs
  use of, 3, 4
  value of, 98–100
Dynamic Formulation, 93–5,
  114, 128–9
  contexts (present and past),
    115–16
  examples, 116–28
  and restricting exploration,
    109–12
  subtext, 115
  text, 115

educative function
  and therapist as teacher, 75,
    151–3
  of therapy, 49–53

ego strengths, 96
emotion, therapist's apparent
    lack of, 70–1
exploration, restricting, 109–12

families, and Contract, 138
first session, opening, 70–4
focal theory, shortcomings of, 4
focal therapy, 96
forecasting, of future breakdown,
    102–4
free association, 81
Freud, Sigmund, resurrected, 3,
    211

goals, setting realistic, 95–7
GP to the Mind
    role as, 37–8, 40–1, 43, 125
    subfunctions of, 82, 92
GPs, permission to consult, 47,
    137
group therapy, restrictions on
    members of, 137–8

identification
    with the aggressor, 19–22
    trial, 14–19
interactional process, 11–12
interpretation
    interventions as, 141–2, 162
    premature, 75, 105
    trial, 104–8
interventions, 33
    'acting in', 165–8, 187
    'acting out', 168–9
    'deep', 144–6
    educative, 53
    expression of, 141–2
    'fingers crossed', 183–4
    functions of, 162–4
    misguided, 162
    by patient, 180–3
    purpose of, 146–8
    reconstructing, 169–73

interventions *cont.*
    reserved, 164–5
    setting as constant, 159–61
    style of, 143–4
    therapist's different roles in,
        148–59
    tidying-up, 163–4
    translating, 173–5
    world-assumptive, 175–9

language
    common, 80–4, 115
    of interventions, 141

management of treatment, 45–9
marriage, discussions of, 182–3

National Health Service, psycho-
    therapy in, 5, 6, 36–8, 68
note-taking, 94–5

palliatives, 96
patient
    appropriate therapy for, 5,
        84–5, 125
    and choice of treatment,
        102–4
    incurable, 96
    interventions by, 180–3
    and management of
        treatment, 45–9
    and psychotherapeutic
        language, 82
    questions and anxieties,
        112–13
    response to interpretation,
        104–6
    self-treatment for new
        symptoms, 96
    use of term, *x*
post-Assessment therapy, 86,
    131
    and change of therapist,
        134–5

post-Assessment therapy *cont.*
  early, 143
  preparation for, 135
prevention, 57–60
projective mechanisms, 22–8
psychiatry, clinical, 38
  value of, 97–101, 102
psychoanalysis, 3, 5, 6, 36–7, 38
  training, 35, 36
psychodynamics, 4, 5
  of transference, 28–9
  *see also* Dynamic Formulation
psychological mindedness, in
    patients, 82–3
psychotherapy
  broad spectrum, 36–8, 212
  limitations of, 100–1
  as poor relation, 3–4, 6, 35–6
  public-sector, 5, 6, 36–8
  training, 6–7, 35–6, 97, 100
pure analysis, unattainable, 3–4

questions, patients', 112–13
  recontextualizing, 32

resistance, 12
resources, measuring, 103–4
restricting exploration, 109–12
revisiting *see* working through
rules of good practice, 57, 157–8,
    180–1

setting, as intervention, 76, 77,
    159–61
silence
  not making interventions,
    183–4
  unasked questions, 112–13
  uses of, 74–80
splitting
  in trial identification, 15
  *see also* transference, split
supervision, of therapists, 34, 60,
    212

Therapeutic Alliance
  and Contract, 131
  difficulties in making, 66, 67,
    177
  ending, 209–10
  forming, 65–6, 69–70
  nature of, 67–8, 153–4
  and post-Assessment, 143–4
  and transference, 85–7, 91–2,
    175
Therapeutic Community, 98–100
therapist
  Achilles' heel, 24
  and being used, 38–43
  changing, 134–5
  and cueing, 12–14
  as Friend, 150
  as God, 148–50
  need for responsible
    judgement, 103–4
  need for rest, 60–2
  own therapy, 9, 60, 154,
    187–90
  as Parent, 153–5
  personal appearance of, 161
  questions about private life,
    181–3
  receptiveness of, 77–8, 91–2
  as Sage, 155–6
  supervision of, 34, 60
  as Surgeon, 150
  as Teacher, 151–3
  use of personal experience, 9,
    126, 193
  well-functioning, 8–10
therapy
  appropriate to patient, 5
  and clinical support, 7–8, 61
  setting goals for, 95–7
  therapist's own, 9, 60, 154,
    187–90
  touching, 157–8, 180–1
training, 6–7, 35–6, 212
  apprenticeship, 60

transference, 28–30, 185
  allowed, 195–8
  attitudinal, 191–3
  confronted, 200–5
  at Contract-making time,
    135–6
  cross, 205–6
  and cueing, 13, 32
  dissolved, 209–10
  in early Assessment, 84–7,
    91–2
  mediated, 193–5
  to the patient, 165, 167–8,
    185
  reciprocated, 186–90
  in silences, 75

transference *cont.*
  split, 89–90, 198–9
  and therapist as teacher, 152
  to things, 206–9
  working with, 31–2
trial identification, 14–19
  by patient, 15
trial interpretation, 104–8
  wonderment, 81

word play, 83–4
working through, 28
world, assumptions about, 175–6

*Index by Auriol Griffith-Jones*